Unity 5.x Animation  Cookbook

A recipe-based guide to give you practical information on
Unity 5.x animation techniques and tools

Maciej Szcześnik

BIRMINGHAM - MUMBAI

Unity 5.x Animation Cookbook

First published: May 2016

Production reference: 1160516

Published by Packt Publishing Ltd.

Livery Place

35 Livery Street

Birmingham B3 2PB, UK.

ISBN 978-1-78588-391-0

www.packtpub.com

Credits

Author

Maciej Szcześnik

Reviewer

Grzegorz Mazur

Commissioning Editor

Amarabha Banerjee

Acquisition Editor

Aaron Lazar

Content Development Editor

Prashanth G Rao

Technical Editor

Murtaza Tinwala

Copy Editor

Sameen Siddiqui

Project Coordinator

Bijal Patel

Proofreader

Safis Editing

Indexer

Rekha Nair

Production Coordinator

Aparna Bhagat

Cover Work

Aparna Bhagat

About the Author

Maciej Szcześnik is an experienced game designer and Unity developer, specializing in gameplay and combat mechanics. His daily responsibilities include motion capture session planning and coordination, creating animation graphs and state machines, and AI design and implementation.

He started his professional career in 2004 at CD Projekt RED—the company best known for the critically acclaimed The Witcher series. Maciej had key roles in the Witcher games, being lead gameplay designer and lead combat designer. He also worked at 11 bit studios, another well-known Polish game development company, famous for the This War Of Mine game.

Maciej gave three talks at the Game Developers Conference and Game Developers Conference Europe. He is also a lecturer at Warsaw Film School, teaching Unity and technical aspects of animation as part of the game development BA course.

I'd like to thank my wife for her support, Kacper Kwiatkowski and Grzegorz Mazur from Vile Monarch for their reviews, Marek Ziemak and Piotr Tomsiński for inspiring discussions about games and animations, and Michał Pieńkowski and Marcin Iwanek for countless RPG and tabletop game sessions. I'd also like to thank all my friends and former coworkers from 11 bit studios and CD Projekt RED for helping me develop my skills.

About the Reviewer

Grzegorz Mazur is a programmer who graduated in information technology from Warsaw University of Technology. He is currently co-boss and technical director at Vile Monarch. Previously, he worked for 11 bit studios, where he was lead programmer of This War of Mine and Sleepwalker's Journey. He specializes in gameplay and AI programming and is a teacher at Warsaw Film School. He is also an amateur musician and board game enthusiast.

www.PacktPub.com

For support files and downloads related to your book, please visit www.PacktPub.com.

eBooks, discount offers, and more

Did you know that Packt offers eBook versions of every book published, with PDF and ePub files available? You can upgrade to the eBook version at www.PacktPub.com and as a print book customer, you are entitled to a discount on the eBook copy. Get in touch with us at customercare@packtpub.com for more details.

At www.PacktPub.com, you can also read a collection of free technical articles, sign up for a range of free newsletters and receive exclusive discounts and offers on Packt books and eBooks.

https://www2.packtpub.com/books/subscription/packtlib

Do you need instant solutions to your IT questions? PacktLib is Packt's online digital book library. Here, you can search, access, and read Packt's entire library of books.

Why subscribe?

- Fully searchable across every book published by Packt
- Copy and paste, print, and bookmark content
- On demand and accessible via a web browser

Free access for Packt account holders

Get notified! Find out when new books are published by following @PacktEnterprise on Twitter or the Packt Enterprise Facebook page.

Table of Contents

Preface   1

Chapter 1: Working with Animations   7
  Introduction   7
  Importing skeletal animations   8
    Getting ready   8
    How to do it…   8
    How it works…   11
    There's more…   11
  Configuring generic and humanoid rigs   12
    Getting ready   12
    How to do it…   13
    How it works…   17
    There's more…   18
  Creating and assigning an Animator Controller   19
    Getting ready   20
    How to do it…   20
    How it works…   21
    See also   22
  Creating animation transitions in Animator Controller   23
    Getting ready   23
    How to do it…   23
    How it works…   24
    There's more…   26
  Using parameters to control the animation flow   27
    Getting ready   27
    How to do it…   27
    How it works…   29
    There's more…   30
  Using animations from multiple assets   31
    Getting ready   31
    How to do it…   32
    How it works…   33
  Looping, mirroring and offsetting the animations   33
    Getting ready   33

How to do it…	33
How it works…	34
There's more…	34
Adjusting the playback speed of animations	**35**
Getting ready	35
How to do it…	35
How it works…	35
There's more…	36
Using override animator controllers to animate different types of characters	**37**
Getting ready	37
How to do it…	37
How it works…	38
Importing object animation from a 3D package	**39**
Getting ready	39
How to do it…	39
How it works…	40
Chapter 2: Working with the Animation View	**41**
Introduction	**41**
Using the Animation View to create a flickering light	**42**
Getting ready	42
How to do it…	42
How it works…	44
There's more…	45
Blending light colors with the Animation View and the Animator Controller	**46**
Getting ready	46
How to do it…	46
How it works…	47
Animating an object's world position – creating a moving platform	**48**
Getting ready	48
How to do it…	48
How it works…	50
There's more…	51
Animating object's local position – creating automatic doors	**52**
Getting ready	53
How to do it…	53
How it works…	58
See also	59

Using the Hierarchy to animate local rotation – creating an orbiting planet   59
    Getting ready   59
    How to do it…   60
    How it works…   61
    There's more…   62
Animating triggers – creating a death trap   62
    Getting ready   62
    How to do it…   63
    How it works…   67
    There's more…   67
Creating an elevator triggered by player input   68
    Getting ready   68
    How to do it…   68
    How it works…   71
    There's more…   72

Chapter 3: 2D and User Interface Animation   75
Introduction   75
Exporting a 2D sprite animation from a 3D package   76
    Getting ready   76
    How to do it…   76
    How it works…   79
    There's more…   80
    See also   80
Creating a frame-by-frame sprite animation with the Animation View   81
    Getting ready   81
    How to do it…   81
    How it works…   82
Creating a 2D sprite doll animation with the Animation View   83
    Getting ready   83
    How to do it…   84
    How it works…   87
Using the Animator Controller to play sprite animations   87
    Getting ready   87
    How to do it…   87
    How it works…   89
    There's more…   90
Creating a fade out – fade in transition with the Animation View   90
    Getting ready   90

How to do it...	91
How it works...	94
Creating a swipe transition with the Animation View	**94**
Getting ready	94
How to do it...	95
How it works...	98
Using filled images for creating animated progress bars	**99**
Getting ready	99
How to do it...	99
How it works...	100
There's more...	100
Using Mecanim states for animating UI button states	**101**
Getting ready	101
How to do it...	101
How it works...	103
There's more...	103
Chapter 4: Character Movement	**105**
Introduction	**105**
Using Blend Trees to blend walk and run animations	**106**
Getting ready	106
How to do it...	106
How it works...	109
There's more...	110
Using root motion to drive Rigid Body characters' movement with animations	**111**
Getting ready	112
How to do it...	113
How it works...	115
There's more...	117
Using root motion to steer a character	**117**
Getting ready	117
How to do it...	118
How it works...	121
Using animations for better looking transitions	**122**
Getting ready	122
How to do it...	122
How it works...	125
There's more...	125
Using root motion for a 180 degrees turn	**125**

Getting ready	126
How to do it…	126
How it works…	128
There's more…	128
Making a character jump with 3-phase animation	**129**
Getting ready	129
How to do it…	129
How it works…	132
There's more…	132
Using root motion to drive a NavMesh Agents' movement with animations	**132**
Getting ready	133
How to do it…	133
How it works…	135
There's more…	135
Using triggers to grab an edge while jumping	**136**
Getting ready	136
How to do it…	137

Chapter 5: Character Actions and Expressions	**141**
Introduction	**141**
Creating an appear or a disappear animation	**142**
Getting ready	142
How to do it…	143
How it works…	143
There's more…	144
Creating background characters and critters with animation-driven behavior	**144**
Getting ready	144
How to do it…	145
How it works…	146
There's more…	146
Using Blend Trees to create randomized actions	**147**
Getting ready	147
How to do it…	148
How it works…	149
There's more…	149
Using Quaternion.LookRotation() and Animator.SetLookAtPosition() methods to make characters follow an object with their gaze	**150**
Getting ready	150

How to do it…	151
How it works…	153
There's more…	153
Action Points – performing an action in a specified spot	154
Getting ready	154
How to do it…	154
How it works…	157
There's more…	158
Synchronizing an animation with objects in the scene	158
Getting ready	159
How to do it…	159
How it works…	160
There's more…	161
Using IK for interacting with scene objects	161
Getting ready	161
How to do it…	162
How it works…	164
See also	164
Animating facial expressions with Blend Shapes	164
Getting ready	165
How to do it…	165
How it works…	166
There's more…	167
Chapter 6: Handling Combat	169
Introduction	169
Using Sub-State Machines in Animator Controller	170
Getting ready	170
How to do it…	170
How it works…	172
There's more…	172
Using Animation Events to trigger script functions	173
Getting ready	173
How to do it…	173
How it works…	177
There's more…	177
Using transitions from Any State to play hit reactions	177
Getting ready	177
How to do it…	178
How it works…	179

Using root motion to create a dodge move   180
  Getting ready   180
  How to do it…   181
  How it works…   182
  There's more…   182
**Checking what Animator state is currently active to disable or enable
player actions**   183
  Getting ready   183
  How to do it…   183
  How it works…   184
  There's more…   184
Using Animation Events to draw a weapon   185
  Getting ready   185
  How to do it…   185
  How it works…   188
Using Avatar Masks and animator controller layers to walk and aim   189
  Getting ready   189
  How to do it…   189
  How it works…   192
  There's more…   193
Using the LookAt() method to aim   193
  Getting ready   193
  How to do it…   194
  How it works…   194
  There's more…   195
Using Blend Trees to aim   195
  Getting ready   196
  How to do it…   196
  How it works…   199
  There's more…   199
Detecting the hit location on a character   199
  Getting ready   199
  How to do it…   199
  How it works…   203
  There's more…   204

Chapter 7: Special Effects   205
  Introduction   205
  Using Animation Events to trigger sound and visual effects   206
    Getting ready   206

How to do it...   206
How it works...   209
There's more...   209
Creating camera shakes with the Animation View and the Animator Controller   209
Getting ready   210
How to do it...   210
How it works...   211
There's more...   211
Using the Animation View to animate public script variables   211
Getting ready   211
How to do it...   212
How it works...   214
Using additive Mecanim layers to add extra motion to a character   214
Getting ready   214
How to do it...   214
How it works...   216
Using Blend Shapes to morph an object into another one   217
Getting ready   217
How to do it...   217
How it works...   218
Using wind emitters to create motion for foliage and particle systems   219
Getting ready   219
How to do it...   219
How it works...   220
Using sprite sheets to animate particles   221
Getting ready   221
How to do it...   222
How it works...   223
Animating properties of a particle system with the Animation View   223
Getting ready   224
How to do it...   224
How it works...   225
Using waveform of a sound clip to animate objects in the scene   225
Getting ready   225
How to do it...   225
How it works...   227
See also   227
Creating a day and night cycle with the Animation View   227

Getting ready   227
How to do it...   228
How it works...   230
There's more...   230

Chapter 8: Animating Cutscenes   231

  Introduction   231
  Using the Animation View to animate the camera   232
    Getting ready   232
    How to do it...   232
    How it works...   233
    There's more...   233
  Changing cameras with animation   233
    Getting ready   234
    How to do it...   234
    How it works...   235
  Synchronizing animation of multiple objects 236
    Getting ready   236
    How to do it...   237
    How it works...   238
    There's more...   238
  Importing a whole cutscene from a 3D package 239
    Getting ready   239
    How to do it...   240
    How it works...   241
    There's more...   242
  Synchronizing subtitles   242
    Getting ready   242
    How to do it...   243
    How it works...   244
  Using root motion to play cutscenes in gameplay   245
    Getting ready   245
    How to do it...   246
    How it works...   249

Chapter 9: Physics and Animations   251

  Introduction   251
  Using cloth   252
    Getting ready   252
    How to do it...   252

How it works…	254
There's more…	255
Using rigid body joints	256
Getting ready	256
How to do it…	257
How it works…	258
Destructible objects	259
Getting ready	259
How to do it…	260
How it works…	262
Creating a humanoid ragdoll with the ragdoll wizard	262
Getting ready	263
How to do it…	263
How it works…	265
Creating a generic ragdoll with character joints	266
Getting ready	266
How to do it…	266
How it works…	268
Applying force to a ragdoll	268
Getting ready	269
How to do it…	269
How it works…	270
There's more…	271
Dismemberment	271
Getting ready	272
How to do it…	272
How it works…	275
There's more…	275
Getting up from a ragdoll	275
Getting ready	275
How to do it…	276
How it works…	282
There's more…	282
Chapter 10: Miscellaneous	283
Introduction	283
Using math to animate an object	283
Getting ready	284
How to do it…	284
How it works…	286

Using the Lerp() function to animate an object   286
  Getting ready   286
  How to do it…   287
  How it works…   289
  See also   290
Using the Rotate() function to animate an object   290
  Getting ready   290
  How to do it…   291
  How it works…   292
  There's more…   292
Preparing motion capture files for humanoid characters   292
  Getting ready   293
  How to do it…   293
  How it works…   297
  See also   298
Adding behaviors to Mecanim states   298
  Getting ready   298
  How to do it…   299
  How it works…   303
Index   305

Preface

This book describes Unity's animation techniques from a designer's point of view. It is focused on achieving interesting gameplay effects and creating game mechanics. Each topic is presented in the form of a short recipe with a list of steps needed to implement the given feature. All the recipes are prepared in the most condensed form—a good basis to build your own solutions on.

This book doesn't cover animating in a 3D package, although you may find some helpful tips regarding Blender 3D in it. A lot of the recipes presented in this book use C# scripting not only for triggering animations, but also for creating interesting motions and effects. If you are a game designer or a Unity developer and would like to know more about what's possible with Unity's animation system, I hope this book will be an interesting read for you. Also, if you have any questions regarding this book or the topics it covers, you can contact me via Twitter (@MaciejSzczesnik). I will be happy to help.

What this book covers

Chapter 1, *Working with Animations*, describes the tools essential for importing animations from 3D packages. It also covers most of the import settings.

Chapter 2, *Working with the Animation View*, covers Unity's built-in animation tool, used to animate almost everything apart from characters.

Chapter 3, *2D and User Interface Animation*, focuses on animating 2D sprites and UI elements.

Chapter 4, *Character Movement*, covers different types of movement, using animations and root motion.

Chapter 5, *Character Actions and Expressions*, is about actions, action points, and facial expressions.

Chapter 6, *Handling Combat*, covers combat-specific topics, such as using animations for aiming and creating a hit-detection system.

Chapter 7, *Special Effects*, is not only about particle systems, but also about animating fog, creating wind zones, and even using sound waveforms for animation.

Chapter 8, *Animating Cutscenes*, describes how to import a cutscene from a 3D package and how to prepare simple cutscenes using Unity's Animation View.

Chapter 9, *Physics and Animations*, shows how to create ragdolls and break stuff.

Chapter 10, *Miscellaneous*, is the last chapter and describes a few solutions to common problems—for instance, working with mocap animations in Blender and Unity.

What you need for this book

You need to install Unity 5.x (preferably 5.3 or greater). You also need to have your own animations or download the provided example project. It contains the assets needed to follow each recipe.

Who this book is for

This book is for Unity developers who have some exposure to Unity game development and want to learn the nuances of animation in Unity. Previous knowledge of animation techniques and mecanim is not necessary.

Sections

In this book, you will find several headings that appear frequently (*Getting ready, How to do it..., How it works..., There's more...,* and *See also*).

To give clear instructions on how to complete a recipe, use these sections as follows:

Getting ready

This section tells you what to expect in the recipe and describes how to set up any software or any preliminary settings required for the recipe.

How to do it...

This section contains the steps required to follow the recipe.

How it works...

This section usually consists of a detailed explanation of what happened in the previous section.

There's more...

This section consists of additional information about the recipe in order to make you more knowledgeable about the recipe.

See also

This section provides helpful links to other useful information for the recipe.

Conventions

In this book, you will find a number of text styles that distinguish between different kinds of information. Here are some examples of these styles and an explanation of their meaning.

Code words in text, database table names, folder names, filenames, file extensions, pathnames, dummy URLs, user input, and Twitter handles are shown as follows: "Simply drag and drop the file to your `Assets` folder."

A block of code is set as follows:

```
using UnityEngine;
using System.Collections;

public class Wave : MonoBehaviour {
//The anim variable is used to store the reference
//to the Animator component of the character.
private Animator anim;
```

New terms and **important words** are shown in bold. Words that you see on the screen, for example, in menus or dialog boxes, appear in the text like this: "Go to **Assets** | **Import new asset** and choose your FBX file."

Warnings or important notes appear in a box like this.

Tips and tricks appear like this.

Reader feedback

Feedback from our readers is always welcome. Let us know what you think about this book—what you liked or disliked. Reader feedback is important for us as it helps us develop titles that you will really get the most out of.

To send us general feedback, simply e-mail feedback@packtpub.com, and mention the book's title in the subject of your message.

If there is a topic that you have expertise in and you are interested in either writing or contributing to a book, see our author guide at www.packtpub.com/authors.

Customer support

Now that you are the proud owner of a Packt book, we have a number of things to help you to get the most from your purchase.

Downloading the example code

You can download the example code files for this book from your account at http://www.packtpub.com. If you purchased this book elsewhere, you can visit http://www.packtpub.com/support and register to have the files e-mailed directly to you.

You can download the code files by following these steps:

1. Log in or register to our website using your e-mail address and password.
2. Hover the mouse pointer on the **SUPPORT** tab at the top.

3. Click on **Code Downloads & Errata**.
4. Enter the name of the book in the **Search** box.
5. Select the book for which you're looking to download the code files.
6. Choose from the drop-down menu where you purchased this book from.
7. Click on **Code Download**.

You can also download the code files by clicking on the **Code Files** button on the book's webpage at the Packt Publishing website. This page can be accessed by entering the book's name in the **Search** box. Please note that you need to be logged in to your Packt account.

Once the file is downloaded, please make sure that you unzip or extract the folder using the latest version of:

- WinRAR / 7-Zip for Windows
- Zipeg / iZip / UnRarX for Mac
- 7-Zip / PeaZip for Linux

The code bundle for the book is also hosted on GitHub at `https://github.com/PacktPublishing/Unity-5.x-Animation-Cookbook`. We also have other code bundles from our rich catalog of books and videos available at `https://github.com/PacktPublishing/`. Check them out!

Downloading the color images of this book

We also provide you with a PDF file that has color images of the screenshots/diagrams used in this book. The color images will help you better understand the changes in the output. You can download this file from `https://www.packtpub.com/sites/default/files/downloads/Unity5xAnimationCookbook_ColoredImages.pdf`.

Errata

Although we have taken every care to ensure the accuracy of our content, mistakes do happen. If you find a mistake in one of our books—maybe a mistake in the text or the code—we would be grateful if you could report this to us. By doing so, you can save other readers from frustration and help us improve subsequent versions of this book. If you find any errata, please report them by visiting `http://www.packtpub.com/submit-errata`, selecting your book, clicking on the **Errata Submission Form** link, and entering the details of your errata. Once your errata are verified, your submission will be accepted and the errata will be uploaded to our website or added to any list of existing errata under the Errata section of that title.

To view the previously submitted errata, go to `https://www.packtpub.com/books/content/support` and enter the name of the book in the search field. The required information will appear under the **Errata** section.

Piracy

Piracy of copyrighted material on the Internet is an ongoing problem across all media. At Packt, we take the protection of our copyright and licenses very seriously. If you come across any illegal copies of our works in any form on the Internet, please provide us with the location address or website name immediately so that we can pursue a remedy.

Please contact us at `copyright@packtpub.com` with a link to the suspected pirated material.

We appreciate your help in protecting our authors and our ability to bring you valuable content.

Questions

If you have a problem with any aspect of this book, you can contact us at `questions@packtpub.com`, and we will do our best to address the problem.

1
Working with Animations

This chapter explains the essentials of working with animations in Unity and covers the following topics:

- Importing skeletal animations
- Configuring generic and humanoid rigs
- Creating and assigning an Animator Controller
- Creating animation transitions in Animator Controller
- Using parameters to control the animation flow
- Using animations from multiple assets
- Looping mirroring and offsetting animations
- Adjusting the playback speed of animations
- Using override Animator Controllers to animate different types of characters
- Importing object animation from a 3D package

Introduction

Unity is a great game engine that implements the *animate everything* philosophy, which allows you to visualize even the most creative gameplay ideas. Through the course of this book, we will learn a variety of recipes that will help you unleash the power of Unity 5.x animation tools and make your games more fun.

In this first chapter, we will get more familiar with using skeletal animations in Unity. It will guide you through the process of importing such animations, editing them, and assigning them to your in game characters. This knowledge is essential for understanding recipes described in further chapters.

Importing skeletal animations

This first recipe shows how to import a skeletal animation from a 3D package. It assumes that you have an animation already prepared. We are going to bring the file to Unity and show where you can adjust the import settings. We will not jump into too much detail for now to make the import process as quick as possible. We will cover all the settings in further recipes.

Getting ready

Most animations are created in external 3D packages such as Maya, 3ds Max, Motion Builder, or Blender 3D. Make sure you have prepared a 3D model with a skeleton, the model is skinned, and you have created at least one animation. You can also download the provided example; open the project in Unity and go to this folder: Chapter 01 Working with animations\Recipe 01 Importing skeletal animations\Sheep Model. You will find an imported FBX file called Sheep.fbx there.

How to do it...

To import a skeletal animation, you need to follow these steps:

1. Export a skinned model and its skeleton (called **rig** in Unity) to FBX format.

    If you are using Blender, you don't have to manually export the file to FBX format. Simply drag and drop the file to your Assets folder. Unity will use Blender FBX exporter in the background. Additionally, you will be able to open the file by double-clicking on it in Unity. After you edit and save it, Unity will reimport it again. It is a very convenient way of editing animations as you don't have to go through the export-import process each time you make a change.

2. Drag and drop the exported file into any subfolder in the Assets folder in your project or go to **Assets | Import new asset** and choose your FBX file.

3. Select the imported file and navigate to the **Inspector** tab. Click on the **Rig** button:

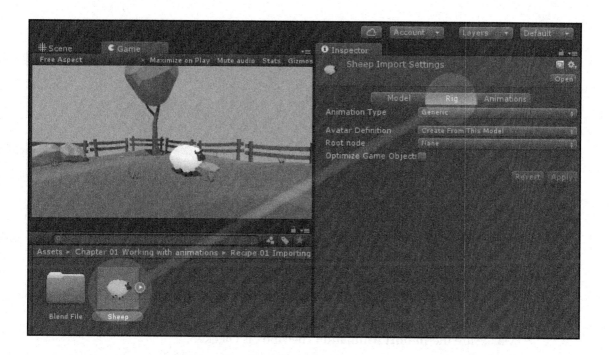

4. Here you can specify the type of the rig to use. For bipedal characters, use the **Humanoid** option, for all the rest choose **Generic**. We use a sheep model in this example, so we need to choose the **Generic** rig. Differences between those options are described in the *How it works* section.

5. Leave all the other inputs as defaults.

6. Click on the **Animations** button. If an **Unapplied import settings** window appears, click on **Apply**.

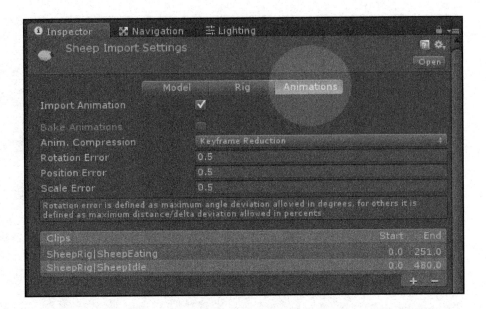

7. Make sure the **Import Animation** checkbox is checked.
8. Click on the **Apply** button in the lower right corner of the **Inspector** (just above the **Animation Preview**). You may need to scroll the **Inspector** down.

9. You should be able to see all imported animation clips as child assets of your imported FBX file.

How it works...

Unity uses four different rig configurations:

- **Generic** rig: This one is used for quadrupeds, spiders, and other non-humanoid characters. It uses Unity's Mecanim system for controlling animation flow. It can use root motion if you provide a **Root node**—a bone responsible for character movement.

- **Humanoid** rig: This one is used for humanoid characters only. It also uses Mecanim system for controlling animation. If you are using **Humanoid** rigs, you have more options for importing animations. The biggest advantage is automatic animation retargeting—you can use the same animation clip on various types of humanoid characters (for example, a dwarf and a troll).

- **Legacy**: This option is used mostly for backward compatibility with previous versions of Unity. It is similar to the **Generic** rig but uses scripts instead of Mecanim for controlling animation flow. I recommend using **Generic** rig instead.

- **None**: This last option turns off the rig and disables animation import.

We will discuss differences between **Generic** and **Humanoid** rigs further in the next recipe.

There's more...

- Imported animation clips are also listed in the **Clips** section of the **Animations** tab.

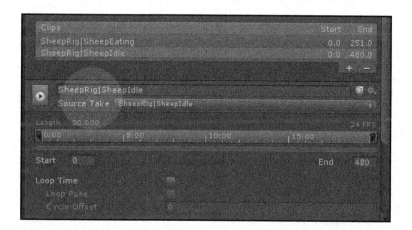

- You can add new clips by clicking on the plus button below the **Clips** section. You can also remove clips by clicking on the minus button.
- You can rename each clip by using the input field above the **Source Take** drop-down menu.
- You can choose the source take (the animation stored in your FBX file) for each animation clip with the **Source Take** drop-down menu.
- You can also trim the animation clip by editing the **Start** and **End** input fields.

If you are using Blender, make sure to rotate the rig *-90* degrees in the *X* axis, apply the rotation in Blender and then rotate it again, *+90* degrees in the *X* axis. The rotation of the rig in Blender should be: *90 X, 0 Y*, and *0 Z*. Your model should be facing the *-Y* axis in Blender (when you change the view to **FRONT**, you should see the face of your character). Blender and Unity use different axes alignment: in Blender, *Z* is up and *Y* is back; in Unity *Z*, is front and *Y* is up. This little trick solves the problem. Your model after import should have 0 rotation and should be facing the *Z* axis. It is important for moving objects (such as characters) and rig configuration. If you don't do this, your model will have *-90 X* rotation after the import.

Configuring generic and humanoid rigs

This recipe shows how to configure two most frequently used rig types: **Generic** and **Humanoid**. We will go through all the available options for both of them.

Getting ready

As previously mentioned, make sure you have prepared two animated characters. One of them should be a humanoid and the other a non-humanoid, a quadruped for instance. You can also download the provided example Unity project and go to the `Chapter 01 Working with animations\Recipe 02 Configuring generic and humanoid rigs\Rigs` directory.

You will find there three FBX files:

- `Generic.fbx`
- `Humanoid.fbx`
- `Quadruped.fbx`

If you are creating your characters from scratch, the bones hierarchy of your humanoid rig is important for Unity to recognize the rig as a humanoid. It should follow this pattern:

```
HIPS -> SPINE -> CHEST -> NECK -> HEAD
HEAD -> EYE (for left and right eyes)
HEAD -> JAW
HIPS -> UPPER LEG -> LOWER LEG -> FOOT -> TOES (for left and right legs)
CHEST -> SHOULDER -> ARM -> FOREARM -> HAND (for left and right hands)
HAND -> PROXIMAL -> INTERMEDIATE -> DISTAL (for five fingers in left and
right hands)
```

The hip bone is the root bone of the humanoid character. Fingers, shoulders, chest, neck, eyes, jaw, and toes are optional bones. Your humanoid character will work without them.

You should also remember to model the character in a T-POSE. It should face the Z axis in Unity (if your 3D software uses different axis alignment from Unity's like Blender, remember about the *-90* and *+90* degrees rotation trick shown in the *Importing skeletal animations* recipe). Hands of the character should be flat, palm down, and parallel to the ground along the X axis. A-POSE characters will also work.

How to do it...

To configure a generic rig you need to follow these steps:

1. Import your animated asset into Unity the same way as in the *Importing skeletal animations* recipe.
2. Select the asset and choose the **Rig** tab in the **Inspector**. Then select the **Generic** option in the **Animation Tab** drop-down menu. If you are using the provided example Unity Project, select the Generic.fbx file in the Chapter 01 Working with animations\Recipe 02 Configuring generic and humanoid rigs\Rigs directory.
3. Choose the **Create From This Model** option from the **Avatar Definition** drop-down menu.
4. Leave the **Root Node** option set to **None**.
5. Leave the **Optimize Game Objects** option unchecked.
6. Click on the **Apply** button to complete the configuration.

Humanoid rig configuration has a lot more options:

1. First, import your skinned humanoid model to Unity the same way as in the *Importing skeletal animations* recipe.
2. Select the asset and choose the **Rig** tab in the **Inspector**. Then select the **Humanoid** option in the **Animation Tab** drop-down menu. If you are using the provided example Unity Project, select the `Humanoid.fbx` file in the `Chapter 01 Working with animations\Recipe 02 Configuring generic and humanoid rigs\Rigs` directory.
3. Choose the **Create From This Model** option from the **Avatar Definition** drop-down menu.
4. Leave the **Optimize Game Objects** option unchecked.
5. Click on the **Apply** button.
6. You should see a **Configure** button with a tick icon near to it.

7. The tick icon shows that Unity was able to automatically recognize the rig hierarchy as a humanoid. If Unity fails to recognize it, automatically a cross will be displayed instead of the tick. If you are using the provided example, you can observe it when you try to set the rig to **Humanoid** for the `Generic.fbx` file.

Some quadruped characters can be mistaken by Unity for humanoids. You can find a `Quadruped.fbx` file in the provided example Unity project. Theoretically, you can set its rig to **Humanoid**, and Unity will recognize it as valid. This, however, is a mistake—all quadruped characters' rigs should be set to **Generic**. Setting them as humanoids can cause problems later.

8. Click on the **Configure** button to enter the **Avatar Configuration Inspector**. A new scene will be opened. You should be able to see your model in the **scene** and bone **mapping** section in the **Inspector** tab.

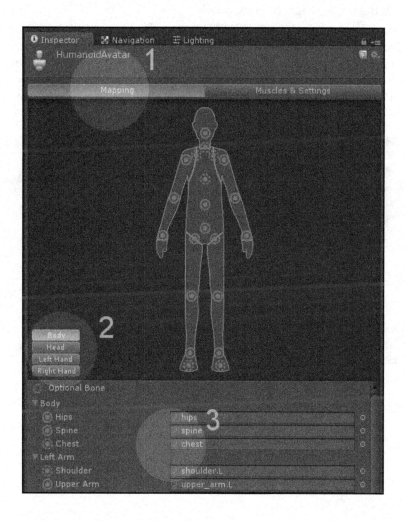

9. Make sure you are in the **Mapping** section (**1**). All recognized and assigned bones are shown as green body parts on the displayed dummy character. If a required bone is missing or is not assigned, it will show up as red. You can navigate between the **Body, Head, Left Hand**, and **Right Hand** sections by clicking on a corresponding button (**2**). All bones are displayed in a list (**3**) for each section. Required bones are marked with circle icons and optional bones are marked with dotted circle icons.

10. You can change the bone assignment by dragging a bone from the **Hierarchy** tab and dropping it onto a corresponding bone slot in the **Inspector** tab. Unity will occasionally miss a bone or two (especially fingers); thus, you should always check the bone assignment manually.

11. If your character is not in a T-POSE (is modeled in an A-POSE for instance), a **Character is not in T-POSE** message will be displayed in the scene view and the character's bones will show up in red. Unity needs the character in a T-POSE for proper humanoid avatar configuration. You can enforce that pose by choosing the **Pose** |**Enforce T-POSE** option, found below the bones **mapping** list.

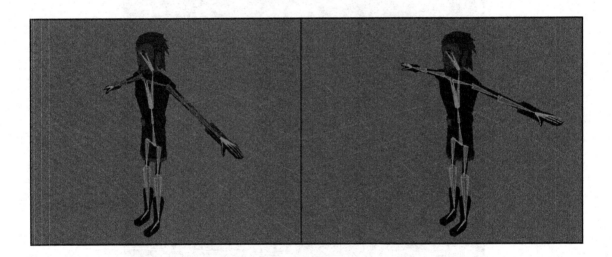

12. Click on the **Apply** button and then the **Done** button to finish configuration.

How it works...

Humanoid rig uses more advanced Mecanim features than the **Generic** rig. You can find the list of such features below:

- **Automatic retargeting**: This is one of the most important differences between those two rigs. The **Humanoid** rig uses automatic retargeting, which means that you can have the same animations on different humanoid characters. Your characters can share a group of animations (basic movement or some common actions). It gives you the possibility to buy your animation assets from the Asset Store and easily use them on your characters. **Generic** rigs don't support this feature. You have to prepare animations for your specific rig or retarget them in a 3D package.

- **Inverse kinematics**: This feature lets you control your characters' feet and hands position with scripting. It is useful for making your characters stand on uneven ground or grab an object in the scene. It is a built-in feature for Humanoid rigs in Unity. **Generic** rigs have to use custom-made solutions.

- **Advanced animation settings**: Humanoid rigs have more settings for animation import, such as the **mirror** option. We will discuss them in depth in the *Looping mirroring and offsetting animations* recipe.

- **Look at**: Unity has a built-in solution for humanoid characters looking at something. You have to write custom systems for generic characters.

- **Additional bones**: A lot of people think that they cannot use additional bones with **Humanoid** rigs. It is not true. If your rig has an animated weapon slot for instance, you can still use it with the **Humanoid** rig. All you need to do is to find the **Mask** section in your animation import settings and enable the additional bone for each animation it is used in (you need to use the **Transform** foldout to find your additional bone).

I highly recommend using **Humanoid** rigs for all humanoid characters in your game.

There's more...

- In the Humanoid rig configuration, you can find the **Muscles & Settings** section, where you can preview and adjust the movement (muscle) range for your character.

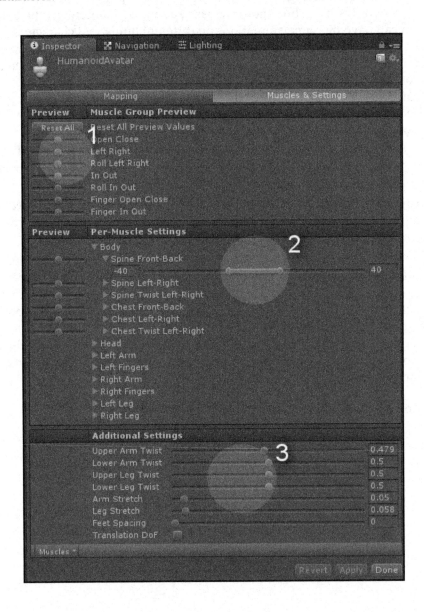

- You can preview the range of movement in the **Muscle Group Preview** section by adjusting the sliders (**1**). You can preview the range of movement per muscle in the **Per-Muscle Settings** section. You can also adjust the range here by unfolding a given muscle foldout and using the slider (**2**). In the **Additional Settings** section, you can adjust more options of your avatar. These are mainly responsible for the *flexibility* of your rig. You can set how much a bone can be stretched during animation for instance.

- The **Translation DoF** option enables animating bones transition in your **Humanoid** rig. It is turned off by default, meaning that only rotation of the bones is used in animation.

- In the **Rig** tab in the **model import settings**, you can find some additional options:

    - **Avatar Definition**: This option is responsible for creating a new avatar or copying the avatar from another model. The second option is useful for storing animations in multiple files. It will be discussed further in the *Using animations from multiple assets* recipe.

    - **Optimize Game Objects**: This option lets you hide all bones from the **Hierarchy** view. The number of game objects in the game has an impact on the performance. You can still choose a number of bones that will be displayed in the **Hierarchy**. It is useful for having exposing weapon slots and similar gameplay-related bones while hiding others.

    - **Root node**: This option is visible only for **Generic** rigs. It lets you choose the bone responsible for root motion calculation. We will discuss it further in `Chapter 4`, *Character Movement*.

Creating and assigning an Animator Controller

Animator Controllers are state machines (graphs) responsible for controlling the flow of animations of any animated object in the game. The same Animator Controller asset can be used by multiple objects or characters. Unity will create an independent runtime copy of the asset for each animated object it is assigned to.

Getting ready

As always, you should have a rigged and animated character ready before we start. Import it into Unity, choose the proper rig type, and put it into a scene. You can download the example Unity project and go to the `Chapter 01 Working with animations\Recipe 03 Creating and assigning an animator controller` directory. There is a scene called `Example.unity` there. If you open it, you'll find a Sheep character in the **Hierarchy**. It has an Animator Controller already created and assigned. You can also use the `Quadruped.fbx` file from the `Chapter 01 Working with animations\Recipe 03 Creating and assigning an animator controller\Rigs` directory to follow the recipe step by step.

How to do it...

To create and assign an Animator Controller, follow these steps:

1. Navigate to the **Project View** (any directory in the `Assets` folder) and press the right mouse button.
2. Choose **Create | Animator Controller** from the menu. A controller asset will be created. You can name it as you wish.
3. Double-click on the created controller. An **Animator** tab will appear. It will show the current selected **Animator Controller**.

4. Here you can add the first animation. Navigate to your imported character in the **Project View**. Unfold it and drag and drop one of the imported animations into the **Animator** window. A new state will be created and will be colored orange, showing that this is the default animation state—the state from which your graph starts.

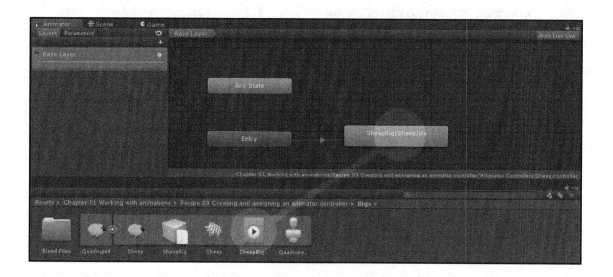

5. Navigate to your character on the scene and select it.

6. Find the Animator component in the **Inspector** tab. All animated objects have an **Animator** component added automatically.

7. Find the **Controller** slot in the **Animator** component inspector.

8. Drag and drop your **Animator Controller** asset into the **Controller** slot of the **Animator** component.

9. Run the game to see your character play the default state animation of your Animator Controller. If the animation is not looped, it will be played just once and then the character will freeze.

10. You can also select your character in runtime and navigate to the **Animator** tab to see what animation state the character is currently in. Current animation state will have a blue progress bar displayed.

How it works...

Every animated object in Unity uses an Animator component and an Animator Controller asset. The component is responsible for playing animations in runtime. It has a number of parameters that we have to set or we can use to tweak the component's functionality:

- **Controller**: This is the field we have to attach the Animator Controller asset to. It determines which animation graph the Animator component will use.

- **Avatar**: In Unity, **Avatars** are rig definitions. For instance, if we have multiple files containing animations with the same **Generic** rig, we should use the same **Avatar** for all of them. You can find more information about it in the *Using animations from multiple assets* recipe.
- **Apply Root Motion**: With this checkbox, we can turn the root motion on and off. It can be useful when we have animations with root motion but don't want to use the root motion definition for a given character.
- **Update Mode**: This parameter tells Unity in which update the animations should be evaluated. The **Normal** option makes the animations synchronized with the normal `Update()` call, the **Animate Physics** option synchronizes animations with the physics `FixedUpdate()` call, and the **Unscaled Time** option synchronizes the animation with the normal `Update()` call, but disables animation time scaling (the animation is played with 100 percent speed regardless of the `Time.timeScale` variable value).
- **Culling Mode**: This parameter tells Unity when to turn off the animation playback on a given Animator. The **Always Animate** option makes the Animator always play animations (event when off-screen), the **Cull Update Transforms** option culls Retarget and IK Transforms when the Animator is not visible on screen, and the **Cull Completely** option disables the animation completely when the Animator is not visible on screen.

The Animator Controller asset stores a graph of animations (animation states) and defines the rules of switching between them, blending them, and so on. The controller (asset) is attached to the component's **Controller** field (the component is attached to a character prefab or a character placed in the scene). Many objects or characters can share the same Animator Controller if they use the same animations (have the same rigs or are humanoid characters).

See also

If you want to learn how to create animation graphs and control their flow, see the next two recipes: *Creating animation transitions in Animator Controller* and *Using parameters to control the animation flow*.

Creating animation transitions in Animator Controller

As mentioned previously, Animator Controllers are state machines containing animations (states). Any given character can be in one such state (play one animation) at a time. To switch between states (animations), you need to create state transitions.

Getting ready

Before we start, you should have an animated model placed on a scene with an Animator Controller assigned. You can find such a model in the provided example Unity project. Go to the `Chapter 01 Working with animations\Recipe 04 Creating animation transitions in Animator Controller` directory. Open the `Example.unity` file. You will find a **Sheep** object in the **Hierarchy**. It has an **Animator Controller** assigned. You can open it by double-clicking on the **Controller** field in the **Animator** component of the **Sheep** game object.

How to do it...

To create a state transition in an Animator Controller, follow these steps:

1. Open the **Animator Controller** asset.
2. Add at least two states by dragging and dropping two animations into the **Animator** window. You can also point the cursor at an empty space in the **Animator** window, press the right mouse button and select **Create State | Empty**, then select the state, and add an animation to the **Motion** field in the **Inspector**.
3. Click on the right mouse button on the state you want to transition from and choose **Make Transition**.
4. Drag the transition onto the state you want to transition to and click the left mouse button.

5. A default transition will be created. The state will switch after its animation has finished playing. To be able to observe it in gameplay, make sure you transition from the default (orange) state, as only the default state will play when the game starts.

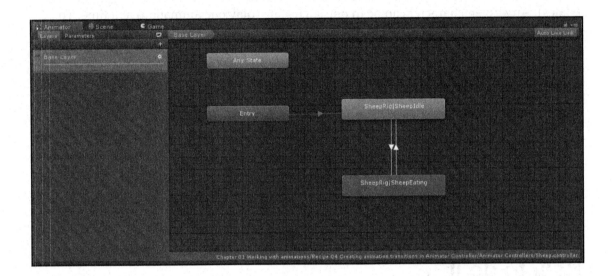

How it works...

State transitions define how we can *travel* through the graph of animations. They are combined with transition conditions based on Animator Controller parameters; we will discuss the parameters in detail in the next recipe: *Using parameters to control the animation flow*. Each transition has a set of properties we can adjust. Click on the transition (white arrow) to select it. You can find the transition properties in the **Inspector** tab (make sure to unfold the **Settings** foldout):

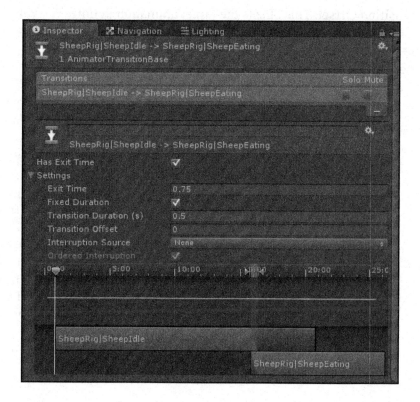

- **Has Exit Time**: If set to true, this enables the transition only after a given percentage of the animation has been already played. If disabled, the transition will take place instantly after its conditions are met. If you want to create a sequence of animations, set it to true.
- **Exit Time**: This is the percentage (0-1 range) of the animation length after which the **Has Exit Time** condition is met. If you set it to 0.5, for instance, the state will transition after 50 percent of the animation was played.
- **Fixed Duration**: This property is combined with the next one, **Transition Duration (s)**. If it's on, the **Transition Duration (s)** is in seconds, and if it's off, the **Transition Duration (s)** is in percentage of the animation time.
- **Transition Duration (s)**: the time of the state transition. This is how long the animations will transition one into another. Animations are being blended together during the transition. Longer transitions are smoother, shorter, are more sharp. A good default value is around 0.25.

- **Transition Offset**: This offsets the target animation in time. The value is in percentage of the animation. Setting it to 0.3 means that the target animation will start from 30 percent of its length instead of the beginning.
- **Interruption Source**: This setting tells Unity whether the transition can be interrupted by other transitions. You can set it to:
  - **None:** the transition cannot be interrupted by any other transition.
  - **Current State:** The transition can be interrupted by transitions from the state we are trying to transition *from*.
  - **Next State:** The transition can be interrupted by transition from the state we are trying to transition *to*.
  - **Current State then Next State:** The transition can be interrupted by the transitions of the state we are trying to transition from or by the transitions of the state we are trying to transition to. The transitions from the state we are trying to transition *from* take the priority.
  - **Next State then Current State:** The transition can be interrupted by the transitions of the state we are trying to transition from or by the transitions of the state we are trying to transition to. The transitions from the state we are trying to transition *to* take the priority.
  - **Ordered Interruption:** If set to false, this lets the transition be interrupted by other transitions independently of their order. If set to true, the order of the transitions matters.

There's more...

When you create an Animator Controller, you can see three more nodes apart from your animation states:

- **Entry and Exit**: This node is used when you transition between state machines (Animator Controllers or substate machines). We will discuss it in detail in the *Using Sub-State Machines in Animator Controller* recipe in Chapter 6, *Handling Combat*.
- **Any state**: This node can be used as a helper to make a transition from any state to a given state. It is used when you have an animation that can be played anytime, for instance, a hit animation. We will discuss it in detail in the *Using transitions from any state to play hit reactions* recipe in Chapter 6, *Handling Combat*.

Using parameters to control the animation flow

You can define a set of parameters in an Animator Controller and use them to control the transitions between animation states in Mecanim. In this recipe, we will show how to use parameters for transition conditions and use scripts to set values of those parameters in runtime.

Getting ready

Before we start, you should prepare an Animator Controller with at least one transition between animation states. The controller should be assigned to a character (its Animator component) placed in a scene. You can also use the provided example Unity project and go to the Chapter 01 Working with animations\Recipe 05 Using parameters to control the animation flow directory. You will find an Example.unity scene there. There is a **Warrior** game object in the scene's **Hierarchy**. If you run the game and press the space bar, the **Warrior** will make a wave gesture. You can select the **Warrior** and open his **Animator Controller**. If you click on the **Idle | Wave** transition, you will be able to see the transition condition.

How to do it...

To use parameters for controlling state transitions, follow these steps:

1. Open the **Animator Controller** asset.
2. Find the **Parameters** tab in the upper left corner of the **Animator** window and click on it.
3. Click on the plus icon in the **Parameters** tab to add a new parameter.
4. Choose the **Trigger** type for the parameter.
5. Type a name of the newly created parameter (in the provided example, the name of the parameter is Wave).
6. Click on the transition between states you want to use parameters for. In the provided example, it is the transition between **Idle** and **Wave** animation states. **Idle** is the default state.
7. Go to the **Inspector** tab and find the **Conditions** section.

8. Click on the plus icon to add a new condition. If you have only one parameter, it will be chosen as the condition automatically. If you have more parameters, you need to choose the proper one from a drop-down list.

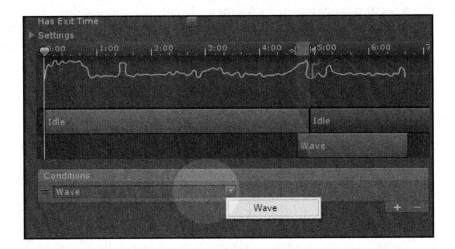

9. If you want to make an immediate transition between your animation states, make sure to disable the **Has Exit Time** option, found above the **Settings** foldout.

10. Your transition will take place only when its conditions are met. You need to set the parameter using scripts.

11. To create a new C# script, click on the right mouse button in the **Project View** and select **Create | C# Script**. Name the script as you wish (in the provided example, it's called `Wave`, the same as the parameter it sets).

12. Open the script and write the following:

```
using UnityEngine;
using System.Collections;

public class Wave : MonoBehaviour {
//The anim variable is used to store the reference
//to the Animator component of the character.
private Animator anim;
void Start () {
//We get the component and assign it to
//the anim variable when the game starts
anim = GetComponent<Animator>();
}
void Update () {
//We check if player pressed the spacebar
```

```
if (Input.GetKeyDown(KeyCode.Space))
{
/*We cal the SetTrigger() function on the
Animator component stored in the anim
variable. The function requires one
parameter - the name of the trigger
parameter set in our Animator Controller
("Wave" in our example). Make sure to match
it with the name of the parameter you've
created in your Animator Controller*/
anim.SetTrigger("Wave");
}
}
}
```

13. Make sure your class name is the same as the file name of the script, as it won't compile otherwise.

14. Assign the script to the character, to the same **Transform** that has the **Animator** component with your **Animator Controller** attached. Play the game and press the space bar; you should see your character switch to the next animation state.

How it works...

You can use several types of parameters and corresponding script functions to set them:

- **Trigger**: This is the simplest parameter. It is set to *true* with the `SetTrigger(string name)` function called on the **Animator** component object. It is reset by the **Animator Controller** after it is consumed (used) by a transition. The `string name` parameter of the function has to match your trigger parameter name set in the **Animator Controller**.

- **Int**: This is an integer parameter. When you use it, you have to specify a logical comparison in the condition. The transition will only occur if the value of the parameter meets the comparison condition with a given number. You can use the **Equal, Greater, Less**, and **Not Equal** options to compare the value of your parameter with the given number. Integer type parameters are set with the `SetInteger(string name, int value)` function. The `string name` parameter needs to match the parameter name set in the controller. The `int value` parameter is the value to set the controller parameter to.

- **Float**: This is a float parameter. It works the same as the integer type, but uses floating point numbers instead of integers. It is set using the `SetFloat(string name, float value)` function.

- **Bool**: This is a Boolean parameter. The condition can check if the parameter is true or false. The value of the parameter is set with the `SetBool(string name, bool value)` function.

There's more...

- You can add more than one condition to a state transition by clicking on the plus icon in the **Conditions** section in the transition **Inspector**. For the transition to occur, all its conditions have to be met. It works as logical *AND* for the conditions.

- You can also create more than one transition between the same states. To do this, right-click on the state you want to transition from and choose the **Make Transition** option, and then select the state you already have a transition to. A multi-transition is marked with three arrows instead of one. If the conditions of any of the transitions are met, the transition will occur. You can use it as logical *OR* for transition conditions.

- If you have more than one transition between states, you can only edit one of them at a time. To edit a transition, select it in the **Transitions** section of the **Inspector**.

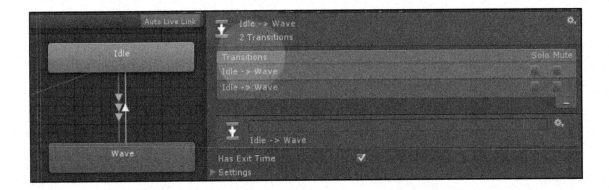

- If you want to remove a transition, select it in the **Inspector** and click on the minus icon, or select it in the **Animator Controller** and press *Delete* on the keyboard. Pressing *Delete* removes all the transitions.

- If you want to remove a condition from a transition, select it in the **Inspector** tab and click on the minus icon. To select a condition, you need to click on the handle to the left of the condition drop-down list (the handle looks like a = sign).
- If you want to remove a parameter from the **Animator Controller**, you need to click on the handle on the left of the parameter and press the *Delete* button on the keyboard. You can also right-click on the parameter and choose the **Delete** option from the context menu.

Using animations from multiple assets

At times it is very convenient to separate animations to multiple assets. A common scenario is to have rigged models separated from animations or different animation types separated from each other (combat from movement, movement from actions, actions from cut scenes, and so on). This recipe shows how to do it for both **Humanoid** and **Generic** rigs.

Getting ready

Before we start, you should prepare and import at least two assets containing animations. If you are using a **Generic** rig, make sure to have the same rig in both assets. You can also use the provided example Unity project and go to the `Chapter 01 Working with animations\Recipe 06 Using animations from multiple assets`. There is a scene called `Example.unity` file there. In the scene **Hierarchy** you can find a **Character** game object. It has an attached **Animator Controller** in which you can find two animations: **Idle** and **Wave**. In the **Rigs** directory, you will find the `Character.fbx` asset containing only a rigged character along with the `Idle.fbx` and `Wave.fbx` assets containing the corresponding animations.

If you are exporting FBX files from Blender, make sure to disable the **Add Leaf Bones** option in the **exporter**. If you are exporting just the rig and animations (without a mesh), add an empty object to the scene. If you will not do this, your rig could be messed up a bit after import.

How to do it...

To use animations from multiple assets, you need to follow these steps:

1. Import the files to Unity.
2. If you are using the Generic rig, you have to set the **Avatar Definition** to **Create From This Model** on your character (or reference character if you plan to have multiple characters with the same rig). For each imported animation asset, set the **Avatar Definition** to **Copy From Other Avatar** and choose the avatar of your character or reference character. To do so, you need to unfold the character asset, find the avatar, and drag and drop it to the **Source** field in the **Inspector** tab.

3. If you are using a **Humanoid** rig, you don't have to copy the **Avatar Definition** (you still can if your rigs are exactly the same; that way you will have fewer avatars in your project, making it easier to find the ones you need).
4. Create or open an **Animator Controller**.
5. Assign animations from different files and build transitions between them.
6. Run the game to see the animations work.

How it works...

All **Generic** rigs can use animations from multiple assets that share the same **Avatar Definition**. To share the same **Avatar Definition**, **Generic** rigs have to have exactly the same rigs (the same hierarchy, the same bone names and transforms). All **Humanoid** rigs can use animations from multiple assets that are also set to **Humanoid**. Additionally, they don't need to have the same rigs because Unity automatically retargets all humanoid animations.

Looping, mirroring and offsetting the animations

Unity allows editing the animations to some extent after they're imported. It can save a lot of work and greatly speed up your workflow.

Getting ready

Before we start, you should prepare and import a **Humanoid** rig with at least one animation. You can also use the provided example Unity project and go to the `Chapter 01 Working with animations\Recipe 07 Looping mirroring and offsetting animations` directory. There is a scene called `Example.file` there. In the scene **Hierarchy**, you can find a **Mirror** game object. It has an attached **Animator Controller** in which you can find two animations: **Wave** and **WaveMirror**. In the **Rigs** directory, you will find the `Mirror.fbx` asset. If you select it and go to the **Inspector**, and to the **Animations** tab, you can find normal and mirrored animation examples, as well as looped animation examples (**Idle** and **IdleMirror**).

How to do it...

To set an animation to *loop*, you need to go through the following steps:

1. Select the animated asset and go to the **Animations** tab.
2. Check the **Loop Time** checkbox and click on the **Apply** button. The animation is looped.
3. If your animation's first and last frames don't match perfectly, you can force them to match with the **Loop Pose** checkbox. It is not recommended to use this option for animations that have matching first and last frames.

To *offset* an animation, you need to go through the following steps:

1. Select the animated asset and go to the **Animations** tab.
2. Select your animation and make it loop (**Loop Time** checkbox).
3. Enter a value in the **Cycle Offset** field, below the **Loop Pose** checkbox.
4. Click on the **Apply** button.

To *mirror* an animation, you need to go through the following steps:

1. Select the animated **Humanoid** asset and go to the **Animations** tab.
2. Find the **Mirror** checkbox on the bottom of the animation settings.
3. Check the **Mirror** checkbox and click on the **Apply** button. The animation is mirrored.
4. Mirroring animations works only for **Humanoid** rigs.

How it works...

- **Looping animations**: This is a common technique used for all cyclic movements (walk and run cycles, idle animations, and so on). If you don't set an animation to loop, it will play once and freeze on the last frame.
- **Offsetting animations**: Sometimes it is convenient to offset the cycle of a looped animation. It is often used with the **Mirror** option for steering animations (clips used to turn the character while moving). We will be showing that in the *Using root motion to steer a character* recipe in Chapter 4, *Character Movement*.
- **Mirroring animations**: This option works only with **Humanoid** rigs. It is used to flip the animation left to right and can save up to 50 percent of steering animations when combined with the **Offset Cycle** option.

There's more...

You can also mirror and offset animation states in the **Animator Controller**. If you select an animation state and go to the **Inspector** tab, you can find the **Mirror** and **Cycle Offset** options. There is also an option to use **Animator Controller** parameters to switch the **Mirror** option on and off and set the **Cycle Offset**. You need to have a Boolean parameter defined for the **Mirror** option and a float parameter for the **Cycle Offset**. Those settings will be automatically synchronized with the parameters. Whenever you change a parameter value, the setting will also be changed.

Adjusting the playback speed of animations

Unity allows you to slow down and speed the animation playback in the **Animator Controller**. You can do it in runtime with scripts to achieve interesting effects, for instance, slow motion.

Getting ready

Before we start, you should prepare and import a rig with at least one animation and create an **Animator Controller** with at least one animation state for it. You can also use the provided example Unity project and go to the Chapter 01 Working with animations\Recipe 08 Adjusting the playback speed of animationsdirectory. There is a scene called Example.unity there. In the scene **Hierarchy**, you can find and **AdjustSpeed** game object. It has an attached **Animator Controller** in which you can find two animation states: **WaveSpeedNormal** and **WaveSpeedIncreased**. There is also an **AdjustSpeedByScript** game object in the scene. You can increase the playback speed of its animations by pressing the **Space** button on your keyboard in runtime.

How to do it...

To change the animation playback speed, follow these steps:

1. Open an **Animator Controller**.
2. Select an animation state.
3. Go to the animation state Inspector and find the **Speed** parameter below the **Motion** field.
4. Enter a number in the **Speed** parameter to change the playback speed.

How it works...

The **Speed** parameter set for an animation state in the **Animator Controller** multiplies the speed playback of the animation state. Setting this parameter to zero will freeze the animation.

There's more...

You can also set the parameter using scripts. Following is an example script (it is used by the `AdjustSpeedByScript` game object in the provided `Example.unity`). You can assign it to your animated game object that has the **Animator** component and an **Animator Controller** attached:

```
using UnityEngine;
using System.Collections;

public class AdjustSpeedByScript : MonoBehaviour {
//This is a variable, in which we store the reference to the
Animator component
private Animator anim;
//We store the wanted animation speed in this variable, the
default value is 2 (200%).

public float newAnimationSpeed = 2f;
void Start () {
//At the start of the game we assign the Animator
component to our anim variable
anim = GetComponent<Animator>();
}
void Update () {
//We check if player pressed the Space button
if (Input.GetKeyDown(KeyCode.Space)) {
//And set the playback speed of the whole Animator
Controller (it multiplies all states animation
playback speed)

anim.speed = newAnimationSpeed;
}
}
}
```

If you want to change the speed of just one animation state, then add a float parameter to your **Animator Controller**, use this parameter in the **Multiplier** field in the animation state **Inspector**, and change the parameter with scripts using the following function:

```
anim.SetFloat(string name, float value);
```

Here name is the name of your parameter in the **Animator Controller** and value is the float value you want to set the parameter and playback speed to.

Using override animator controllers to animate different types of characters

If you have multiple types of character in your game, most probably you would like to be able to share the animation states logic between them and just replace the animation clips. Imagine that you have several types of enemies, and their combat logic is the same (they have attacks, movement, hit reactions, and so on) but they use different animation clips. For such situations, **Override Animator Controllers** come in handy.

Getting ready

You should have at least two characters with different animation clips ready and imported into Unity. You can also download the provided example Unity project and go to the `Chapter 01 Working with animations\Recipe 09 Using override animator controllers to animate different types of characters` directory. There is a scene called `Example.unity` there. If you open it, you'll find **Warrior** and **Spider** game objects in the **Hierarchy**. They have **Override Animator Controllers** attached, and you can examine them. If you run the game, the characters will play attack animations. The underlying logic is defined in the **HumanCombat** controller (found in the **Animator Controllers** directory). The **Warrior** game object uses the **HumanCombat** controller without overriding it, the **Spider** game object uses a **SpiderCombat** override controller.

How to do it...

To use **Override Animator Controllers**, follow these steps:

1. Create a normal **Animator Controller** that will be used as the reference controller containing the logic of animation states. In the provided example, it is the **HumanCombat** controller, created with **Warrior** animations.
2. You can attach this controller to your first character (its **Animator** component) and use it as previously.
3. Create an **Override Animator Controller** by right-clicking on the **Project View** and choosing **Create | Override Animator Controller**.
4. Select the newly created override controller and go to the **Inspector** tab.
5. Drag and drop your original/reference **Animator Controller** to the **Controller** field of the newly created override controller.
6. You will see all your original animation clips listed on the left and fields for overriding those animation clips.

7. Drag and drop the animation clips from your second character to the override fields corresponding with original animation clips of your first character. In the provided example, **Human** animations are replaced with **Spider** animations.

8. Assign the **Override Animator Controller** to the **Controller** field of the **Animator** component of your second character.

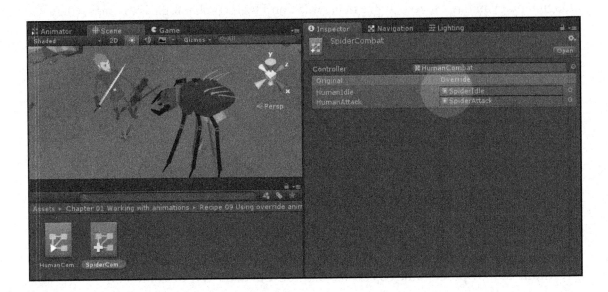

How it works...

Override Animator Controller only replace animation clips from your original **Animator Controller**. The logic of the original controller stays the same (so you can also use the same scripts to set the same parameters and so on). It is extremely useful for creating NPC characters in your games. You create the **Animator Controller** once, you write the scripts driving the controller once and only change the animations.

Your original **Animator Controller** has to have animation clips. You cannot override empty animation states.

Importing object animation from a 3D package

In Unity, you can import not only skeletal animation but also object transform animation. It can be useful for creating complex movements, for instance, an object following a path.

Getting ready

You have to animate an object's translation, rotation, or scale in a 3D package, then export the object as FBX file. You can also download the provided example Unity project and go to the `Chapter 01 Working with animations\Recipe 10 Importing object animation from a 3D package` directory. There is a scene called `Example.unity` there. This object has a follow path animation created in Blender and exported to FBX file. It has a normal Animator Controller with that animation as default state (looped). You can run the game to see the object animate.

How to do it...

To import object animation, follow these steps:

1. Animate an object in a 3D package (translation, rotation, and scale animations are supported).
2. Import the object into Unity and select the **Generic** rig type.
3. You can adjust animation settings normally (loop an animation for instance).
4. Create an **Animator Controller** and drag and drop one of the imported animations into the **Animator** window to create a default animation state.
5. Place your animated object into a scene and assign the controller to the **Animator** component of the object.
6. If you run the game, the object will be animated.

How it works...

Unity imports translation, rotation, and scale animation of 3D objects from a 3D package. It makes it easy to create complex animations and use advanced features of a chosen 3D software. Make sure to bake your animations into frames before importing them to Unity (Blender bakes the exported animations to frames by default). Importing mesh animation (vertices movement) is not supported (you have to use **Blend Shapes** instead; we will discuss them in detail in the *Animating facial expressions with Blend Shapes* recipe in `Chapter 5`, *Character Actions and Expressions*).

2
Working with the Animation View

This chapter explains the **Animation View**, which is an essential tool in Unity's animation workflow, and the following topics are covered in this chapter:

- Using the Animation View to create a flickering light
- Blending light colors with the Animation View and the Animator Controller
- Animating object's world position – creating a moving platform
- Animating object's local position – creating automatic doors
- Using the Hierarchy to animate local rotation – creating an orbiting planet
- Animating triggers – creating a death trap
- Creating an elevator triggered by player input

Introduction

In the first chapter, we imported animations from external 3D packages to Unity. Now we will learn how to use Unity's powerful built-in tool called the Animation View. It allows us to animate almost everything within the editor and can be used to create interesting gameplay mechanisms. Knowledge of this tool is essential to learn future recipes as we will use Animation View a lot.

Using the Animation View to create a flickering light

This first recipe shows how to make a basic animation inside Unity. We will animate a light-intensity value to create an interesting flickering light effect, which is often found in horror or sci-fi games.

Getting ready

Before we start, you need to have a scene with geometry and at least one light. You can also download the example provided; open the project in Unity and go to the folder Chapter 02 Working with the animation view\Recipe 01 Using the animation view to create a flickering light. You will find a scene called Example.unity there, with a point light that has already been animated.

How to do it...

To use the Animation View and create a flickering light, follow these steps:

1. Open the scene and select a light you want to animate.
2. With the light selected, go to **Window** | **Animation**. The Animation View will open.
3. To create a new animation, click on the **Create** button, as shown in the following screenshot:

4. A **Create New Animation Clip** will appear. You can choose a directory and the animation name. Then, click the **Save** button.

5. A new, empty animation will be created, an **Animator** component will be added to the selected game object (a light in this example), and an Animator Controller will be created in the same directory as the animation clip.

6. To animate the light intensity, we need to add an **Intensity** property. Click on the **Add Property** button in the Animation View, then choose **Light | Intensity**, and then click on the + icon next to it, as shown in the following screenshot:

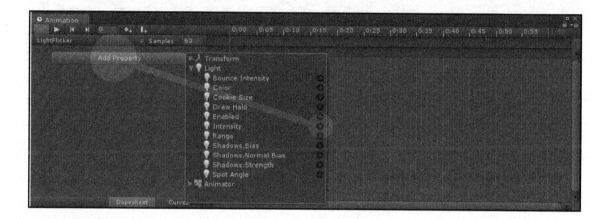

7. Two key frames will be added. You can click and drag on them to adjust their position in time. You can also add new key frames by changing any property in the light game object's **Inspector** (make sure to have the record button clicked in the upper-left corner of the **Animation** View).

8. Add several key frames with different values of light intensity.

9. Close the **Animation** View when the animation is done. Any changes will be saved automatically.

10. Play the game to see the effect.

How it works…

The Animation View is divided into three main parts, as shown in the following screenshot:

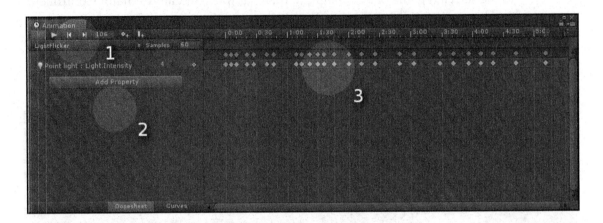

- **Playback buttons** (1): Here you can play back the animation on your scene (you do not have to enter **Play Mode** to see your animation). On the right to the play back buttons, you can find an **Insert Key Frame** button and an **Insert Animation Event** button. You can use the first one to insert key frames; the second one inserts **Animation Events** that allow to call script functions from an animation (Animation Events will be covered later in Chapter 6, *Handling Combat*). Just below the playback buttons, you can find a drop-down menu, with which you can switch between this object's animations and add new ones.

- **Animated properties** (2): Here you can find all the properties of the game object used by this animation. You can also click on the **Add Property** button to add new properties to the animation.

- **Timeline (3)**: It represents the time in the animation. You can find all the key frames (and animation events) here. You can click on the timeline header (the one with time displayed in seconds) to go to the frame you clicked on. If you click on a key frame instead, the timeline will automatically jump to that exact key frame.

When you create an animation in the Animation View for the first time for a given game object, a new **Animation Clip** and an Animation Controller are created. The Animator Controller is automatically assigned to the game object you are animating and the Animation Clip is added to the Animator Controller. Any new animation created for the same game object will be added to the same Animator Controller automatically.

There's more...

The timeline of the Animation View has two modes (you can switch between them by clicking on the corresponding buttons on the bottom of the properties section):

- **Dope Sheet**: This mode displays key frames in the timeline.
- **Curves**: With this mode, you can adjust the interpolation curves of the animation. When you click on a property, its animation curves will be displayed. You can manipulate the handles to adjust the shape of the curves. You can also right-click on any handle to change its tangent type, as shown in the following screenshot:

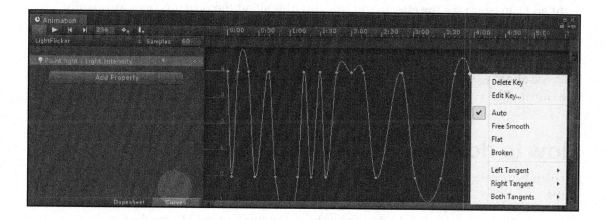

- All Animation Clips created in the Animation View are looped by default. To change this, find the Animation Clip asset, select it, and disable the **Loop Time** checkbox in its **Inspector**.
- All the animations are created for selected game objects in the Hierarchy. To view an object animation, you need to select it and open the **Animation** View.
- If you have multiple Animator components in your object's **Hierarchy**, a new Animator Controller will be created for each Animator component. It may be useful to create different animations for different objects in the **Hierarchy** and play them simultaneously. For example, you can have a 2D sprite character with its head and body as separate game objects. You can use two Animator components: one for the body, one for the head. If you choose so, you will be able to create facial expressions independently of the body animation.

Blending light colors with the Animation View and the Animator Controller

This recipe shows how to use Animation Controllers with the clips created in Animation View.

Getting ready

We will animate the light color in this example. You need to have a scene with at least one light and a mesh to see the effect. You can also download the provided example Unity project and go to the `Chapter 02 Working with the animation view\Recipe 02 Using the animation view and the animator controller to blend light colors` directory. You will find a scene called `Example.unity` there, with a direction light that has already been animated. In this example, we also animate the background color of the camera (the camera is a child object of the directional light).

How to do it...

To blend animations (colors in this example) of a game object, you need to follow these steps:

1. Open the scene and select the light game object in the **Hierarchy**.
2. With the light selected, go to **Window | Animation** to open the **Animation** View and create at least two animations the same way as in the *Using Animation View to create a flickering light recipe,* but this time set the color property instead of the light's intensity. In our example, we have two Animation Clips: **Day** and **Night**. They just set the color of the directional light: **Day** sets it to bright yellow and **Night** to dark blue. There is no change in the light color over time. Each animation has two key frames with the exact same color value in each key frame (this color is different for each animation). Each animation lasts for about 7 seconds.
3. An Animator Controller will be created automatically.

4. Open the Animator Controller and create two transitions between our animations, one going from **Day** to **Night** and one from **Night** to **Day**, as shown in the following screenshot:

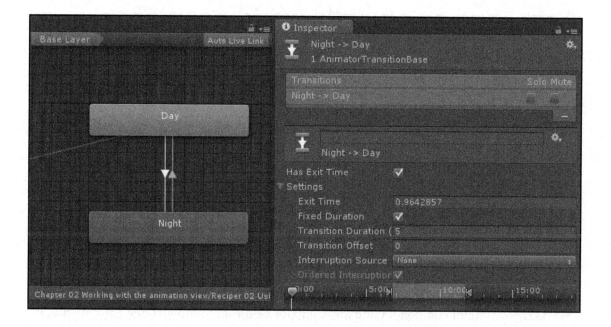

5. Those animations are looped, so you can set the **Transition Duration** to around 5 seconds to make the effect more subtle. You can set the **Transition Duration** in the **Settings** foldout in the **Inspector** after you select the transition.

6. Make sure that the **Has Exit Time** option is selected as we do not use any other conditions in this example. You can also add your own conditions and use scripts to trigger them.

7. Play the game to see the effect.

How it works...

The purpose of this recipe is to show one very important feature of the Unity animation system: the Animator Controller can blend Color, Vector3, Quaternion, bool, and float values stored in Animation Clips. The Int and string values are not supported and cannot be animated. You can only animate public MonoBehaviour script variables and Unity component properties.

You do not have to always animate the properties of a game object. Using the transitions in the Animator Controller will create a smooth blend between them.

Animating an object's world position – creating a moving platform

In this recipe, we will create a very common gameplay mechanism: a moving platform. We will use a Rigid body for our character and an animated, kinematic Rigid body for the platform.

Getting ready

Before we start, you should have a scene with your character and a platform you want to animate. You can use the example project; go to the `Chapter 02 Working with the animation view\Recipe 03 Animating objects world position – creating a moving platform` directory. There is a scene called `Example.unity` there. If you open it, you will find a **Sheep** character in the **Hierarchy**. This is our character, using the **Rigidbody** component and a Simple Move script to move. There is also a **Moving Platform** game object in the **Hierarchy**. This is the kinematic rigid body with a `Platform` script attached to it. It also has an Animator component and an Animator Controller with just one animation in it. This animation makes the platform move.

How to do it...

To create and assign an animated moving platform, follow these steps:

1. Select your platform game object in the **Hierarchy**.
2. Open the **Animation** View.
3. Make sure the record button is pressed (in the upper-left corner of the **Animation** View).
4. Move the platform to the desired position in the first frame.
5. Adjust the timeline a few seconds forward and move your platform to new destination.

6. To make the animation loop, select the first key frame and press *Ctrl + C* (*cmd + C* on Mac). Then adjust the timeline forward from the second key frame, the same amount of seconds like the previous step. If the first key frame is on the 0 seconds mark and the second on the 10 seconds mark, set the timeline to 20 seconds mark. Press *Ctrl + V* to paste the copied key frame. In our example, the platform is going from one floating island to another and back. It also has some pauses on each end to make it easier for the player to jump on to it.

7. When you are happy with your animation, exit the **Animation** View.

8. An Animator Controller will be created and an Animation Clip will be assigned to it automatically. Also, an Animator component will be added to the platform game object.

9. Find the Animator Controller on the platform game object and set the **Update Mode** property to **Animate Physics**. Set the **Culling Mode** to **Always Animate**.

10. Add a **Rigidbody** component to the platform and select the **Kinematic** checkbox.

11. Add a collider component (a **Mesh Collider** or a **Box Collider**) to your platform. If you are using a **Mesh Collider**, make sure to select the **Convex** checkbox.

12. Create a new script, and name the file `Platform.cs`.

13. Open the script and write the following code:

```
using UnityEngine;
using System.Collections;

public class Platform : MonoBehaviour {

/*This function is called by Unity every time this object
starts to collide with any other game object with a Collider
component attached.The Collision collisionInfo object
parameter stores the information about the collision and the
object we are colliding with.*/

    void OnCollisionEnter(Collision collisionInfo)
    {
/*We are checking if the object we are colliding with
has a RigidBody component and the RigidBody is not set
to kinematic. Optionally we can also check the tag of
the object we are colliding with here (to make it work
only for the player for instance).*/
        if (collisionInfo.rigidbody != null
        && !collisionInfo.rigidbody.isKinematic)
        {
/*We are setting the parent of the object we are
colliding with to the platform game object (the
object out script is attached to).This will make
our character move with the platform instead of
```

```
    slide from it.*/
        collisionInfo.transform.parent = transform;


    }
}

/*This function is called by Unity every time this object stop
colliding with any object with a Collider component attached.
The CollisionInfo collision info parameter stores the same
information as in the OnCollisionEnter function.*/

    void OnCollisionExit(Collision collisionInfo)
    {

/*We are checking the same conditions as before*/

        if (collisionInfo.rigidbody != null
        && !collisionInfo.rigidbody.isKinematic)
        {
        /*We are setting the parent of the object we are
colliding with to null. The object has no parent
        at all and stops moving with the platform*/
            collisionInfo.transform.parent = null;
        }
    }
}
```

14. Attach the script to the platform game object and play the game to see the effect.
15. This moving platform will work with characters using **Rigidbody** components to move. You can import the `ThirdPersonCharacter` prefab from Unity's `Standard Assets`. You can also write your own simple character movement. To do so, see the *There's more section*.

How it works...

This is the most simple but working moving platform solution. It uses a few key elements:

- **Animation-driven movement**: The platform is moved only by the Animation Clip created with the Animation View. This allows you to experiment with the movement easily.

- **Kinematic Rigid body**: To animate a game object with a **Rigidbody** component attached, you need to set the **Kinematic** checkbox to true. It completely disables the physics of the Rigid Body. You can still animate the object with **Kinematic** set to false, but physics will still have an impact on the movement (the object will not be able to penetrate other objects, it will rotate on collisions, and so on).

- **Animate Physics option**: Set in the **Update Mode** parameter of the **Rigidbody** component. This option makes the Rigid body to be animated in the physics loop (you can think of it as the `FixedUpdate()` function equivalent). It prevents the Rigid Bodies colliding with this object to jitter and behave in strange ways.

- **Animation in world space**: Our platform is animated in world coordinates. This means that the animation sets the object's position regarding the scene's 0x, 0y, 0z point. It does not matter where the object is placed in the scene; after playing the animation, it will be placed in the positions stored in the animation's key frames. We will discuss local space animation in the *Animating object's local position – creating automatic doors* recipe.

- **Moving platform as a parent to the character**: We are setting the platform as the parent to the in-game character, which collides with it. Rigid bodies parented to other **Transforms** try to move with them in game. This is the easiest and rather bulletproof way of making our character move with/relative to the platform game object. And because the platform moves with the **Update Mode** set to **Animate Physics**, no jittering will occur. Instead of parenting the character to the platform, you could also experiment with creating a physical material with appropriate friction, or write your own custom solution that would add the platform's speed to the character's speed.

There's more...

In the provided example, we created our own script for moving the character using a **Rigidbody** component. You can find the script in the `Shared scripts` directory. It is called `SimpleMove.cs`. To make your character move:

1. Add a collider component (we use a **Sphere Collider** in the example) and a **Rigidbody** component to it.
2. Create a zero friction `Physics Material` and assign it to the collider component.
3. Set the **Rigidbody** component **Constraints** to **Freeze Rotation** in the X, Y, and Z axes.
4. Create an empty game object, position it around 0.2 units above the character's feet, and parent it to the character. Name it `GroundCheck` for clarity.

5. Attach the script to the character's game object. Attach the `GroundCheck` game object to the `Ground Check Transform` field of the `Simple Move` script component.

6. If you want your character to have an animation, create an Animator Controller with `float Speed`, `bool Ground`, and `Trigger Jump` parameters. Prepare idle, walk, and jump animations. Idle and walk should be looped, jump should end in the air.

7. Create a transition between idle and run using the `Speed` parameter with the `Speed > 0.1` condition.

8. Create a transition between run and idle using the `Speed` parameter with the `Speed < 0.1` condition.

9. Create transitions from run and idle to jump using the `Jump` trigger parameter.

10. Create transitions from jump to run and idle using the `Ground` and `Speed` parameters. Conditions should check if `Ground` is true and if `Speed < 0.1` (transition to idle) or `Speed > 0.1` (transition to run).

11. Attach the Animator Controller to your character.

12. Parent the game camera to your character or use the provided `CameraFollow.cs` script found in the Shared scripts directory. You can also use one of the camera scripts found in Unity's **Standard Assets.**

Animating object's local position – creating automatic doors

In this recipe, we will learn how to animate an object's local position to be able to use the same animated object in multiple locations in the scene. We will create another common gameplay mechanism, automatic door, as an example.

Getting ready

To make an animated door, you should have two objects ready: the **Door Frame** and the **Door**. The **Door** should be a child of the **Frame** in the **Hierarchy**. It should be placed in the *closed position*. We assume that our **Door** will slide upward when opening. You should also have a player character with the `Player` tag assigned. The character should use a **Rigidbody** component to move or have a kinematic **Rigidbody** component. We will use triggers for our doors, and triggers react to Rigid bodies only. You can also go to the `Chapter 02 Working with the animation view\Recipe 04 Animating objects local position - creating automatic doors` directory and find the `Example.unity` scene there. If you open it, you can find **Automatic Door** game object in the **Hierarchy** and a **Sheep** game object that will work as our player (it has the `Player` tag). If you run the game and go near the door, it will open.

How to do it...

To create automatic doors, follow these steps:

1. Select your **Door Frame** game object, and add an Animator component to it. To do so, click on the **Add Component** button in the **Inspector** and choose **Animator**. Make sure to add the component to the **Door Frame** instead of the **Door** (the parent instead of the child). Set the **Update Mode** of the **Animator** component to **Animate Physics**.

2. With the **Door Frame** game object selected, go to **Window | Animation** to open the **Animation** View.

3. Create a new Animation Clip and call it `Closed`; this will be our animation for the closed door. To create a new clip, click on the drop-down list below the playback buttons and choose the **Create New Clip** option.

4. Click on the **Add Property** button and find your **Door** object in the list (a child of the **Door Frame** game object).

5. Unfold the **Door** game object foldout and find the **Transform** section. Unfold it and click on the plus icon near the **Position** property, as shown in the following screenshot:

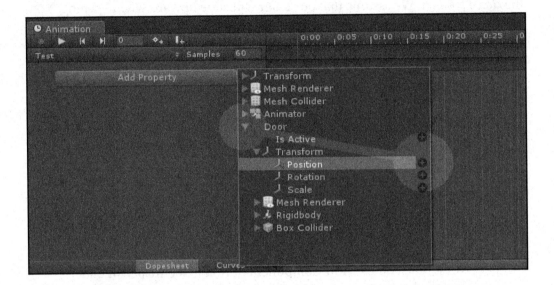

6. Two key frames will be added for the **Door** game object's local position. We are not going to adjust them (assuming that the **Door** is in the closed position).

7. Add another Animation Clip and name it Door Opening.

8. Click on the **Add Property** button, choose your door game object, and add the **Transform | Position** key the same way as in step 5.

9. Move the second key frame to around the 3 second mark.

10. Select the **Door** game object (the child of the **Door** Frame).

11. Move it up to the open position. Make sure the record button is active (in the upper-left corner of the **Animation** View). If you play the animation, it should move the **Door** game object up.

12. Select the last frame of the **Door** Opening animation (in the **Animation** View). Go to the **Inspector** and copy the Door's **Transform** component. To do so, click on the small gear icon in the upper right corner of the component and choose the **Copy Component** option.

13. Create a new Animation Clip and name it `Opened`. Add the key frames to the **Door** child object the same way as in step 5. If your **Door** object moved, select it, click on the gear icon near the **Transform** component in the **Inspector**, and choose **Paste Component Values**. That will paste our copied **Transform** properties from the last frame of the `Door Opening` animation.

14. Make sure both frames in the animation have the same position.

15. Create one more Animation Clip (the last one) and name it `Door Closing`.

16. Make the animation of the **Door** game object slide down from open to closed positions. Remember that you can copy the Door's **Transform** component from appropriate animation frames and paste them in the animation you are working on.

17. Preview all the animations with the **Animation** View. You can switch between animations using the drop-down list below the playback buttons.

18. If you are happy with your animations, close the **Animation** View. Select your **Door Frame** game object and find its Animator component in the **Inspector**.

19. Click on the **Controller** field, which will show you the automatically created Animator Controller in the **Project** View. Double-click to open it.

20. Create a `bool` parameter and call it `Open`.

21. Create a loop of transitions between the animation states: **Closed | Door Opening | Open | Door Closing | Closed**. See the following screenshot:

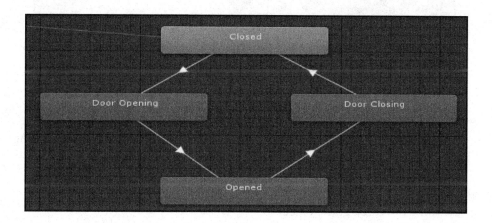

22. Select the **Closed | Door Opening** transition. Add a condition to it, choose the `Open` parameter, and set the condition to true. Disable the **Has Exit Time** option in the transition.

23. Select the **Opened | Door Closing** transition. Add a condition to it, choose the `Open` parameter, and set the condition to false. Disable the **Has Exit Time** option in the transition.

24. Leave the **Door Opening | Opened** and **Door Closing | Closed** transitions without a condition. Make sure the **Has Exit Time** option is enabled in both those transitions.

25. Close the Animator Controller.

26. Select the Door Frame game object in the scene's Hierarchy.

27. Add a **Cube** child object to the Door Frame game object. To do so, right-click on the **Door Frame** game object and choose **Create | 3D Object | Cube**. This will be our trigger.

28. Select the **Cube** and scale it so that it stands out on both sides of the Door Frame. See the following screenshot for reference:

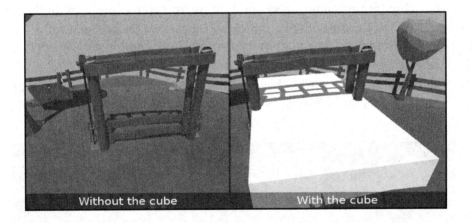

29. Remove the **Mesh Renderer** and **Mesh Filter** components from the **Cube**. To do so, click on the small gear icon in the upper-right corner of the given component and choose the **Remove Component** option. That will leave only the **Transform** and **Box Collider** components on the Cube.

30. Enable the **Is Trigger** checkbox on the Cube's **Box Collider** component.

31. Rename the Cube game object to `Trigger`.

32. Select the **Door Frame** game object and add a **Mesh Collider** component to it.

33. Select the **Door** game object and add a **Box Collider** component (or a **Mesh Collider** set to **Convex**) and a **Rigidbody** component. Enable the **Is Kinematic** option in the **Rigidbody** component.

34. Create a new C# script and name it `AutomaticDoors.cs`. Open it and write the following code:

```csharp
using UnityEngine;
using System.Collections;

public class AutomaticDoor : MonoBehaviour
{

    /*The anim variable is used to store the reference
    to the Animator component*/

    private Animator anim;

    void Start ()
    {
        /*We assign the Animator component of the parent object
          because this script is attached to the trigger, which
          is the child object of our animated doors*/

        anim = transform.parent.GetComponent<Animator> ();
    }
    /* This function is called when a Rigidbody intersects with
    the collider attached to our game object for the first time.
    Our collider has to be set to trigger. The Collider other
    parameter stores information about the object which collided
    with our trigger (entered the trigger).*/
        void OnTriggerEnter (Collider other)
        {

            //We check the tag of the object entering the trigger
            if (other.gameObject.CompareTag ("Player")) {

                /*If the tag equals "Player", we set the
                      bool parameter "Open" to true in our
                Animator Controller - that plays the open
                animation and opens the doors*/

                anim.SetBool ("Open", true);
            }
        }
    /* This function is called when a Rigidbody exists the trigger
       (stops colliding with our trigger collider).*/
```

```
void OnTriggerExit (Collider other)
{

    /*Again, we check if the object was the player*/
    if (other.gameObject.CompareTag ("Player")) {

        /*If it's true, we set the bool parameter "Open"
        to false in our Animator Controller. That plays
        the close animation and closes the doors.*/

        anim.SetBool ("Open", false);
    }
}
}
```

35. Assign the script to your **Trigger** game object and make sure your character has a **Rigidbody** component and the `Player` tag.

36. Play the game and approach the door; it should open. It should close when you exit the trigger.

How it works...

This recipe illustrates a very important feature of Unity's animation workflow, the possibility to animate objects in local space. If we animate child game objects, their position, rotation, and scale will be animated in relation to their parent game objects. This makes it possible to create animated game objects, save them as prefabs, and reuse them in our games.

There are a few key elements of this recipe:

- **Door as a child of Door Frame**: We have two objects: an animated, moving **Door** and a stationary **Door Frame**. The **Door** game object is the child of the **Door Frame** game object in the **Hierarchy**. If we animate it, an Animator component will be added to the **Door Frame** game object (the parent), and the **Door** (the child) will be animated relative to the **Door Frame** (the parent).

- **Bool parameter "Open"**: This parameter is used by the door Animator Controller to switch between Opened and Closed states. We set it in the script attached to the trigger game object. When player enters the trigger, it sets the `Open` parameter to true, which tells the **Door** Animator Controller it should play the `Door Opening` animation. When the player exits the trigger, it sets the `Open` parameter to false, so the **Door** Animator Controller plays the `Door Closing` animation.

- **Animation-driven movement**: The **Door** game object is animated to open (move up) and close (move down), depending on the **bool Open** parameter. The `Door` game object has a collider to prevent any Rigid body going through it. It also has a **Rigidbody** component set to **Is Kinematic**. All moving colliders should be kinematic Rigid bodies for optimization reasons.
- **Trigger game object**: The **Door Frame** has also a trigger game object as a child. A trigger is a game object with a collider set to **Is Trigger**. It recognizes when an object with a **Rigidbody** component enters or exits the collider and calls the `OnTriggerEnter` and `OnTriggerExit` functions, respectively. We set the value of the `bool Open` parameter in those functions.

See also

The concept of animating game objects in local space will be used multiple times throughout the course of this book. We are going to create an interesting example in the next recipe.

Using the Hierarchy to animate local rotation – creating an orbiting planet

In this recipe, we will explore local transform animations further. We will use the **Hierarchy** and create smart parent-child relationships between our game objects to make an interesting effect of orbiting planets. Learning how to animate an object's local position and rotation and use the **Hierarchy** to our advantage is key to getting the most of Unity's animation system.

Getting ready

Before we start, you need to prepare at least two objects to animate. We are using planets in this example. You can also use the example Unity project provided and go to the `Chapter 02 Working with the animation view\Recipe 05 Using the hierarchy to animate local rotation – creating an orbiting planet` directory. You will find an `Example.unity` scene there. There is a **Planets** game object with an Animator component and an Animator Controller assigned. If you select the **Planets** game object and go to **Window | Animation**, you can edit the animation of orbiting planets.

How to do it...

To use Hierarchy to animate an object's local rotation, follow these steps:

1. Put your planet models into the scene.
2. One of our planets will be the parent of our little "planetary system." Call it **Planet1** (as we will refer to it in this recipe a lot).
3. Add an empty child game object to **Planet1** and name it **Planet2Orbit**. The **Planet2Orbit** game object should be placed in the center of the **Planet1** game object.
4. Parent your second planet game object (let's call it **Planet2**) to the **Planet2Orbit** game object.
5. Set the position of the **Planet2** game object to 0x, 0y, 0z to place it exactly in the same position as the **Planet2Orbit** (and **Planet1**) game object.
6. Move your **Planet2** object to the desired distance from **Planet1**. Use only one axis (X, Y, or Z). See the following screenshot :

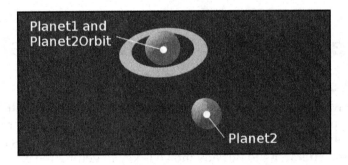

7. Add an Animator component to the root game object of our planetary system (**Planet1**).
8. Open the **Animation** View with the **Planet1** game object selected (go to **Window | Animation**).
9. Create a new Animation Clip by clicking on the **Create** button.
10. Make sure the record button is pressed (upper-left corner of the **Animation** View).
11. Select the **Planet2Orbit** game object from the **Hierarchy**.

12. Rotate the **Planet2Orbit** a bit in one axis (choose *Y* for instance) to create a new key frame. After you rotate it, the **Rotation** property of that object will be added automatically to the **Animation** View. Find the **Rotation** section, in the **Transform** component in the **Inspector** of the **Planet2Orbit** game object, and enter 0 in the axis you chose (*Y* in this example).

13. Move the timeline in the **Animation** View a few seconds forward to create the second key frame.

14. Make sure the **Planet2Orbit** game object is still selected and the record button is pressed.

15. Type 360 in the rotation section in the `Transform` component of the **Planet2Orbit** game object. Remember to type it in the same axis you chose before (*Y* in this example). This will create the second key frame and the animation will be perfectly looped.

16. Play the game to see the effect of an orbiting planet.

How it works...

The key element of this recipe is the **Hierarchy** of our game objects. All animations created with Unity's **Animation** View are made in local space, which means that if you animate a parent object's position or rotation, its child objects will also move or rotate, respectively.

Our Hierarchy looks like this: **Planet1 | Planet2Orbit | Planet2**:

- **Planet1:** This is our root game object. We can move it in space and our animation will still work perfectly.

- **Planet2Orbit:** This game object is the child of the **Planet1** game object. It is placed in the center of **Planet1**. Only this object is animated in the whole **Hierarchy**. We use this empty game object because we may want to rotate the root planet (**Planet1**) and we need another object in the **Hierarchy** to desynchronize the rotation of **Planet1** with the orbiting movement of **Planet2**.

- **Planet2**-This game object is the child of **Planet2Orbit.** It is translated in the local space of **Planet2Orbit** in one axis only. The rotation of the **Planet2Orbit** game object makes **Planet2** move in circles, which creates the orbiting planet effect.

There's more...

- You can add more planets to our planetary system. In the provided example, there is also a **Moon** game object orbiting **Planet2**.
- You can also have nested game objects with their own Animator components attached. That will make it possible to have multiple Animator Controllers driving animations of different parts of the **Hierarchy**.

Animating triggers – creating a death trap

In this recipe, we will animate a trigger position and use it to create a death trap. You can use Unity's Animation View to create various game play mechanisms with minimum scripting.

Getting ready

Before we start, you should prepare a death trap model. We are using a "press trap" as an example. It contains two identical moving elements. See the following screenshot:

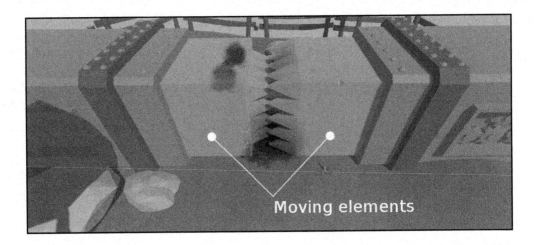

The model is not skinned and has no rig; instead, the moving elements are separate objects. We will animate them with Unity's **Animation** View. You can also use the example Unity project provided and go to the `Chapter 02 Working with the animation view\Recipe 06 Animating triggers - creating a death trap` directory. You will find an `Example.unity` scene there. If you play the game, you can see the trap working. If you open the scene, you will find the **Trap** game object with the **LeftTrap** and **RightTrap** game objects as its children. Those child objects are the only ones animated in this example. They have trigger objects as their children. Those trigger objects kill the player when he enters them. All other child objects of the **Trap** game object are only decorations and are optional.

How to do it...

To animate the trigger position and create a death trap, follow these steps:

1. Create an empty object in the scene and name it **Trap**. It will be a parent object for our moving parts.
2. Put your models into the scene and parent them to the **Trap** game object. The models should have descriptive names, for instance, **LeftTrap** and **RightTrap**.
3. Add an Animator component to your **Trap** game object (the root object of our death trap). Set the **Update Mode** to **Animate Physics**.
4. Go to **Window | Animation** and open the **Animation** View.
5. Create a new Animation Clip by clicking on the **Create** button.
6. Select the **LeftTrap** game object and make sure the record button is pressed (in the upper-left corner of the **Animation** View).
7. Move the **LeftTrap** game object to the open position.
8. Adjust the timeline a few seconds forward and move the **LeftTrap** game object to the closed position.
9. Adjust the timeline a few seconds again and move the **LeftTrap** game object to the open position again to create a looping animation.
10. Repeat steps 7-9 for the **RightTrap** game object.
11. You should have a looping animation of the trap opening and closing. You can adjust the animation until you're happy with it. You can add a pause in the open position to make it easier for the player to go through the trap without being killed.
12. Close the **Animation** View.

13. We need to write a script for our character to be able to harm them with our death trap. Create a new C# script and call it `Character.cs`. Write the following code:

```csharp
using UnityEngine;
using System.Collections;

public class Character : MonoBehaviour
{

/*We are going to store the reference to a blood effect prefab
   in this variable*/
    public GameObject bloodEffect;

  /*This variable is set to true when the character object was
    already killed*/
    bool isKilled = false;

    /*This function is called by the death
    trap, when we enter it*/
    public void Kill ()
    {
        /*If the character was already killed by the trap,
        we don't want to do anything*/
        if (isKilled) {
            return;
        }
        /*If it was not killed, we set the isKilled
        variable to true*/
        isKilled = true;

       /*We check if the character has a Rigidbody component*/
        Rigidbody rb = GetComponent<Rigidbody> ();

        if (rb != null) {

            /*If we find the component, we need to set it to
            kinematic to prevent our character from being
            launched in the air by the collision with our
            trap*/
            rb.isKinematic = true;
        }

        /*Here we spawn a blood effect prefab stored in the
        bloodEffect variable*/
        GameObject.Instantiate (bloodEffect, transform.position
                + Vector3.up * 2f, Quaternion.identity);
```

```
/*We are getting all the Renderer components of our
character*/

Renderer[] r = GetComponentsInChildren<Renderer> ();

for (int i = 0; i < r.Length; i++) {
    /*We are turning all the renderers of, making the
    object dissapear*/
    r [i].enabled = false;
}

/*We are also checking if our character uses our
SimpleMove script if so, we are turning it off to
prevent player from moving the character after death*/
SimpleMove move = GetComponent<SimpleMove> ();

if (move != null) {
    move.enabled = false;
}


    }
}
```

14. Select the **LeftTrap** game object and add a **Box Collider** component to it.

15. Adjust the collider shape so that it will not cover the spikes section (we plan to add a trigger there). To do so, click on the **Edit Shape** button in the **Box Collider** component. Shapes handles will appear on every face of the **Box Collider** in the **Scene** View. You can click on the handle and move it to adjust the shape.

16. Add a **Rigidbody** component to the **LeftTrap** game object and set it to **Is Kinematic**.

17. Right-click on the **LeftTrap** game object and choose **3D Object | Cube** to add a Cube child object to it. It will become our trigger.

18. Scale the Cube to cover the spikes with it. See the following screenshot:

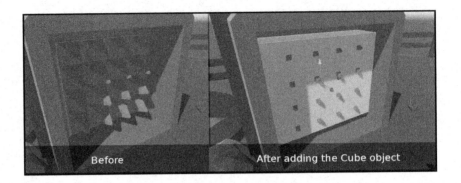

| Before | After adding the Cube object |

19. Remove the **MeshRenderer** and **MeshFilter** components from the **Cube**. Give the **Cube** a descriptive name, for instance, **LeftTrapTrigger**.
20. Check the **Is Trigger** option in the **Box Collider** of the **LeftTrapTrigger**.
21. Repeat steps 14-20 for the **RightTrap**.
22. Now we need to write a script for the death trap itself. Create a new C# script and call it `DeathTrap.cs`. Open the script and write the following code:

```
using UnityEngine;
using System.Collections;

public class DeathTrap : MonoBehaviour
{

    /*This function is called when a Rigidbody
    enters the trigger object*/
    void OnTriggerEnter (Collider other)
    {

    /*We are checking if the object which entered the
trigger has a Character script, if so we are calling the
    Kill() method on it*/
        Character characterScript =
        other.gameObject.GetComponent<Character> ();

        if (characterScript != null) {
            characterScript.Kill ();
        }
    }
}
```

23. Attach the `DeathTrap.cs` script to the **LeftTrapTrigger** game object and the **RightTrapTrigger** game object.
24. Make sure your character has a **Rigidbody** component (the **ThirdPersonCharacter** prefab from Unity's Standard assets will work).
25. Add the `Character.cs` script to your character.
26. Create a blood particle effect and save it as a prefab. Name it **BloodSplash**.
27. Assign the **BloodSplash** prefab to the **Blood Effect** field of the **Character** script component in your character.
28. Play the game and enter the trap to see the effect. Your character should disappear and the **BloodSplash** effect should be spawned.

How it works...

In this recipe, we attach triggers (game objects with **Box Collider** components set to **Is Trigger**) as child objects of our trap's moving parts. The `OnTriggerEnter()` method in our `DeathTrap.cs` script is called whenever an object with a **Rigidbody** component enters one of our trigger objects. It does not matter if the object or the trigger is moving. The animation of the moving parts of our trap also moves the child trigger objects. You can use it to create some really spectacular traps in your games.

There's more...

In our example, the character will die whenever it touches the spikes of our trap. We can add some more realism by using Animation Events to enable the triggers when the trap is closing and disable them when it opens. It would prevent us from killing the character when the trap is not closing on them. You can learn more about Animation Events in `Chapter 6`, *Handling Combat*.

Remember that you can also rotate the triggers, similar to how we did it in the *Using the Hierarchy to animate local rotation – creating an orbiting planet* recipe. Scaling the triggers is also possible.

You should not use this concept for moving normal colliders. Always try to use a Rigid body set to **Is Kinematic** when you want to move a collider (for optimization reasons).

Creating an elevator triggered by player input

In this last recipe, we will use player input to create a simple elevator.

Getting ready

Before we start, you should prepare an elevator model to contain the objects: the root object called **Elevator**, the **Lift** object (this one will be animated), and the **ElevatorFrame** object, which will work as decoration. The **Lift** and **ElevatorFrame** objects should be children of the empty **Elevator** object. You can also use the example Unity project provided and go to the Chapter 02 Working with the animation view\Recipe 07 Creating an elevator triggered by player input directory. You will find an Example.unity scene there with the **Elevator** game object and its children **Lift** and **ElevatorFrame** objects. The **Elevator** is already animated in the example assets.

How to do it...

To create an elevator triggered by player input, follow these steps:

1. Select the root **Elevator** object and assign an Animator component to it. Set the **Update Mode** to **Animate Physics**.
2. Open **Window** | **Animation** and create a new Animation Clip by clicking on the **Create** button. Call it **ElevatorGoingDown**.
3. Make sure the record button is pressed (in the upper-left corner of the **Animation View**).
4. Select your **Lift** game object and move it to the up position.
5. Adjust the timeline a few seconds forward and move the **Lift** game object to the down position. Your **Lift** game object should animate going from the maximum up position to the minimum down position.
6. Create another Animation Clip by selecting the **Create New Clip** option from the animations drop-down list (you can find it below the playback buttons). Call it **ElevatorGoingUp**.
7. Animate your **Lift** game object to go from the down position to the up position.
8. Create another Animation Clip and call it **ElevatorDown**. Create a one-second looping animation for the **Lift** game object in the down position.

9. Create another Animation Clip and call it **ElevatorUp**. Create a one-second looping animation for the **Lift** game object in the up position.

10. Close the **Animation** View.

11. Navigate to the **ElevatorGoingUp** and **ElevatorGoingDown** assets in the **Project** View. Select them and uncheck the **Loop Time** option in the **Inspector**.

12. Select the **Elevator** game object in the **Hierarchy** and find its Animator component in the **Inspector**.

13. Double-click on the **Controller** field to open the automatically created Animator Controller asset.

14. Create a new trigger parameter and call it Move.

15. Create a loop of transitions, as shown in the following screenshot:

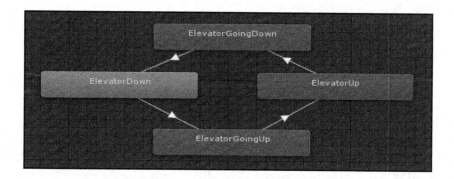

16. Make sure the **ElevatorDown** state is the default one. If not, right-click on it and choose the **Set as Layer Default State** option.

17. The **ElevatorDown | ElevatorGoingUp** and **ElevatorUp | ElevatorGoingDown** transitions should both have the **Move** trigger set as the condition and the **Has Exit** option set to false.

18. The **ElevatorGoingDown | ElevatorDown** and **ElevatorGoingUp | ElevatorUp** transitions should have the **Has Exit Time** option set to true and should have no additional conditions.

19. Create a new C# script and call it `Elevator.cs`. Write the following code:

```
using UnityEngine;
using System.Collections;

public class Elevator : MonoBehaviour
{

    // Update is called once per frame
    void Update ()
    {

        /*When the player presses the E key, we are setting the
        Move trigger on the Animator component. We are assuming
        the Animator component is present on the game object our
        script is attached to*/
        if (Input.GetKeyDown (KeyCode.E)) {
            GetComponent<Animator> ().SetTrigger ("Move");
        }

    }
}
```

20. Assign the `Elevator.cs` script to the **Elevator** game object.
21. Select the **ElevatorFrame** game object and add a **Mesh Collider** component to it.
22. Select the **Lift** game object and add three **Cube** game objects to it by choosing the **3D Object | Cube** from the right-click menu. Use the cubes to encapsulate the floor and two barriers of the **Lift** (the number of the cubes may vary in your particular case). See the following screenshot:

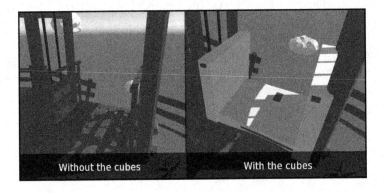

23. Remove the **Mesh Renderer** and **Mesh Filter** components from the cubes, leaving just the **Box Collider** components. Give the cubes proper names, for example, `FloorCollider`, `LeftCollider`, and `RightCollider`.

24. Select the **Lift** object again. Add a **Rigidbody** component to it and set it to **Is Kinematic**.

25. Add the `Platform.cs` script to the **Lift** game object. You can find the script in the *Animating an object's world position – creating a moving platform* recipe, the *How to do it* section, step 13.

26. This simple elevator will work for characters using **Rigidbody** components. You can use the **ThirdPersonCharacter** prefab from Unity's Standard Assets or use the one in the Unity example project provided.

27. Run the game and press the *E* button on the keyboard to trigger the elevator.

How it works...

This recipe has a few key elements that make it work:

- **Animated Lift game object**: The **Lift** game object uses animations to go from the up to the down position.

- **Lift as a child game object**: The **Lift** game object is a child of the **Elevator** game object, which makes it possible to copy the **Elevator** and use it in multiple places in the scene.

- **Platform.cs script**: We are using the same `Platform.cs` script as in the *Animating an object's world position – creating a moving platform* recipe. This script parents the character to the **Lift**. This way the character is forced to move with the **Lift**, which prevents it from jittering (you can try removing the `Platform.cs` script from the **Lift** game object and going down in the **Elevator**: the character will jump up and down).

- **Player input**: We are using player input to set the `Move` trigger parameter in the Animator Controller of the **Elevator**. That plays the animation (**ElevatorGoingUp** or **ElevatorGoingDown**, depending on the state in which the Elevator is currently in).

There's more...

Right now, the **Elevator** will move after every player input, regardless of whether the player is standing in the **Lift** or not. You can use a **Box Collider** component set to **Is Trigger** and write a script to check whether the player is in the **Lift**, and only then allow the player to use the input. Here is an example `LiftCheck.cs` script that would do it (you can find the script in the example Unity project provided in the `Chapter 02 Working with the animation view\Recipe 07 Creating an elevator triggered by player input\Scripts` directory):

```
using UnityEngine;
using System.Collections;

public class LiftCheck : MonoBehaviour
{
    Elevator elevatorScript;
    // Use this for initialization
    void Start ()
    {
        /*We try to find the Elevator script on the root
        transform (we are assuming this is the Elevator game
        object)*/
        elevatorScript = transform.root.GetComponent<Elevator> ();
    }
    // This function is called when our character
    enters the trigger
    void OnTriggerEnter (Collider other)
    {
        /*We check if we've found the Elevator script*/
        if (elevatorScript != null) {
            /*We check if the object which entered
            the trigger is the Player*/
            if (other.gameObject.CompareTag ("Player")) {
                /*We enable the Elevator script
                (and enable the input)*/
                elevatorScript.enabled = true;
            }
        }
    }
    // This function is called when our character
    exits the trigger
    void OnTriggerExit (Collider other)
    {
        /*We check if we've found the Elevator script*/
        if (elevatorScript != null) {
            /*We check if the object which exited the
            trigger is the Player*/
```

```
if (other.gameObject.CompareTag ("Player")) {
    /*We disable the Elevator script (and ,
    disable the input)*/
    elevatorScript.enabled = false;
}
        }
    }
}
```

3

2D and User Interface Animation

In this chapter, we are going to cover the following topics:

- Exporting a 2D sprite animation from a 3D package
- Creating a frame-by-frame sprite animation with the Animation View
- Creating a 2D sprite doll animation with the Animation View
- Using the Animator Controller to play sprite animations
- Creating a fade out-fade in transition with the Animation View
- Creating a swipe transition with the Animation View
- Using filled images for creating animated progress bars
- Using Mecanim states for animating UI button states

Introduction

In the previous chapter, we were working with the Animation View, which is an essential tool for authoring animations in Unity. This chapter explains the **2D and user interface animation pipeline**. We will continue to use the Animation View to create various 2D and UI animation in this chapter.

Exporting a 2D sprite animation from a 3D package

Drawing animated 2D sprites can be a challenge. Some artists create their characters in a 3D package and export them as 2D sprites to make the animation process easier. In this first recipe, we will create such a character and export it's animation as a sprite sheet.

Getting ready

Before we start, you need to have an animated model in your chosen 3D package (we are using Blender). You can also download the provided example; open the project in Unity; go to the `Chapter 03 2D and user interface animation\Recipe 01 Exporting a 2d sprite animation from a 3d package` folder. You will find a scene called `Example.unity` there, with an animated coin sprite. In the `Animation` directory, you can find exported frames and a sprite sheet containing them. You can also find a `*.blend` file with the coin model; set to render out the animation.

How to do it...

To export a 2D sprite animation from a 3D package and import it into Unity, follow these steps:

1. Create an animated object in your chosen 3D package.
2. Set the camera to render out the animated object. The camera can be perspective or orthographic, depending on what you would like to achieve. In this example (a rotating coin), it is set to perspective to better show the animation. Try to have the center of your object in the center of the frame.
3. Render the animation into separate frames with a transparent background (often 12 frames per second is enough for a good quality sprite animation). Use a logical naming convention (for example, `frame_01.png`, `frame_02.png`, and so on). All the frames should have the same size in pixels.
4. Create a new image in a chosen image editing software (we are using GIMP in this recipe). The image should have a transparent background.

5. Count all your rendered frames and set the size of the newly created image to be big enough to contain all the rendered frames, one next to another (in columns and rows). For example, an image of 512 × 512 pixels size can contain up to 8 frames of 256 × 256 size, 16 frames of 128 × 128 size, or 32 frames of 64 × 64 size.

6. Place all the frames next to each other on the newly created image (in columns and rows), starting from the first frame, as shown in the following screenshot:

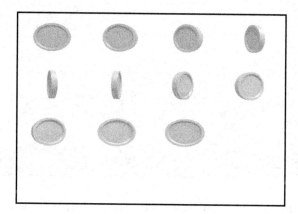

7. Export the image as a *.png file with transparent background.

8. Import the image to Unity (drag and drop it to the **Project** View or go to **Assets | Import New Asset** and choose the image file in the explorer).

9. Select the imported file in the **Project** View and go to the **Inspector**. Set the **Texture Type** to **Sprite (2d and UI)**, as shown in the following screenshot:

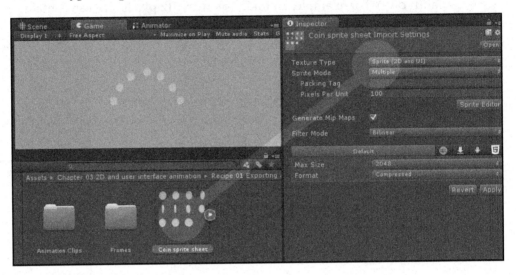

10. Set the **Sprite Mode** to **Multiple**, click on the **Apply** button (to save the settings), and then click on the **Sprite Editor** button.

11. The **Sprite Editor** window will open, as shown in the following screenshot:

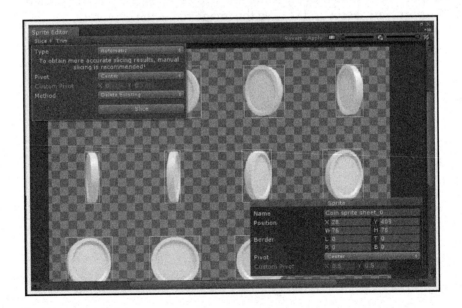

12. Click on the **Slice** button, a dialog with additional settings will appear.
13. Set the **Type** to **Automatic**, **Pivot** to **Center**, and click on the **Slice** button.
14. To finish the editing, click on the **Apply** button and close the **Sprite Editor** window.
15. The texture asset will be turned into a sprite asset with all the frames as separate children: sprites with numbers added to their names, as shown in the following screenshot:

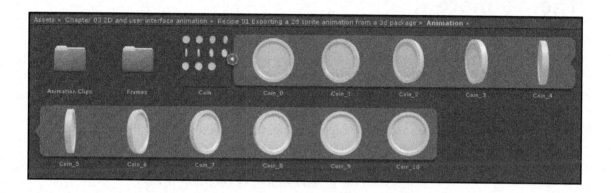

16. You can use those children sprites as static 2D graphics or create an animation in the **Animation** View.

How it works...

You can use animation frames rendered from a 3D package to create 2D sprites in Unity as long as those frames have transparent background. Combining those frames into a sprite sheet saves precious draw calls (sprites are treated as one texture) and makes your game run smoother on lower end devices. It is also easier to organize your project files if you combine sprites into sprite sheets. Unity can automatically split a sprite sheet with transparency into multiple sprites. It recognizes *empty pixels* (transparent pixels) and isolates individual objects (or animation frames) quite effectively.

Unity can also automatically pack the sprites into a sprite sheet using the sprite packing feature. To pack sprites into an atlas, first make sure that packing is enabled. To do so, go to **Edit | Project Settings | Editor** and check the **Sprite Packer Mode**. You should change it to **Always Enabled**. Then select the sprites you want to pack into one atlas and give them the same **Packing Tag**. Finally, open the **Sprite Packer** (go to **Window | Sprite Packer**) and click on the **Pack** button. All sprites with the same **Packing Tag** will be packed together.

There's more...

There are a few other, interesting options in the **Sprite Editor**:

- In the **Slice** dialog, you can set the **Type** to:
  - **Automatic**: Unity will try to automatically slice the sprite sheet into individual sprites.
  - **Grid By Cell Size**: Unity will slice the sprite sheet into a grid with defined size of every cell in pixels. You can slice the sprite sheet into 64 × 64 pixel cells for instance
  - **Grid By Cell Count**: Unity will slice the sprite sheet into a grid of sprites with the given number of cells and rows
- You can also set the **Pivot** of each sprite in the **Slice** dialog. There are multiple options available for setting the pivot of each created sprite to the center of the sprite, right corner, left corner, and so on.
- You can also trim each sprite manually when you select it. To do so, click on the border of the sprite and drag it.
- You can adjust the pivot of each sprite in a similar way. Select the sprite in the **Sprite Editor**, click on its pivot (the blue circle), and drag it to change its position.

See also

To create a sprite animation, see the next recipe.

Creating a frame-by-frame sprite animation with the Animation View

This recipe shows how to use the Animation View to create sprite animations from previously rendered (or hand drawn) frames.

Getting ready

To create a frame by frame sprite animation in Unity, you should first draw or render out the animation frames from a 3D package, combine them into a sprite sheet, and import the sprite sheet into Unity (see the *Exporting a 2D sprite animation from a 3D package* recipe). You can also download the provided example Unity project and go to Chapter 03 2D and user interface animation\Recipe 02 Creating a frame by frame sprite animation with the animation view directory. You will find a scene called Example.unity there, with a **Coin** game object that has been already animated. You can select it and go to **Window** | **Animation** to see how the animation was prepared.

How to do it...

To create a frame by frame sprite animation in Unity, follow these steps:

1. Select your sprite sheet asset in the **Project** View.
2. Unfold the sprite sheet to see the individual sprites (children objects of the sprite sheet asset).
3. Select one of the sprites, and then drag and drop it into the scene's **Hierarchy**.
4. You can rename the created game object.
5. With the game object selected, go to **Window** |**Animation**.
6. Click on the **Create** button in the **Animation** View to create a new Animation Clip.

7. Adjust the **Samples** to the number of frames per second your animation was created with (12 in this example), as shown in the following screenshot:

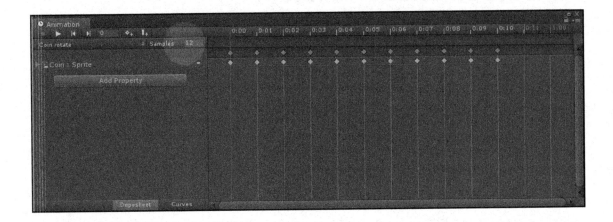

8. Make sure the record button is pressed. In the **Project** View, select all the frames (child sprites) in your sprite sheet asset and drag them into the **Animation** View.
9. A frame by frame sprite animation will be created. Click on the **Play** button in the **Animation** View or run the game to see the effect.

How it works...

Unity can animate the public **Sprite** field in the **Sprite Renderer** component of a game object. This is exactly what we did in this recipe. We are changing the sprites each frame to create a frame by frame animation. We have changed the **Samples** number to lower the frame rate of the animation. That allows us to use less frames per second. In standard 2D frame by frame animation, we use 12 or 24 frames per second, and Unity's default **Samples** number is 60.

In some cases, you can use even lower **Samples** values: try experimenting with 8 frames per second.

Creating a 2D sprite doll animation with the Animation View

In this recipe, we will use a different approach: a 2D sprite doll animation. It is based on creating a 2D doll character with all its limbs as separate sprites and then animating those sprites using Unity's **Hierarchy** and the **Animation** View.

Getting ready

To create a 2D doll animation, first you need to prepare your character sprite sheet with all the limbs as separate sprites. See the following screenshot for reference:

You can also use the example project, and go to the `Chapter 03 2D and user interface animation\Recipe 03 Creating a 2d sprite doll animation with the animation view` directory. You can find the `Example.unity` scene there, with a **Warrior** character already animated in the scene's **Hierarchy**. In the `Animation` directory, you can find a `Warrior.png` sprite sheet with all the body parts of the character.

How to do it...

To create a 2D sprite doll style animation, follow these steps:

1. Import your character sprite sheet with all the body parts into Unity.
2. Select the sprite sheet and go to its **Inspector**.
3. Set the **Sprite Mode** to **Multiple** and click on the **Apply** button.
4. Click on the **Sprite Editor** button to open the **Sprite Editor**.
5. Click on the **Slice** button in the **Sprite Editor**. The **Slice** dialog will appear.
6. Set the **Type** do **Automatic**.
7. Click on the **Slice** button in the bottom of the **Slice** dialog.
8. In the **Sprite Editor**, adjust all the pivot points of the character's body parts. Body parts will be rotated around those pivot points in our animation. Try to have the pivot points in the joints of the limbs, as shown in the following screenshot:

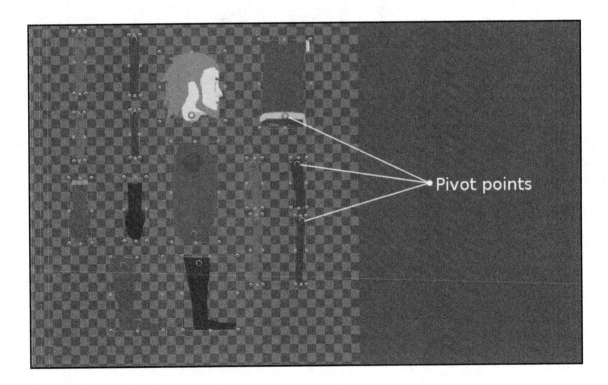

9. Click on the **Apply** button in the **Sprite Editor**.

10. Create an empty game object in the scene's **Hierarchy** and give it a descriptive name (`Warrior` in our example).

11. Drag and drop all the body parts from your character sprite sheet onto **Warrior** game object (you have to drag and drop one body part at a time because dragging multiple sprites will create an Animation Clip).

12. Rename the body parts for better clarity. In our example, we have `Hips`, `Chest`, `Head`, `FrontUpperArm`, `FrontLowerArm`, `Front Hand`, `BackUpperArm`, `BackLowerArm`, `BackHand`, `FrontUpperLeg`, `FrontLowerLeg`, `FrontFoot`, `BackUpperLeg`, `BackLowerLeg`, and `BackFoot`.

13. Build a humanoid hierarchy from all the body parts in the scene's **Hierarchy**, with the **Warrior** game object as the root. In our example, the hierarchy looks like the following:

```
Warrior | Hips | Chest | Head
Chest | FrontUpperArm | FrontLowerArm | FrontHand
Chest | BackUpperArm | BackLowerArm | BackHand
Hips | FrontUpperLeg | FrontLowerLeg | FrontFoot
Hips | BackUpperLeg | BackLowerLeg | BackFoot
```

14. Adjust the **Order in Layer** field for every **Sprite Renderer** component in every body part. In our example, body parts have this order:

0	BackUpperArm
1	BackLowerArm
2	BackHand
3	BackUpperLeg
4	BackLowerLeg
5	BackFoot
6	FrontUpperLeg
7	FrontLowerLeg
8	FrontFoot
9	Head
10	Chest
11	Hips

12	FrontUpperArm
13	FrontLowerArm
14	FrontHand

15. Move the body parts to their "anatomical" positions to form the character, as shown in the following screenshot:

16. Select the **Warrior** game object (the root game object containing all the body parts).
17. Go to **Window** | **Animation**.
18. Create a new Animation Clip by clicking on the **Create** button in the **Animation View**.
19. Make sure the record button is pressed (upper left corner of the **Animation View**).
20. Animate the character by rotating its individual body parts.

How it works...

Creating a 2D doll animation uses the same concept as shown in the *Using the Hierarchy to animate local rotation – creating an orbiting planet* recipe in Chapter 2, *Working with the Animation View*. The key element of this recipe is the **Warrior** root game object containing all the body parts of our character as children game objects. When we select this object and open the **Animation** View, we can animate all its children game objects. The saved Animation Clip will be used by the **Warrior** game object's Animator Controller. That allows us to create complex hierarchical animations (such as this one) and save them as single Animation Clips.

Using the Animator Controller to play sprite animations

In this recipe, we will create an Animator Controller to play 2D animations of a character. Unity's animation system is using the same principles for both 2D and 3D animation clips, which makes it quite intuitive to use.

Getting ready

First, you should have at least two sprite animations (or 2D sprite doll animations) ready. You can also go to the Chapter 03 2D and user interface animation\Recipe 04 Using the animator controller to play sprite animations directory and open the Example.unity scene. You will find an already animated **Warrior** game object there. If you play the game, you can use the arrow keys (left and right) to move the character. It will play 2D animations accordingly.

How to do it...

To create an Animator Controller for 2D animation, follow these steps:

1. Import your 2D sprite sheets to Unity the same way as in the *Exporting a 2D sprite animation from a 3D package* recipe.
2. Drag and drop one of the child sprites (not sprite sheets) into the **Hierarchy**.
3. Select the sprite game object and give it an appropriate name (it is named **Warrior** in this example).

4. With the **Warrior** game object selected, go to **Window** | **Animation** to open the **Animation** View.

5. Create the required Animation Clips using the **Animation** View (the same way as in the *Creating a frame-by-frame sprite animation with the Animation View* recipe). In this example, we use two animations: **Warrior2dIdle** and **Warrior2dWalk**.

6. An Animator Controller will be automatically created and assigned to the Animator component on the **Warrior** game object.

7. Open the created Animator Controller (you can easily do it by selecting the **Warrior** game object in the **Hierarchy** and going to **Window** | **Animator**).

8. Create a new `float` parameter in the Animator Controller and name it `Speed`. We will use it for controlling the animation flow.

9. Create two transitions: from **Warrior2dIdle** to **Warrior2dWalk** and from **Warrior2dWalk** to **Warrior2dIdle**. The first one should have a condition of Speed greater than 0.1 and the second should have a condition of **Speed** less than 0.1. See the following screenshot:

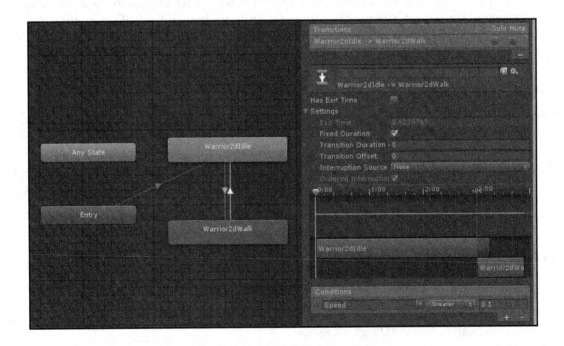

10. Set the **Has Exit Time** to false and the **Transition Duration** to 0 in both transitions (you cannot blend frame by frame sprite animations).

11. Write a script to set the **Speed** parameter based on the player input. You can also find and use the `Warrior2dMove.cs` script in the provided Unity project in the `Scripts` directory of this recipe.

12. In this script's `Update()` function, we take the `Horizontal` axis as the input. Then we set the **Speed** variable to be the absolute value of the input because in our Animator Controller, we check only if it's greater or less than 0.1, and the `Horizontal` axis can have values between−1 and 1. We use the `speed` variable to set the **Speed** parameter in our Animator Controller. The `animator` variable holds reference to the Animator component on the same game object (we set this reference in the `Start()` function):

```
hor = Input.GetAxis("Horizontal");
speed = Mathf.Abs(hor);
animator.SetFloat("Speed", speed);
```

13. This will make the character play the **Warrior2dWalk** animation when the user presses the left or right arrow on the keyboard and **Warrior2dIdle** animation when player is not pressing any button.

How it works...

There are a few key elements of this recipe:

- **Animator Controller for 2D animations**: Controlling 2D animations playback works very similar to 3D and skeletal animations in Unity. You can create Animator Controllers as usual, with all required states and transitions between them.

- **Transition Duration set to 0**: The **Transition Duration** parameter only makes sense with animations that can be blended together to create a smooth transition. In 2D frame by frame animation, this is not possible (Unity cannot create "in between sprites" automatically). This is the reason to set the parameter to 0 and have a sharp, immediate transition. In case of the parameter value being greater than 0, the transition will still look sharp but also be delayed.

There's more...

We have used a simple trick in our `Warrior2dMove.cs` script to lower the number of required animations. Our character can move left and right, but we use only one animation: **Warrior2dWalk** (in which the character is moving right). In the script's `Update()` function, we check if the player `Horizontal` axis input is greater than 0 or less than 0 and set the local X scale of the character to 1 or-1, depending on the movement direction. This flips the character and saves us around 50 percent of the animations:

```
if (hor > 0f)
{
    transform.localScale = Vector3.one;
}
else if (hor < 0f)
{
    transform.localScale = new Vector3(-1f, 1f, 1f);
}
```

Creating a fade out – fade in transition with the Animation View

Every game has some sort of fade in/fade out transitions: between the levels, or when you enter a dialog or a cutscene, and so on. In Unity, we can create such transitions very easily using the Animation View.

Getting ready

You don't have to prepare anything for this recipe; everything is created in Unity from scratch. You can open the provided example Unity project and go to the `Chapter 03 2D and user interface animation\Recipe 05 Creating a fade out – fade in transition with the animation view` directory. You will find an `Example.unity` scene there. Play the game and press the space bar to see the fade in/fade out effect.

How to do it...

To create a fade in/fade out effect, follow these steps:

1. Open a scene.
2. Create an **Image** in the **Hierarchy**. To do so, go to **Game Object | UI | Image** menu on the top of the screen.
3. **Image** and **Canvas** game objects will be created in the **Hierarchy**.
4. Select the **Image** game object and set its name to `BlackScreen`.
5. Right-click on the **Canvas** game object and choose **Create Empty** to create an empty game object.
6. Set the name of the newly created game object to `FadeAnimator`. This object will animate the effect.
7. Set the **Anchor Preset** of the **BlackScreen** and **FadeAnimator** game objects to stretch in both *X* and *Y* coordinates, as shown in the following screenshot:

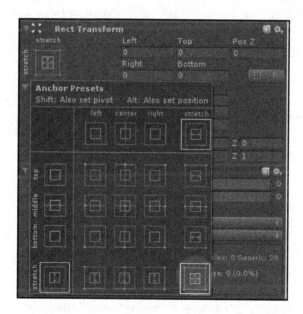

1. Set the **Left, Top, Right,** and **Bottom** position parameters to 0 in both the **BlackScreen** and **FadeAnimator** game objects. That will make the **BlackScreen** and **FadeAnimator** game objects cover the whole screen.
2. Parent the **BlackScreen** game object to the **FadeAnimator** game object in the **Hierarchy**.

3. Select the **FadeAnimator** game object and go to **Window** | **Animation** to open the **Animation** View.

4. Create a new Animation Clip by clicking on the **Create** button. Name the clip Alpha_0; this will be our default animation.

5. Make sure the record button is pressed and select the **BlackScreen** game object. Set its color to black with alpha channel set to 0 (also black). Also disable the **BlackScreen** game object. This Animation Clip should only have one key frame on the frame ; delete any unwanted key frames. Disable the **BlackScreen** game object in this animator (set is as inactive). This way the object will not render when its alpha is 0 percent.

6. Select the **FadeAnimator** game object again and create another Animation Clip. Name it Alpha_100. The object in this animation should be enabled.

7. Make sure the record button is pressed and select the **BlackScreen** game object. Set its color to black and the alpha channel to 100 percent (white). Enable the **BlackScreen** game object (make sure a **Game Object.Is Active** property shows in the **Animation** View, and, if not, click on the game object's **enable** checkbox twice). This Animation Clip should also have only one key frame on the frame 0; remove any other key frames.

8. Select the **FadeAnimator** game object again and create another animation. Name it FadeIn. With the record button pressed, select the **BlackScreen** game object and create two key frames: one on frame 0 and one on 1-second mark. The **BlackScreen** game object should have a black color with alpha set to 0 percent (black) on the first frame and a black color with alpha set to 100 percent (white) on the second key frame. This is meant to be our fade to black animation. You should also enable the **BlackScreen** game object at frame 0 to make it render.

9. Select the **FadeAnimator** game object again and create another animation. Name it FadeOut. With the record button pressed, select the **BlackScreen** game object and create two key frames: one on frame 0 and one on 1-second mark. The **BlackScreen** game object should have a black color with alpha set to 100 percent (white) on the first frame and a black color with alpha set to 0 percent (black) on the second key frame. This is meant to be our fade from black animation. You should also disable the **BlackScreen** game object on the second key frame to prevent it from rendering despite its alpha is 0 percent.

10. Open the Animator Controller assigned to the **FadeAnimator** game object.

11. Create a Trigger parameter and call it Fade.

12. Create a loop of transitions (see the following screenshot for reference):

- **Alpha_0 | FadeIn** with the trigger **Fade** set as condition and **Has Exit Time** set to `false`.
- **FadeIn | Alpha_100** with no conditions and **Has Exit Time** set to `true`.
- **Alpha_100 | FadeOut** with the trigger **Fade** set as condition and **Has Exit Time** set to `false`.
- **FadeOut | Alpha_0** with no conditions and **Has Exit Time** set to `true`.

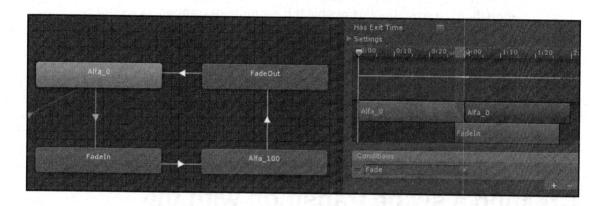

13. Write a script to set the **Fade** `Trigger` parameter in the Animator Controller. In this example, we use player input to set the **Fade** parameter. Whenever a player presses the space bar button, the **Fade** `Trigger` is set. You can find the `Fade.cs` script in the provided example Unity project in the `Chapter 03 2D and user interface animation\Recipe 05 Creating a fade out - fade in transition with the animation view\Scripts` directory:

```
if (Input.GetKeyDown(KeyCode.Space))
{
    animator.SetTrigger("Fade");
}
```

14. Attach the script to the **FadeAnimator** game object.

How it works...

This recipe animates the color of an **Image** component (a part of Unity's UI). We can animate the alpha parameter to fade the transparency of an**Image**. It allows us to create a fade in/fade out effect very easily. This recipe has some other key elements:

- **FadeAnimator empty game object**: Our**BlackScreen** game object (containing the**Image** component) is a child of an empty game object (named**FadeAnimator** in this example). The empty game object has the Animator component attached. This way we can disable and enable the**BlackScreen** game object in our animations (it wouldn't be possible if the Animator component would be attached to the same**BlackScreen** game object).
- **Disabling and enabling the BlackScreen game object**: It is a good practice to disable our black screens because they can block mouse input for UI elements if they are enabled (even if they are fully transparent).
- **BlackScreen in the bottom of the Hierarchy**: Out**BlackScreen** object should be placed in the very bottom of the**Hierarchy** to cover all other UI elements in our game.

Creating a swipe transition with the Animation View

In this recipe, we will create a bit more creative transition effect. A lot of the steps are similar to the previous recipe, but the final result is completely different. This recipe's goal is to encourage you to experiment with animating different UI properties to achieve interesting effects.

Getting ready

Similar to the previous recipe, we will create everything from scratch in Unity; you don't have to prepare anything beforehand. You can open the provided example Unity project and go to the `Chapter 03 2D and user interface animation\Recipe 06 Creating a swipe transition with the animation view` directory. You will find an `Example.unity` scene there. Play the game and press space bar to see the swipe transition effect.

How to do it...

To create a swipe transition effect, follow these steps:

1. Open a scene.
2. Create an **Image** in the **Hierarchy**. To do so, go to **Game Object | UI | Image** menu on the top of the screen.
3. **Image** and **Canvas** game objects will be created in the **Hierarchy**.
4. Select the **Image** game object and set its name to `BlackScreen`.
5. Right-click on the **Canvas** game object and choose **Create Empty** to create an empty game object.
6. Set the name of the newly created game object to `FadeAnimator`. This object will animate the effect.
7. Set the **Anchor Preset** of the **BlackScreen** and **FadeAnimator** game objects to stretch in both X and Y coordinates the same way as we did in the previous recipe.
8. Select the **Canvas** game object and add a **Canvas Scaler** component to it. We will need it to scale our effect when players change the screen resolution in our game.
9. Set the **UI Scale Mode** in the **Canvas Scaler** component to **Scale With Screen Size** to scale the whole canvas, depending on the screen resolution.
10. Set the **Left, Top, Right,** and **Bottom** position parameters to 0 in both the **BlackScreen** and **FadeAnimator** game objects the same way as we did in the previous recipe.
11. Set the color of the **Image** component in the **BlackScreen** game object to fully opaque black.
12. Parent the **BlackScreen** game object to the **FadeAnimator** game object in the **Hierarchy**.

13. Make sure the **Scene** View is set to 2D. Set the **Right** position parameter in the **BlackScreen** game object to –20 pixels and the Left position parameter to a number bigger than your current **Game** View screen resolution. The **BlackScreen** game object should be visible as a very thin strip on the right of the **Canvas** in the **Scene** View, as shown in the following screenshot:

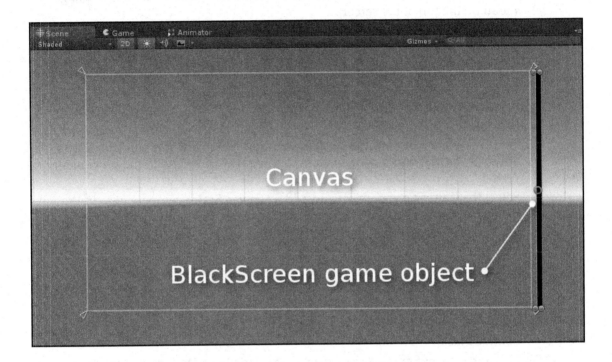

14. Select the **FadeAnimator** game object and go to **Window** | **Animation** to open the **Animation** View.

15. Create a new Animation Clip by clicking on the **Create** button. Name the clip **Alpha_0**; this will be our default animation.

16. Make sure the record button is pressed and select the **BlackScreen** game object. Click on the **Left** position input field in the **Inspector** and enter the same value again. It should insert the key frame for all position values. Disable the **BlackScreen** game object; it should also create a key frame. This Animation Clip should only have one key frame on the frame 0; delete any unwanted key frames.

17. Select the **FadeAnimator** game object again and create another Animation Clip. Name it `Alpha_100`.

18. Make sure the record button is pressed and select the **BlackScreen** game object. Set the **Right** and **Left** positions to 0. Enable the **BlackScreen** game object (make sure a **Game Object.Is Active** property shows in the **Animation** View, and, if not, click on the game object's **enable** checkbox twice). This Animation Clip should also have only one key frame on the frame 0; remove any other key frames. The whole **Game** View should show a black screen.

19. Select the **FadeAnimator** game object again and create another animation. Name it **FadeIn**. With the record button pressed, select the **BlackScreen** game object and create two key frames: one on frame 0 and one on 1-second mark. The **BlackScreen** game object's position on frame 0 should be set to the same values as in the **Alpha_0** animation (**Right** to –20 and **Left** to a number bigger than the **Game** View screen resolution). On the 1-second frame, the position should be set to **Left** 0, **Right** 0. Also enable the game object in both frames. When you play the animation in the **Animation** View, you should see the **BlackScreen** game object swipe from right to left (from a clear game screen to a complete black screen).

20. Select the **FadeAnimator** game object again and create another animation. Name it `FadeOut`. With the record button pressed, select the **BlackScreen** game object and create two key frames: one on frame 0 and one on 1-second mark. The position of the **BlackScreen** game object in frame 0 should be set to Left 0 and Right 0. In the 1-second mark frame, the **Left** position should be set to –20 and the **Right** position to a number higher than the **Game** View's screen resolution. Also make sure to enable the **BlackScreen** game object in both key frames. When you play the animation in the **Animation** View, you should see the **BlackScreen** game object swipe from right to left (from a full black screen to a clear game screen).

21. Open the Animator Controller assigned to the **FadeAnimator** game object.

22. Create a `Trigger` parameter and call it **Fade**.

23. Create a loop of transitions:

   - **Alpha_0 | FadeIn** with the trigger **Fade** set as condition and **Has Exit Time** set to `false`
   - **FadeIn | Alpha_100** with no conditions and **Has Exit Time** set to `true`
   - **Alpha_100 | FadeOut** with the trigger **Fade** set as condition and **Has Exit Time** set to `false`
   - **FadeOut | Alpha_0** with no conditions and **Has Exit Time** set to `true`

24. Set every **Transition Duration** to 0.

25. Write a script to set the **Fade** `Trigger` parameter in the Animator Controller. In this example, we use the same script as in the previous recipe. Whenever player presses the space bar button, the **Fade** `Trigger` is set. You can find the `Fade.cs` script in the provided example Unity project in the `Chapter 03 2D and user interface animation\Recipe 05 Creating a fade out - fade in transition with the animation view\Scripts` directory:

```
if (Input.GetKeyDown(KeyCode.Space))
{
    animator.SetTrigger("Fade");
}
```

26. Attach the script to the **FadeAnimator** game object.

How it works...

This recipe is very similar to the previous one but uses a different concept for the black screen animation. Instead of animating the color value, we are animating the position of the black screen to create the swipe effect. This recipe has several key elements that are different from the precious recipe:

- **Animating Left and Right positions**: Our UI **BlackScreen** game object has its anchors set to stretch in both X and Y coordinates to make it cover the whole screen. With this anchor type, **Left**, **Right**, **Top**, and **Bottom** position parameters work as offsets from the screen edge. So setting them to 0 means that the game object will cover the whole screen. The goal of setting the **Right** position to -20 pixels and the **Left** position to a number bigger than the **Game View** screen resolution was to put our **BlackScreen** game object completely off screen on the right. This way we were able to hide it in game and animate its position later.
- **Canvas Scaler**: We were using a new component, the Canvas Scaler. This component's job is to scale the whole UI canvas to fill the whole screen. If we didn't use this component, our black screen wouldn't cover the whole screen after changing the screen resolution.

Using filled images for creating animated progress bars

In this recipe, we will create a very common UI mechanism: progress bar. The same concept can also be used for creating health bars, cooldown indicators, and so on.

Getting ready

Before we start, you should prepare at least one sprite image and import it to Unity. You can also use the provided example Unity project and go to the `Chapter 03 2D and user interface animation\Recipe 07 Using filled images for creating animated progress bars` directory. You will find an `Example.unity` scene there. Open it and play the game to see the effect.

How to do it...

To create an animated progress bar, follow these steps:

1. Import the progress bar image to Unity and set its type to **Sprite (2d and UI)**.
2. Open a scene and create a new **Image** by using the **Game Object | UI |Image** command.**Canvas** and **Image** game objects will be created.
3. Select the **Image** game object and change its name to **ProgressBar**.
4. Find the **Image** component in the **ProgressBar** game object's **Inspector**.
5. Set the **Image Type** property to **Filled**, the **Fill Method** to **Horizontal**, and the **Fill Amount** to 0, as shown in the following screenshot:

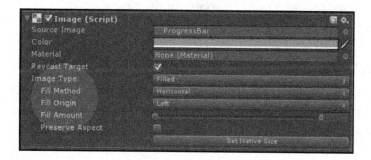

6. By changing the **Fill Amount,** value you can animate a progress bar. You can do it with an **Animation** View, but it makes more sense to use a script here.

7. Create a new script and call it `ProgressBars.cs` (you can also use the same script provided with the example Unity project; you can find it in the `Scripts` directory of this recipe). Make sure to include the `UnityEngine.UI` namespace in the script. Write the following line in the `Update()` function:

```
image.fillAmount += Time.deltaTime * fillSpeed;
```

8. The `image` object is a reference to the **Image** component on the same game object. We assign it in the `Start()` function by calling the line:

```
image = GetComponent<Image>();
```

9. The `fillSpeed` variable is a `public float` variable that describes the fill amount increment per second.

10. In this simple script, we increase the **Fill Amount** of the **Image** component in time.

11. Assign the script to the **ProgressBar** game object and play the game to see the effect.

How it works...

This recipe has a few key elements that make it work:

- **Image Type set to Filled**: Unity provides the **Filled Image** type for the UI Image components. It fills the image from left to right (or in any other desired direction).

- **Fill Amount reference in scripts**: The fill amount of an image can be changed through scripts: it's a public variable of the `Image` class.

There's more...

Try experimenting with different Fill Types. You can find an example of a Fill Type set to Radial360 in the provided example Unity project.

Using Mecanim states for animating UI button states

Unity has a very powerful built in UI system. An important part of it is buttons. Buttons have four states: **Normal**, **Highlighted**, **Pressed**, and **Disabled**. You can use the default **Color Tint** option to visualize those states, but there is a more interesting option: the animation transition. This recipe covers it.

Getting ready

You don't need to prepare anything before hand as we will create animated buttons from scratch in Unity. You can also use the provided example Unity project and go to the Chapter 03 2D and user interface animation\Recipe 08 Using Mecanim states for animating UI button states directory. You will find an Example.unity scene there. Open it, play the game, and click on the buttons to see the effect.

How to do it...

To create an animated button, follow these steps:

1. (Optional) Import the **Button** graphic to Unity.
2. Open a scene and create a new **Button** by using the **Game Object | UI | Button** command. **Canvas** and **Button** game objects will be created.
3. Select the **Button** game object and find the **Button** component in **Inspector**.
4. Set the **Transition** to **Animation**.

5. Click on the **Auto Generate Animation** button, as shown in the following screenshot:

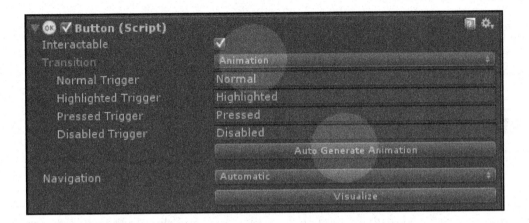

6. Four empty Animation Clips will be created, one for each button state.
7. With the button selected, open the **Animation** View.
8. Select each animation in the **Animation** View (their names correspond with button states) and change the appearance of the **Button** game object with the record button pressed in the **Animation** View. You can change the size of the button, its color, text, and so on. Even one frame of the animation is enough for creating a smooth transition because Unity will smoothly transition between those animations when the game changes the **Button** state.
9. When you finish your animations, close the **Animation** View and play the game to see the effect.

How it works...

This recipe has a few key elements that make it work:

- **Button Animator Controller**: When you click on the **Auto Generate Animation** button, not only the Animation Clips are created, but also an Animator Controller is. It is also automatically assigned to the button (along with an Animator component). All the transitions between animation states in the Animator Controller are also already set up. Unity also creates parameters in the Animator Controller for you-those are the `Trigger` parameters used for transitions between the button states.
- **Calling the Triggers**: You can find four properties in the Button component: **Normal Trigger**, **Highlighted Trigger**, **Pressed Trigger**, and **DisabledTrigger**. Unity will try to call those triggers in the Button's Animator Controller to transition to a proper button state. If you change the `Trigger` names in the Animator Controller, make sure to change them also in the **Button** component.

There's more...

You don't have to make one frame animations for button states. In fact, your animations can be as long and complex as you please. Remember that you can also add child objects to your buttons and animate them the same way we did in the *Exporting a 2D sprite animation from a 3D package* recipe. Try experimenting! You can achieve awesome results with this simple system.

4
Character Movement

This chapter explains the usage of animations for character movement and covers the following recipes:

- Using Blend Trees to blend walk and run animations
- Using root motion to drive Rigid Body characters' movement with animations
- Using root motion to steer a character
- Using animations for better looking transitionWe've seen a lot of "hovering" monsters in games in the past, but creatures flying s
- Using root motion for a 180 degrees turn
- Making a character jump with 3-phase animation
- Using root motion to drive Nav Mesh Agents' movement with animations
- Using triggers to grab an edge while jumping
- Changing the character's collision while crouching
- Adding animation to off-mesh links
- Using root motion for climbing
- Using root motion to create flying characters

Introduction

Character movement is an essential part of almost every game. In this chapter, we will explore different possibilities, from simple walk and run blending to complex animation-driven movement.

Using Blend Trees to blend walk and run animations

In this first recipe, we will get familiar with **Blend Trees** (a new type of states in the Animator Controller). Blend Trees allow to smoothly blend multiple animations together. A common example for using them is blending walk and run cycles.

Getting ready

Before we start, you should have a character with at least three looped animations: idle, walk (in place), and run (also in place). You can download the provided example; open the project in Unity and go to the `Chapter 04 Character movement\Recipe 01 Using blend trees to blend walk and run animations` folder. You will find a scene called `Example.unity` there, with an animated humanoid character. If you play the game, you can click on the ground to move the character, and if you press *Shift* while moving, the character will blend to run animation smoothly. In the `Rigs` directory, you can find the `Humanoid.fbx` asset with the required animations.

How to do it...

To create a smooth blend between walk and run animations, follow these steps:

1. Import your animated character with **Idle**, **Walk**, and **Run** animations. **Walk** and **Run** animations should be done "in place".
2. Set the animations to **Loop Time** in the character asset's **Inspector** in the **Animation** tab. If your character's rig is set to **Humanoid**, you may also need to set all the **Bake Into Pose** options to true for each animation and all the **Based Upon** options to **Original**, as shown in the following screenshot:

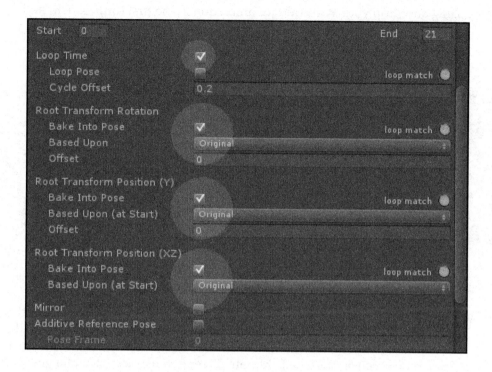

Settings of in place Idle, Walk and Run animations

3. Create an Animator Controller for your character.
4. Drag and drop the **Idle** animation into the Animator Controller to make it the default state.
5. Add a `float` **Speed** parameter in the Animator Controller.
6. Right-click on the empty space in the Animator Controller and choose **Create State | New From Blend Tree**. This will create an empty **Blend Tree**.
7. Click on the **Blend Tree** and change its name in the **Inspector** to something meaningful; we use **WalkAndRunBlend** in this example.
8. Double-click on the **Blend Tree**. It will open the **Blend Tree** settings.
9. Click on the plus button (marked with number **1** in the following screenshot) and choose the **Add Motion Field** option twice. Two **Motion** fields will be added.

10. Drag and drop your **WalkInPlace** animation in the first (upper) field and your **RunInPlace** animation in the second (lower) field. Fields are marked with number **2**, as shown in the following screenshot:

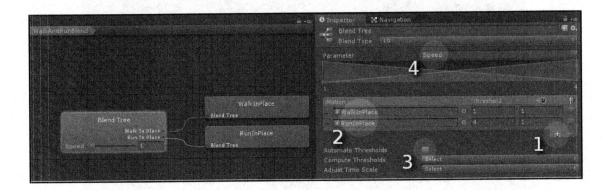

Blend Tree properties

11. Unselect the **Automate Thresholds** option (**3** in the preceding screenshot). This will make the **Threshold** field available for each **Motion** field. These are the thresholds of the **Parameter** used by the **Blend Tree** (marked with **4** in the preceding screenshot). If the **Parameter** is set to the exact value of a given threshold, the animation corresponding to that threshold is played. If the **Parameter** is set to a value between two thresholds, both animations are played with appropriate weights (and are blended together).

12. Set the **Thresholds** to 1 for the **WalkInPlace** motion and 4 for the **RunInPlaceMotion** (you may need to adjust these values later).

13. Click on the **Play** button in the **Preview** window, below the **Blend Tree** settings.

14. Find the **Speed** parameter slider on the **Blend Tree** node, and move it to see the animations blending smoothly, depending on the **Speed** parameter value.

15. Double-click on the empty space in the Animator Controller to get out of the **Blend Tree** settings.

16. Create two transitions:

    - **Idle | WalkAndRunBlend** with the condition set to **Speed** parameter greater than 0.5, **Has Exit Time** set to false, and **Transition Duration** set to 0.2 seconds.
    - **WalkAndRunBlend | Idle** with the condition set to **Speed** parameter less than 0.5, **HasExitTime** set to false, and **TransitionDuration** set to 0.2 seconds.

17. Write a script to move your character and set the **Speed** parameter value according to the movement speed of your character. We are using point and click movement in this example. You can find two scripts in the provided Unity project, `ClickToMove.cs` in the `Shared` scripts directory and `SetSpeedFromAgent.cs` in the `Scripts` directory of this recipe. The first one is used to set the destination for the Nav Mesh Agent component attached to the character.

18. In the `Update()` function of the `SetSpeedFromAgent.cs` script, we use the `desiredVelocity` of the **NavMeshAgent** to set the **Speed** parameter in our Animator Controller:

```
anim.SetFloat("Speed", agent.desiredVelocity.magnitude,
0.2f, Time.deltaTime);
```

19. The `anim` variable stores the reference to the Animator component of the character and the `agent` variable stores the reference to the Nav Mesh Agent component.

20. We are also adjusting the `agent.speed` variable in the `Update()` function to set the maximum speed of the **NavMeshAgent**. This allows us to make the character run when player holds the *Shift* button and walk when player releases the *Shift* button:

```
if (Input.GetKey(KeyCode.LeftShift) ||
Input.GetKey(KeyCode.RightShift))

{

    agent.speed = 4f;
}
else
{
    agent.speed = 1f;
}
```

How it works...

Blend Trees blend multiple animations based on the chosen Animator Controller parameter value and **Motion** fields' thresholds. In the standard Blend Tree, always only two animations are blended at the same time: the animation with a lower **Threshold** and the animation with a higher **Threshold**. Each animation is blended with the weight corresponding to the distance between the actual parameter value and the **Threshold** of the animation. For instance, if your **Walk** animation **Threshold** is set to 1, your **Run** animation **Threshold** is set to 2, and your current **Speed** parameter value equals 1.5, both **Walk** and **Run** animations will be played with 50 percent weight, which will most likely result in your character jogging slowly.

When blending **Walk** and **Run** animations, make sure to have the contact poses in the same normalized time in both animations. For instance, if the **Walk** animation has contact poses in 0 percent, 50 percent, and 100 percent of the animation, the **Run** animation should also have contact poses in 0 percent, 50 percent, and 100 percent of the animation. That will assure proper and smooth blending between the animations.

There's more...

There are a few other interesting options in the **Blend Tree** settings:

- You can set the **Blend Type** of a **Blend Tree** to the following:
    - **1D**: A simple Blend Tree using one parameter to define the weight of a currently played animation.
    - **2D Simple Directional**: This option uses two parameters for blending the animations, such as the X axis and Y axis. It is best used for motions representing different movement directions, for instance, walk forward, walk left, walk right, and walk back. It shouldn't be used with multiple animations representing movement in the same direction (such as walk forward and run forward).
    - **2D Freeform Directional**: This option is similar to the previous one, but you can use multiple animations representing movement in the same direction (such as walk and run). You need to add a single animation representing the motion in the 0, 0 position (such as idle).
    - **2D Freeform Cartesian**: This option is similar to the preceding one, but is used when your animations don't represent movement in different directions. It can be used to blend multiple versions of the idle animation, for instance.
    - **Direct**: You can control the weight of each of the nodes (Motion fields) directly. This type is often used while blending facial expressions (see the *Animating facial expressions with Blend Shapes* recipe in `Chapter 5`, *Character Actions and Expressions*).

- You can set a few additional **Motion** field options:
  - **Time Scale**: You can alter the playback speed of each animation in the **Blend Tree** by changing the number in the **Time Scale** field: the one with a clock icon. It is set to 1 (100 percent) by default.
  - **Mirror**: You can mirror any of the animations in the **Blend Tree** by checking the **Mirror** option, the one with a mirrored humanoid icon.

- You can also check the **Automate Thresholds** option, which will distribute the **Motion** fields' **Thresholds** evenly throughout the whole parameter's range. For instance, if your parameter's range is 0 to 9 and you have four animations, the first one will have a **Threshold** of 0, the second one 3, the third one 6, the fourth one 9. You can change the parameter range by clicking on the 0 and 1 numbers below the blending graph.
- You can also use the **Compute Thresholds** option (**Automate Thresholds** have to be set to **false**). This option will compute the **Thresholds** based on the root motion information from your animations (speed magnitude, velocity in the X axis, velocity in the Y axis, velocity in the Z axis, angular speed in radians, and angular speed in degrees). We will cover root motion in the next recipe.

Using root motion to drive Rigid Body characters' movement with animations

This recipe describes a very important concept called root motion. It allows the extraction of translation and rotation data from an animation and applies it to our character in the game.

Getting ready

To use root motion, first you need to create a character with a walk or run animation, that has translation in it; see the following screenshot:

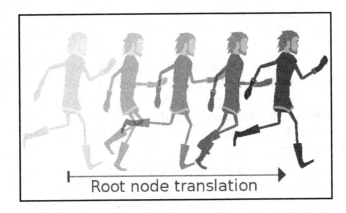

Frames of a run animation using root motion. The character is animated with root node translation

If you are using a **Humanoid** character, the hip bone is used as the root node, the one describing root motion. So hip translation will describe the translation of the character in game (you can still have motion in the *Y* axis as we can then adjust it in the **Import** settings). Its rotation will describe character rotation in the game. If you are using a Generic character, you need to choose the **Root Node** manually in the **Import** settings. Select the model, go to **Inspector**, click on the **Rig** tab, set the **Animation Type** to **Generic**, and select the **Root Node** from its drop-down menu (it contains the whole bone hierarchy of your rig).

You can also download the provided example Unity project and go to `Chapter 04 Character movement\Recipe 02 Using root motion to drive rigid body characters movement with animations` directory. You will find a scene called `Example.unity` there, with a **Humanoid** game object in the **Hierarchy**.

If you play the game, you can move the character with *WSAD* or the arrow keys and run with *Shift*. The movement is described by root motion, but steering is done with scripts (we simply rotate the character). In the `Rigs` directory, you can find the imported `Humanoid.fbx` file with all the required animations.

How to do it...

To move a using animations, follow these steps:

1. Import your character with root motion animations into Unity. We are using three animations in this example: **Idle**, **WalkRoot**, and **RunRoot**.

2. Select the character asset file and go to the **Inspector**. Make sure the Animation Type is set properly for your character (**Generic** or **Humanoid**). If you are using a **Generic** character, make sure to set its **Root Node**.

3. Go to the **Animation** tab and select the **Idle** animation. Select all the **Bake Into Pose** options. This bakes all the root motion data into the animation and makes it completely stationary. We don't want the **Idle** animation to move or rotate our character. You may also set the **Base Upon** option of the **Root Transform Rotation** to **Original**. This will make your character stand in the same pose as authored in the 3D software.

4. For **WalkRoot** and **RunRoot** animations, select the same options as for the Idle animation, but uncheck **Bake Into Pose** for **Root Transform Position (XZ)**. This will make our character move in the X and Z axes only. The Y movement of the root node and its rotation will be baked into the animation and will not be stored as root motion anymore.

5. Set the **Loop Time** options to true for all animations.

6. Apply the **import** settings.

7. Place your character onto a scene.

8. Select it in the **Hierarchy** and add a **Capsule Collider** to it. You may need to adjust the **Capsule Collider** properties to better fit your character. In our examples, we need to set the **Height** property to 2 units and the Y axis in the **Center** property to 1 unit.

9. Add a **Rigidbody** component to the character and set its **Constraints** to **Freeze Rotation** in every axis.

10. Navigate to the Animator component of the character (it is added automatically for animated game objects). Set **Update Mode** to **Animate Physics**. Make sure the **Apply Root Motion** option is checked in the Animator component.

11. Create an Animator Controller asset for the character.

12. Drag and drop the **Idle** animation into the Animator Controller to make it the default state.

13. Create a `float` **DesiredSpeed** parameter in the Animator Controller.

14. Right-click on the empty space in the Animator Controller and choose **Create State | New From Blend Tree**.

15. Click on the **Blend Tree** and change its name in the **Inspector** to **WalkAndRun**.

16. Double-click on the **Blend Tree** to open its settings.

17. Click on the **Plus** button and choose the **Add Motion Field** option twice.

18. Drag and drop your **WalkRoot** animation in the first (upper) field and your **RunRoot** animation in the second (lower) field.

19. Uncheck the **Automate Thresholds** option.

20. Set the **WalkRoot** animation **Threshold** to 1 and **RunRoot** animation **Threshold** to 2.

21. Double-click on the empty space in the Animator Controller to get out of the **Blend Tree** settings.

22. Create two transitions:
    - **Idle | WalkAndRun** with the condition set to **DesiredSpeed** parameter greater than 0.5, **Has Exit Time** set to false, and **Transition Duration** set to 0.2 seconds.
    - **WalkAndRun | Idle** with the condition set to **DesiredSpeed** parameter less than 0.5, **Has Exit Time** set to false, and **Transition Duration** set to 0.2 seconds.

23. Write a script to set the **DesiredSpeed** parameter and assign it to the character. Play the game to see the effect (make sure your scene has a floor with a collider to prevent your character from falling down).

24. You can also use the `MoveAndSteer.cs` script from the `Scripts` directory in this recipe. In the `Update()` function, we get the player input and save the values in `hor` and `ver` variables:

```
hor = Input.GetAxis("Horizontal");

ver = Input.GetAxis("Vertical");
```

25. Then we use the `Rotate()` method to rotate our character in the global *Y* axis (`Vector3.up`) based on the `hor` variable and a `public float rotationSpeed` variable (set to 90 degrees per second):

```
transform.Rotate(Vector3.up * hor * rotationSpeed *
Time.deltaTime);
```

26. We modify the `desiredSpeed` variable based on player input (we check if the player holds the *Shift* key):

```
if (Input.GetKey(KeyCode.LeftShift) ||
Input.GetKey(KeyCode.RightShift))
{
```

```
        desiredSpeed = 2f;
    }
    else
    {
        desiredSpeed = 1f;
    }
```

27. Finally, we use the vertical axis input stored in the `ver` variable and our `desiredSpeed` value to set the **DesiredSpeed** parameter in the Animator Controller (which moves our character using root motion):

```
anim.SetFloat("DesiredSpeed", desiredSpeed * ver, 0.2f,
Time.deltaTime);
```

28. We use the `SetFloat()` method with the `dampTime` parameter set to 0.2 seconds. That smooths out the changes of the parameter, which results in smoother blends between run and walk animations. The `anim` variable stores the reference to the Animator component and is set in the `Start()` function.

How it works...

The traditional approach to animation in games required all the movement animations to be done "in place." Characters were only moved with code (in Unity, with the `transform.Translate()` and `transform.Rotate()` methods, by changing the `rigidbody.velocity` vector, or by using the `rigidbody.ApplyForce()` method). Animations were merely visual effects and the game could work without a single animation being played. In the root motion approach, animations drive the movement of a character. The translation and rotation data is captured from the root node (a bone in the rig's hierarchy) and applied to the whole character in game. There are a few pros and cons to each approach:

Traditional approach	Root motion approach
Pros • Small number of animations • You can prototype without a single animation • You can adjust the speed of the character easily	Pros • Looks more natural, there is no foot sliding • You can create complex moves and even game mechanics with animations • You can have irregular movements such as a wounded or zombie walk

Cons	Cons
• Hard to remove foot sliding • Special attacks and evasion moves have to be programmed • Looks "last gen"	• Requires a bigger number of animations • You can't move your character without an animation • Longer prototyping iterations

There are a few important options regarding root motion in the **Animation Import Settings**:

- **Root Transform Rotation**: This option captures the rotation of the root node and applies it to the whole game object. You can set it to **Bake Into Pose** to disable the root motion rotation. With this option selected, the rotation will be treated as a visual effect of the animation and will not be applied to the game object. You should set it to true for every animation that shouldn't rotate the character. You can set the **Based Upon** option to one of the following options:
    - **Original**: This is the original root node rotation from the animation file.
    - **Body Orientation**: This alters the original rotation to make the character's upper body face the *Z* axis of the game object (the forward axis). You can also set the **Offset** option to offset the rotation.
- **Root Transform Position Y**: This option captures the vertical movement of the root node and applies it to the whole game object. You can set it to **Bake Into Pose** to disable the root motion in the *Y* axis. With this option selected, the *Y* axis motion will be treated as a visual effect of the animation and will not be applied to the game object. You should set it to true for every "on ground" animation (unless it's a jump). You can set the **Based Upon** option to the following options:
    - **Original**: This is the original root node *Y* axis motion from the animation file.
    - **Center Of Mass**: This aligns the center of mass with the root node vertical position.
    - **Feet**: This keeps the feet aligned with the vertical root node position. You can also set the **Offset** option to offset the vertical root node position.

- : This option captures the horizontal (XZ) movement of the root node and applies it to the whole game object. You can set it to **Bake Into Pose** to disable the root motion in the *X* and *Z* axis. With this option selected, horizontal motion will be treated as a visual effect of the animation and will not be applied to the game object. You should set it to true for all stationary animations (such as **Idle**). You can set the **Based Upon** option to the following options:

    Root Transform Position XZ: This option captures the horizontal (XZ) movement of the root node and applies it to the whole game object. You can set it to Bake Into Pose to disable the root motion in the X and Z axis. With this option selected, horizontal motion will be treated as a visual effect of the animation and will not be applied to the game object. You should set it to true for all stationary animations (such as Idle). You can set the Based Upon option to the following options: Original: This is the original root node horizontal motion from the animation file.

    - **Center Of Mass**: This aligns the center of mass with the root node horizontal position. You can also set the **Offset** option to offset the horizontal root node position.

There's more...

In Unity, you can combine root motion and traditional approaches very easily. In fact, we are doing it in this recipe. We control the movement of our character with root motion but we steer it with the `transform.Rotate()` method. You can also create a character with traditional movement ("in place" animations with all the **Bake Into Pose** options set to true for walk and run animations) and root motion actions such as attacks and evade moves.

Using root motion to steer a character

In this recipe, we will use animations to move and steer our character.

Getting ready

To use root motion for steering, you need to prepare a character with at least four animations: **Idle**, **WalkForward**, **WalkLeft**, and **WalkRight**. **WalkRight** and **WalkLeft** should make the character walk in circles (clockwise and counterclockwise). You don't need to create a full circle, just make sure that the start and end poses of the animation look similar. As always, all the animations should have contact points of the feet in the same normalized time. Make sure not to switch the left and right foot. If you start the **WalkForward** animation with the left foot forward, both **WalkLeft** and **WalkRight** animations should also start with the left foot forward, as shown in the following screenshot:

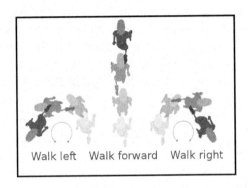

Steering animations using root motion

You can also use the example project; go to the Chapter 04 Character movement\Recipe 03 Using root motion to steer a character directory. You can find the Example.unity scene there, with a **Humanoid** character already animated in the scene's **Hierarchy**. You can start the game and use the *WSAD* keys to move the character relative to the camera. In the Rigs directory, you can find the Humanoid.fbx character with all the required animations.

How to do it...

To use root motion for steering, follow these steps:

1. Import your character with **Idle**, **WalkForward**, **WalkLeft**, and **WalkRight** root motion animations into Unity.
2. Select the character asset file and go to the **Inspector**. Make sure the **Animation Type** is set properly for your character (**Generic** or **Humanoid**). If you are using a **Generic** character, make sure to set its **Root Node**.
3. Go to the **Animation** tab and select the **Idle** animation. Select all the **Bake Into Pose** options and set the **Base Upon** option of the **Root Transform Rotation** to **Original**.
4. For the **WalkForward** animation, select the same options as for the **Idle** animation, but uncheck **Bake Into Pose** for **Root Transform Position (XZ)**.

5. For the **WalkLeft** and **WalkRight** animations, set all the option the same as for the **WalkForward** animation, but additionally uncheck the **Bake Into Pose** option for **Root Transform Rotation**.

6. Set the **Loop Time** options to true for these animations.

7. If your animations don't loop perfectly, you can try out the **Loop Pose** option. It will force the start and end poses to loop.

8. Apply the **import** settings.

9. Place your character into a scene.

10. Select it in the **Hierarchy** and add a **Capsule Collider** to it. You may need to adjust the **Capsule Collider** properties to better fit your character. In our examples, we need to set the **Height** property to 2 units and the Y axis in the **Center** property to 1 unit.

11. Add a **Rigidbody** component to the character and set its **Constraints** to **Freeze Rotation** in every axis.

12. Navigate to the Animator component of the character (it is added automatically for animated game objects). Set **Update Mode** to **Animate Physics**. Make sure the **Apply Root Motion** option is checked in the Animator component.

13. Create an Animator Controller asset for the character.

14. Drag and drop the **Idle** animation into the Animator Controller to make it the default state.

15. Create `float` **Speed** and `float` **Direction** parameters in the Animator Controller.

16. Right-click on the empty space in the Animator Controller and choose **Create State | New From Blend Tree**.

17. Click on the **Blend Tree** and change its name in the **Inspector** to **Steering**.

18. Double-click on the **Blend Tree** to open its settings.

19. Click on the plus button and choose the **Add Motion Field** option three times.

20. Set the **Parameter** of the **Blend Tree** to **Direction**; we will only use the **Direction** parameter for blending walk animations.

21. Drag and drop the **WalkLeft** animation in the first (upper) field, the **WalkForward** in the second (middle) field, and **WalkRight** in the third (lower) field.

22. Uncheck the **Automate Thresholds** option.

23. Set the **WalkLeft** animation **Threshold** to -45, **WalkForward** animation **Threshold** to 0, and the **WalkRight** animation **Threshold** to 45.

24. Double-click on the empty space in the Animator Controller to get out of the **Blend Tree** settings.

25. Create two transitions:
    - **Idle | Steering** with the condition set to **Speed** parameter greater than 0.5, **Has Exit Time** set to false, and **Transition Duration** set to 0.2 seconds.
    - **Steering | Idle** with the condition set to **Speed** parameter less than 0.5, **Has Exit Time** set to false, and **Transition Duration** set to 0.2 seconds.

26. Write a script to set the **Speed** and **Direction** parameters of our Animator Controller and assign that script to the character.

27. You can find the script in the provided Unity project in the `Scripts` directory of this recipe. It is called `RootMotionSteering.cs`.

28. In this script, we make the character move relative to the camera. In the `Update()` function, first we get and store player input in two variables, `hor` (for `Horizontal` input) and `ver` (for `Vertical` input):

```
hor = Input.GetAxis("Horizontal");

ver = Input.GetAxis("Vertical");
```

29. As we want to move the character relative to the camera, we're using the camera's forward and right axis to build a desired movement vector. Our camera is not completely horizontal (it can face slightly down, for instance), so first we need to calculate `cameraHorizontalForward` by taking the normal camera forward vector, setting its Y axis to 0, and normalizing the vector (so it has a length of 1):

```
cameraHorizontalForward = new
Vector3(cameraTransform.forward.x,
0f, cameraTransform.forward.z).normalized;
```

30. In this script, `cameraTransform` is a `public Transform` variable to which we attach our in-game camera.

31. Next we calculate the `desiredMoveDirection`: this is a vector pointing in the direction that we would like to move our character. This vector points directly to the right axis of the camera when the player holds the right arrow, to the left of the camera when player holds the left arrow, to the horizontal version of camera's forward axis (`cameraForwardHorizontal`) when the player holds the up arrow, and to the opposite direction of that vector when player holds the down arrow:

```
desiredMoveDirection = ver * cameraHorizontalForward + hor *
cameraTransform.right;
```

32. Next we calculate the angle between our character's forward vector and our `desiredMoveDirection` vector. We will use this value to set the **Direction** parameter in the Animator Controller. The `Vector3.Angle()` method returns an angle between two vectors. This angle is always positive (greater than 0). Therefore, we use the dot product of the `desiredMoveDirection` and `transform.right` (our character's right axis) vectors to determine whether the `desiredMoveDirection` points to the right or to the left of the character (the dot product is greater than 0 for vectors pointing in the same direction and less than 0 for vectors pointing in the opposite direction). We use the `Mathf.Sign()` method to make sure our dot product value equals -1 or 1. The result is an angle from -180 to 180 degrees; we store the value in the `float direction` variable:

```
direction = Vector3.Angle(transform.forward,
desiredMoveDirection) *
Mathf.Sign(Vector3.Dot(desiredMoveDirection,
transform.right));
```

33. Then we calculate a `float speed` variable's value; it is simply the magnitude of our `desiredMoveVector`. The `speed` variable is used to set the **Speed** parameter in our Animator Controller:

```
speed = desiredMoveDirection.magnitude;
```

34. Lastly, we use the calculated `direction` and `speed` values and set them in our Animator Controller, with a `dampTime` parameter of the `SetFloat()` method set to 0.2 seconds to smooth out the blends. The `anim` variable stores the reference to the Animator component of our character and is set in the `Start()` function:

```
anim.SetFloat("Direction", direction, 0.2f, Time.deltaTime);
anim.SetFloat("Speed", speed, 0.2f, Time.deltaTime);
```

How it works...

Root motion steering works the same way as the root motion movement. We are using the rotation of the root bone to rotate the character. In our example, the character is walking in circles, so its hips are rotating during the animation. That data is then used to rotate the whole character.

Again, to make the walk animations blend properly, you have to make sure that they all start with the same leg and that the feet contact poses are in the same normalized time as the animation.

If you are using a **Humanoid** rig, it is enough to create only forward and left animations. Then you can create a new animation clip in the character **Import Settings** in the **Animation** tab (you need to click on the plus button in the **Clips** section). When you choose the **WalkLeft** animation as the source, set it to **Mirror** and set its **Cycle Offset** to 0.5; you should get a proper **WalkRight** animation.

Using animations for better looking transitions

You've probably already noticed that sometimes when our character stops walking, it blends to the **Idle** animation in a strange way (with sliding feet). That is mostly visible when legs in the **Walk** animation are in a pose that looks like a mirrored Idle pose. We are going to fix this problem in this recipe.

Getting ready

You should use the same character as in the previous recipe and prepare one additional animation that will be a transition from a mirrored Idle pose to a normal Idle pose. You can also go to the Chapter 04 Character movement\Recipe 04 Using animations for better looking transitions directory and open the Example.unity scene. You will find our Humanoid character working the same way as in the previous recipe, but with a **ToIdle** animation added. You can also find the rig with all required animations in the Rigs directory.

How to do it...

To use additional animations for a better-looking transition, follow these steps:

1. First, follow all the points from the *Using root motion to steer a character* recipe to have a working character driven by root motion animations.
2. In the **Animation Import Settings** of the character, find your additional **ToIdle** animation. You may need to add it as a new clip by clicking on the plus button in the **Clips** section (**Animations** tab) and choosing the **ToIdle** animation as the source.

3. Check the **Bake Into Pose** option for **Root Transform Rotation** and **Root Transform Position (Y)** in the **ToIdle** animation.

4. Open the Animator Controller (this should be the same controller as in the previous recipe), add another float parameter, and call it **ToIdle**.

5. Go back to the **Animation Import Settings** and find the **WalkForward** animation.

6. In its import settings, go down to the **Curves** section, unfold it, and click on the plus icon to add a new **Animation Curve**.

7. Name it `ToIdle` (its name should match exactly the parameter we created in the Animator Controller in step 4). Click on the curve (it's a flat green line at the moment) to open the **Curve Editor**. Curves are described by float values on the vertical axis and normalized animation time on the horizontal axis.

8. Create a square-shaped curve with its maximum value equal to 1 and its minimum value equal to 0 (point **1** in the following screenshot). You can add curve control points by clicking on the curve. You can select points by clicking on them. You can remove points with the *Delete* key. To adjust the handles and interpolation types of a point, right-click on it. To set a square curve, choose **Both Tangents | Constant**. You can save a **Curve Preset** for later use by clicking on the small gear icon in the lower left corner of the **Curve Editor** (see point **2** in the following screenshot). When you scrub through the timeline (point **3** in the following screenshot), you can see where your curve starts in the normalized animation time (point **4** in the following screenshot):

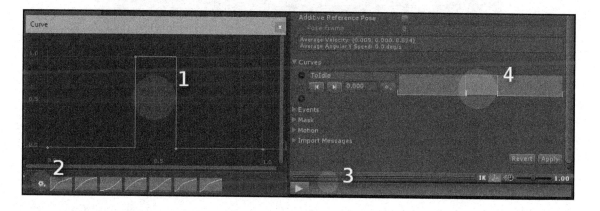

Animation Curve and the Curve Editor

9. In our example, the **Idle** animation has its left foot in front and our **ToIdle** animation starts with its right foot in front. During the animation, the character makes a small step to go back to the proper **Idle** pose with its left foot in front. In the **WalkForward** animation settings, try to set the curve value to 1, on the passing pose, when the right foot passes the left foot (and will be in front of the character few frames later).

10. Save the curve as a **Curve Preset** and add it to the **WalkLeft** and **WalkRight** animations. Set their curves names to **ToIdle** as well.

11. Go to the Animator Controller.

12. Add the **ToIdle** animation and create new state transitions:
    - **Steering | ToIdle** with two conditions, the **Speed** parameter less than 0.5 and the **ToIdle** parameter set to greater than 0.5. **Has Exit Time** should be set to false and **Transition Duration** should be set to 0.2 seconds.
    - **ToIdle | Idle** with no conditions, **Has Exit Time** set to true, and **Transition Duration** set to 0.2 seconds.

13. Alter the **Steering | Idle** transition by adding a second condition to it: the **ToIdle** parameter set to less than 0.5. See the following screenshot:

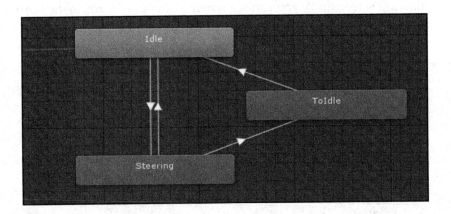

Animator Controller using an additional ToIdle transition animation

14. Start the game and try walking and stopping the character in different time of the walk animation. You should see that the character plays the **ToIdle** animation to prevent foot sliding in the most visible case of the walk pose being a mirrored idle pose.

How it works...

There are a few key elements of this recipe:

- **Animation Curves**: You can add curves to your animations (multiple curves per animation clip) in the **Import Settings, Animation** tab. Curves assign arbitrary float values to the animation frames. If the name of the curve is the same as the name of a parameter in the Animator Controller, the value of the parameter will be set to the value of the curve in any given frame of the animation.
- **Using curve values**: We are using the **ToIdle** value set by the **Animation Curves** in the **WalkForward**, **WalkLeft**, and **WalkRight** animations to trigger the transition from **Steering** to **Idle** (when the **ToIdle** value is less than 0.5) or from **Steering** to **ToIdle** animation (when the **ToIdle** parameter is greater than 0.5). This allows us to control the state transitions in the Animator Controller depending on the poses in the animations.

There's more...

We've covered the most simple (yet most visible) case in this recipe. You can add more stop animations (or any transition animations) from different walk and run poses. You may need to add a stop animation for walk and run passing poses and for all the extremes, depending on your Idle pose. To do so, add more curves to your animations and react to them in the Animator Controller. For instance, you may have curves for `LeftFootExtreme`, `RightFootExtreme`, `LeftFootPassing`, and `RightFootPassing`; use them in your **Walk** and **Run** animations to trigger appropriate stop animations.

You can also check the value of an **Animation Curve** in runtime by checking the corresponding parameter value of the Animator Controller in scripts. To do so, use the `animator.GetFloat()` method, where `animator` is the reference to the Animator component.

Using root motion for a 180 degrees turn

In the previous recipe, we've added a stop animation for a better transition to the idle state. We can add even more animations to our movement to make it more accurate and responsive. An example of such animation is a 180-degree turn.

Getting ready

Use the same character as in the previous recipe. Add a 180-degree turn animation, starting with the Idle pose and ending with the Idle pose rotated by 180 degrees in the vertical axis. Name the animation `180Turn` for clarity. You can open the provided example Unity project and go to the `Chapter 04 Character movement\Recipe 05 Using root motion for a 180 degrees turn` directory. You will find an `Example.unity` scene there. Play the game and try to walk in the direction opposite to the one the character is facing (press the down arrow). You can find the `Humanoid.fbx` asset in the `Rigs` directory with all the required animations.

How to do it...

To make a 180-degree turn, follow these steps:

1. Create four transitions (see the following screenshot):
2. Drag and drop your **180Turn** animation into the Animator Controller to create a new state.
3. Open the Animator Controller (this should be the same controller as in the previous recipe), add two float parameters, and call them `DirectionRaw` and `SpeedRaw`.
4. Check the **Bake Into Pose** option for the **Root Transform Position (Y)** in the **180Turn** animation.
5. In the **Animation Import Settings** of the character, find your additional **180Turn** animation. You may need to add it as a new clip by clicking on the plus button in the **Clips** section (**Animations** tab) and choosing the **180Turn** animation as the source.
6. Import the character and repeat all the steps from the *Using root motion to steer a character* and *Using animations for better looking transitions* recipes to have a character that is able to walk.
    - **Idle | 180Turn** with two conditions: The **SpeedRaw** parameter should be greater than 0.5 and the **DirectionRaw** parameter should be greater than 160. **Has Exit Time** should be set to false and **Transition Duration** should be set to around 0.1 seconds.
    - **Idle | 180Turn** (a second one) with two conditions: The **SpeedRaw** parameter should be greater than 0.5 and the **DirectionRaw** parameter should be less than -160. **Has Exit Time** should be set to false and **Transition Duration** set to around 0.1 seconds. We have two transitions between the same states because we want them to work as a

logical OR operator; if any of them is met, the transition will be triggered.

- **180Turn | Idle** with one condition: **Speed** parameter less than 0.5. **Has Exit Time** should be set to true and **Transition Duration** set to around 0.1 seconds.

- **180Turn | Steering** with one condition: **Speed** parameter greater than 0.5. **Has Exit Time** should be set to true and **Transition Duration** set to around 0.1 seconds.

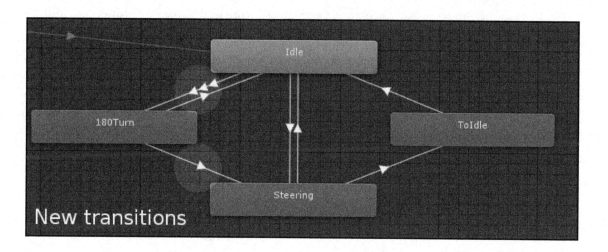

Animator Controller with additional 180Turn transition animation

7. Edit the **Idle | Steering** transition by adding two more conditions: **DirectionRaw** parameter greater than -160 and **DirectionRaw** parameter less than 160. Multiple conditions in the same transition work as an AND logical operator; all of them have to be met to trigger the transition.

8. The Animator Controller is set up, but we need to set the **SpeedRaw** and **DirectionRaw** parameters from scripts. We've created those two additional parameters because we need raw values here (not damped in time). First, open the script in which we calculate and set the `direction` and `speed` parameters. In this example, it is called `RootMotionSteering.cs`; you can find it in the `Chapter 04 Character movement\Recipe 03 Using root motion to steer a character\Scripts` directory.

9. We have two `float` variables there: `direction` and `speed`. They are being calculated every frame. We just need to make them `public` to be able to read them in another script (they are already public in the example script).

10. Write another script and call it `SetRawDirectionAndSpeed.cs` (you can find it in the `Scripts` directory of this recipe). To set the **DirectionRaw** and **SpeedRaw** parameters, we use the following lines in the `Update()` function:

```
anim.SetFloat("DirectionRaw", steeringScript.direction);
anim.SetFloat("SpeedRaw", steeringScript.speed);
```

11. In the preceding lines, the `anim` variable is the reference to the Animator component, the `steeringScript` variable is the reference to the **RootMotionScript** component (we set it with the `steeringScript = GetComponent<RootMotionSteering>()` line in the `Start()` function), and the `steeringScript.direction` and `steeringScript.speed` variables are the calculated raw direction and speed values.

> Alternatively, you can call the `anim.SetFloat("DirectionRaw", direction)` and `anim.SetFloat("SpeedRaw", speed)` methods directly in the `Update()` function of the `RootMotionSteering.cs` script (without writing another script).

12. Assign the script to the character, play the game, and try to walk in the direction opposite to the direction the character is facing. The character should start with an **180Turn** animation first.

How it works...

This recipe adds a start animation that works as a transition between the **Idle** and **Steering** states. We use the **SpeedRaw** and **DirectionRaw** parameters to check the raw player input (not damped). Using damped values wouldn't work in this case because the damped **Direction** parameter always starts from 0 and increases in time to the raw input direction value. This would always trigger the **Idle** | **Steering** transition before the **Idle** | **180Turn** transition as the **Idle** | **180Turn** transition checks if the direction is greater than 160 or less than -160 degrees.

There's more...

To make it simple, this recipe shows just one case of a start animation: the 180 degrees turn. You may require more start animations (-90 and +90 degrees turn or even -45, +45, -270, and +270 turns). You may also need to add a 180 degree turn transition from walking/running to make the character react to the input faster. In such a case, you may need to use **Animation Curves** to determine the walk/run position

(LeftPassing, RightPassing, LeftExtreme, RightExtreme) and play an appropriate turn animation accordingly (starting with the LeftPassing, RightPassing, LeftExtreme, or RightExtreme pose).

Making a character jump with 3-phase animation

In this recipe, we will make our character jump. Jumping is best done with physics, so we will use this approach.

Getting ready

Before we start, you should add three more animations to your character: a short **Jump** animation starting on the ground in a pose similar to **Idle**; an **InAir** animation, a looped animation of the character being in the air; and a **Land** animation starting when the character touches the ground with his feet and ending with the **Idle** pose. All those animations should be done "in place" without root node translation. You can open the provided example Unity project and go to the Chapter 04 Character movement\Recipe 06 Making a character jump with 3-phase animation directory. You will find an Example.unity scene there. Play the game and press the space bar to see the character jump. You will find all the animations needed in the Rigs directory.

How to do it...

To make the character jump, follow these steps:

1. Import the character and repeat all the steps from the *Using root motion to steer a character, Using animations for better looking transitions,* and *Using root motion for a 180 degrees turn* recipes to have a character that is able to move properly.

2. In the **Animation Import Settings** of the character, find your additional **Jump**, **InAir**, and **Land** animations. You may need to add them as new clips by clicking on the plus button in the **Clips** section (**Animations** tab) and choosing the appropriate animation as the source.

3. Check all the **Bake Into Pose** options for in **Jump**, **InAir**, and **Land** animations.

4. Open the Animator Controller (this should be the same controller as in the previous recipe) and add two parameters: a Trigger called **Jump** and a bool called **OnGround**.

5. Drag and drop your **Jump, InAir,** and **Land** animations into the Animator Controller.

6. Create these transitions, as shown in the following screenshot:
    - **Any State | Jump** with a **Jump** trigger parameter. **Has Exit Time** should be set to false and **Transition Duration** set to around 0.1 seconds.
    - **Jump | InAir** with no conditions: **Has Exit Time** should be set to true and **Transition Duration** set to around 0.1 seconds.
    - **InAir | Idle** with one condition: **OnGround** parameter set to true. **Has Exit Time** should be set to false and **Transition Duration** set to around 0.1 seconds.

7. Create a new script and call it `Jump.cs` (you can find it in the `Scripts` directory of this recipe).

8. In the `Update()` function of the script, we check if player pressed the space bar and if the character is on the ground: the `onGround` variable is set by the `GroundCheck()` function. If the player presses space bar and the character is on ground, we save the current game time as our `lastJumpTime` (this variable is used in the `GroundCheck()` function). Then we disable root motion on the Animator component by setting the `anim.applyRootMotion` variable to `false`. We set the `onGround` variable to `false` because our character is jumping. We add force to the **Rigidbody** component of the character and set the `Trigger` Jump in our Animator Controller. Lastly, we call the `GroundCheck()` function, which will be described later:

```
if (Input.GetKeyDown(KeyCode.Space) && onGround)
{
    lastJumpTime = Time.time;
    anim.applyRootMotion = false;
    onGround = false;
    rb.AddForce(Vector3.up* jumpForceUp +
transform.forward * jumpForceForward, ForceMode.Impulse);
    anim.SetTrigger("Jump");
}
GroundCheck();
```

9. The `anim` variable stores the reference to the Animator component. The `rb` variable stores the reference to the **Rigidbody** component. Both variables are set in the `Start()` function. The `jumpForceUp` and `jumpForceForward` are `public float` variables that control the applied force magnitude.

10. In the `GroundCheck()` function, we check if the current game time is bigger than our `lastJumpTime` plus the value of the `public float groundCheckPauseTime` variable. It this is not true, we are setting the `onGround` variable to false (we are assuming that the character is always in the air for a short moment after the player presses the jump button). Then we use the `Physics.Raycast()` method to check if our character stands on the ground. This method casts a ray from the `groundCheck` transform down. We set the maximum ray cast length with a `public float` variable, `maxGroundCheckDistance`. If the character is standing on ground, we set the `onGround` variable to true and we enable the root motion in the Animator component. We also set the `OnGround` parameter in our Animator Controller to the value of the `onGround` variable:

```
    void GroundCheck()
    {
       if(Time.time > lastJumpTime + groundCheckPauseTime        &&
Physics.Raycast(groundCheck.position, Vector3.down,
       maxGroundCheckDistance))
       {
            onGround = true;
            anim.applyRootMotion = true;
       }
       else
       {
            onGround = false;
       }
       anim.SetBool("OnGround", onGround);
    }
```

11. Assign the script to our character.
12. Create an empty child object of the character and call it `GroundCheck`. Set its local position to X = 0, Y = 0.1, and Z = 0. Make sure it is a child object of the character game object.
13. Assign the `GroundCheck` game object to the Ground Check field of the `Jump` script attached to the character.
14. Play the game and press the space bar to see the result.

How it works...

In this recipe, we are using physics to make the character jump. To do it properly, we need to turn off root motion in the Animator component when the character is in the air to make it fully controlled by the physics engine instead of our animations. We are allowing the character to jump only when it's standing on the ground. To avoid setting the `onGround` variable to true just after the jump, we temporarily disable the ground checking function after the player presses the jump button.

Jump animation is divided into three parts:

- **Jump**: In this animation, our character starts to jump
- : This is a long looped animation of the character being in the air (or falling down)

InAir: This is a long looped animation of the character being in the air (or falling down)
Land: This animation is played when the character touches the ground after being in the air

There's more...

Again, this recipe shows the most basic jump setup. You may want to add more start jump animations from different poses (run and walk extremes, passing poses, and another one from the idle animation). To do so, create Animator Controller parameters for each of those poses and **Animation Curves** with the same names as the parameters you've created. Use the **Animation Curves** in the walk and run animations to tell Unity which pose is the animation currently in (left/right extreme or left/right passing pose). Use the parameters in the Animator Controller to set the appropriate transitions between the animations. You may also need to add more landing animations that would transition to idle, walk, or run, depending on the current character **Speed** parameter value (player input).

Using root motion to drive a NavMesh Agents' movement with animations

In this recipe, we will use root motion to move and steer a character with a Nav Mesh Agent component. This can be used to get rid of foot sliding in this type of character.

Getting ready

We are going to use the same character as in the previous recipe with all its animations. You should have a character with at least the **Idle**, **WalkLeft**, **WalkForward**, and **WalkRight** animations ready and set up in the Animator Controller the same way as in the *Using root motion to steer a character* recipe. You can also go to the `Chapter 04 Character movement\Recipe 07 Using root motion to drive Navmesh Agents movement with animations` directory. You will find an `Example.unity` scene there. Open it, play the game, and click on the ground to make the characters move using **NavMesh** Agents and root motion.

How to do it...

To use root motion for moving and steering a character with Nav Mesh Agent component, follow these steps:

1. Import the character with the **Idle**, **WalkLeft**, **WalkForward**, and **WalkRight** animations and set it up the same way as in the *Using root motion to steer a character* recipe, but don't write the `RootMotionSteering.cs` script as we will create a new one.

2. Add the Nav Mesh Agent component to the character. Make sure it also has the **Capsule Collider** component and the **Rigidbody** component with frozen rotation in every axis. Also make sure that the Animator component's **Apply Root Motion** option is set to true and **Update Mode** set to **Animate Physics** (the same way as in the *Using root motion to steer a character* recipe).

3. Bake the **NavMesh** in the scene. To do so, make sure your ground model has a collider attached (you can use the **Mesh Collider** component). Then go to **Window | Navigation**. Select the ground in your scene and set it to **Navigation Static** in the **Object** tab of the **Navigation** window. Click on the **Bake** button at the bottom of the **Navigation** window. After a short while, **NavMesh** should be baked (it is visible in the scene as a light blue, semitransparent mesh covering the ground model). It is needed for our **NavMesh** Agent to work.

4. If your character is using any scripts from this book, remove them from its **Inspector** (we don't need the **Jump**, **RootMotionSteering**, and **SetRawDirectionAndSpeed** scripts).

5. Create a new script and call it `NavMeshAgentWithRigidBody.cs`. We will use both the **NavMesh** Agent and the **Rigidbody** components in this script.

6. In the `Update()` function of the script, we first disable updating rotation and position in the **NavMesh** Agent. That will prevent the agent from moving our character's transform. Then we calculate the `float direction` variable's value. We do it in a very similar way to what we did in the *Using root motion to steer a character* recipe, but instead of creating our own `desiredMoveDirection` vector, we are using the **NavMesh** Agent's `desiredVelocity` vector. This vector describes the speed and direction the agent would like to move with:

```
agent.updatePosition = false;
agent.updateRotation = false;

direction = Vector3.Angle(transform.forward,
agent.desiredVelocity) *
Mathf.Sign(Vector3.Dot(agent.desiredVelocity,
transform.right));
```

In the preceding code `agent` is the variable in which we store the reference to the Nav Mesh Agent component. We set this reference in the `Start()` function.

7. Next we calculate the `float speed` variable value: it's simply the magnitude of the `agent.desiredVelocity` vector. We also set the **Direction**, **Speed**, **DirectionRaw**, and **SpeedRaw** parameters in our Animator Controller using the `anim` variable that stores the reference to the Animator component. The `anim` variable is set in the `Start()` function. Lastly, we set the `agent.nextPosition` to be the same as our transform position every frame. This prevents the agent from moving away from our character's transform.

8. Save the script and attach it to the character.

9. We also need a script to tell the **NavMesh** Agent where we want to go. There is a `ClickToMove.cs` script in the `Shared Scripts` folder in the provided Unity example. In the `Update()` function, we use the `agent.SetDestination()` method when the player presses the left mouse button. A ray is cast from the mouse cursor position in the main camera's forward direction. If the ray hits a collider, the hit position is used to set the new destination for the **NavMesh** Agent:

```
if (Input.GetKeyDown(KeyCode.Mouse0))
{
    if (Physics.Raycast(Camera.main.ScreenPointToRay(
    Input.mousePosition), out hit))
    {
        agent.SetDestination(hit.point);
    }
}
```

In the preceding code `agent` is a `public NavMeshAgent` variable that stores the reference to the Nav Mesh Agent component. We assign this reference manually in the **Inspector** by dragging the game object with the Nav Mesh Agent component to the **Agent** field of the script. The `hit` variable is a global `RaycastHit` variable that is used by the `Physics.Raycast()` method to store the ray cast result.

10. Save the script and attach it to the character. Drag and drop the character game object to the **Agent** field of the script (the script is attached to the same game object but can be attached to any game object).
11. Play the game and click on the ground to see the character move using both **NavMesh** Agent and root motion.

How it works...

This recipe has a few key elements that make it work:

- **NavMesh and NavMesh Agent**: Nav Mesh Agent component is used to navigate in the game level with a baked **NavMesh**. Without one of those elements, our character wouldn't be able to move effectively with point and click input.
- **Disabling the agent's updateRotation and updatePosition**: By default, **NavMesh** Agents update the rotation and position of a game object. To use root motion, we need to disable this feature and update the game object's position and rotation with the root node animation instead.
- **Rigid Body and Animator with Apply Root Motion set to true**: We use Rigid Body to have collisions between all the objects in the game (not only other **NavMesh** Agents) and we use the **Apply Root Motion** option in the Animator to make the character move with root node animation.

There's more...

In the `Scripts` directory of this recipe, you can also find a `NavAgent.cs` script that uses root motion without the **Rigidbody** component. The `Update()` function of the script is very similar to the `NavMeshAgentWithRigidBody.cs` script that we were using in this recipe, but we enable updating the position by the Nav Mesh Agent component. We only disable rotation updating. We add a `OnAnimatorMove()` function to the script. This method is called every frame after Unity finishes evaluating all the states in the Animator.

In that function, we set the `agent.velocity` vector to be the same as the velocity of the root node. We also update the transform rotation to be the same as the root node's rotation:

```
void OnAnimatorMove()
{
    agent.velocity = anim.deltaPosition /
    Time.deltaTime;
    transform.rotation = anim.rootRotation;
}
```

Using triggers to grab an edge while jumping

Grabbing an edge while jumping is a common feature, especially in platform games. It is easily done in Unity with a small amount of scripting. This recipe covers a simple edge grab functionality.

Getting ready

You need three new animations for our character: **EdgeGrab**, **EdgeGrabLoop**, and **EdgeGrabClimb**. The first one is a transition from the **InAir** animation to the **EdgeGrabLoop** animation. It should have minimum movement in the root node if possible. The second one is a looped animation of hanging on the cliff's edge. The last one is an animation that uses root motion to climb the cliff's edge and ends with an **Idle** pose. See the following screenshot for reference:

Frames of the EdgeGrabClimb animation using root motion to climb over the cliff's edge

EdgeGrab and **EdgeGrabLoop** animations should have all **Bake Into Pose** options selected in **Import Settings**. **EdgeGrabLoop** should also have the **Loop Time** option selected. You can also use the provided example Unity project and go to the `Chapter 04 Character movement\Recipe 08 Using triggers to grab an edge while jumping` directory. You will find an `Example.unity` scene there. Open it, play the game, and press the space bar to jump towards the edge. After the character grabs it, press the up arrow to climb over the edge.

How to do it...

To be able to grab a cliff's edge while jumping, follow these steps:

1. Import your character to Unity. Make sure your character can move and jump (follow the *Making a character jump with 3-phase animation* recipe if needed). The character should use a **Rigidbody** component for moving and jumping. You can still use root motion to move and steer the character.

2. Place the character in your scene and make sure it has the `Player` tag set.

3. You need to have a cliff to be able to grab its edge. Import a suitable model or use a Cube from the **Game Object | 3D Object | Cube menu**. The cliff game object should have a collider (**Mesh Collider** for example) because we use a Rigid Body character.

4. Add a trigger game object (an empty game object with a **Box Collider** component set to **Is Trigger**). Name it `GrabTrigger` for clarity. Place the trigger near the edge of the cliff. The trigger is marked with the number **1**, as shown in the screenshot after step 5.

5. Add another empty game object and name it **RootTarget**. Place it in the position where your character's transform should be when it grabs the edge. It is marked with the number **2**, as shown in the following screenshot. You can adjust the exact position later.

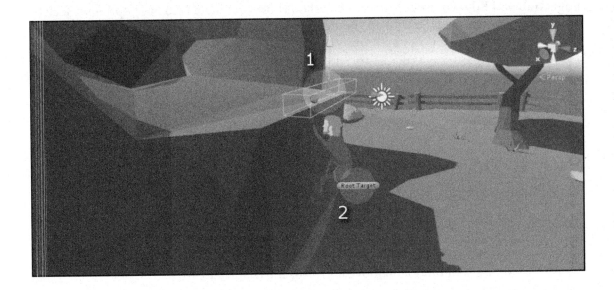

GrabTrigger and RootTarget game objects' placement

6. Open the character's Animator Controller. Drag and drop your **GrabEdge**, **GrabEdgeLoop**, and **GrabEdgeClimb** animations into the controller.

7. Add a `Trigger` **GrabEdge** parameter and a `Trigger` **PullUp** parameter to the controller.

8. Create these transitions:
   - **Jump** | **GrabEdge** with one condition: **GrabEdge** trigger parameter. **Has Exit Time** should be set to false and **Transition Duration** set to around 0.2 seconds.
   - **InAir** | **GrabEdge** with one condition: **GrabEdge** trigger parameter. **Has Exit Time** should be set to false and **Transition Duration** set to around 0.2 seconds.
   - **GrabEdge** | **GrabEdgeLoop** with no conditions. **Has Exit Time** should be set to true and **Transition Duration** set to around 0.2 seconds.
   - **GrabEdgeLoop** | **GrabEdgeClimbing** with one condition: **PullUp** trigger parameter. **Has Exit Time** should be set to false and **Transition Duration** set to around 0.2 seconds.
   - **GrabEdgeClimbing** | **Idle** with no conditions: **Has Exit Time** should be set to true and **Transition Duration** set to around 0.2 seconds.

9. Close the Animator Controller and assign it to the character's Animator component.

10. Create a new script and call it `EdgeGrab.cs` (you can find the finished script in the `Scripts` directory of this recipe). The goal of this script is to play appropriate animation when we touch the edge of the cliff. We also need to disable collisions and physics and make sure our character will be in the right place while playing the animation (in the **RootTarget** game object's position).

11. First we need a `Grab()` function to handle the situation when player starts touching the edge (we will call this function from our **GrabTrigger** game object later):

```
public void Grab (Transform target) {
    grabTarget = target;

    if (grabTarget != null)
    {
        anim.SetTrigger("GrabEdge");
        adjustPosition = true;
        steeringScript.enabled = false;
        jumpScript.enabled = false;
        rb.isKinematic = true;
        anim.applyRootMotion = true;
    }
}
```

12. This function has a `target` parameter which will hold the reference to the **RootTarget** game object. We assign this parameter to a class member variable `grabTarget` (we will use it later). We are starting to play the **GrabEdge** animation by setting the **GrabEdge** `Trigger` in the controller. We are also setting a flag (class member) `adjustPosition` to `true`. This flag is used later to determine whether we should match our character's position with the **RootTarget** game object's position. Then we disable two scripts stored in `steeringScript` and `jumpScript` variables. We are doing it only because we don't want them to interfere with our edge grab action. We are also setting the `isKinematic` option on our **Rigidbody** component (the `rb` variable stores the reference to it) to disable collisions and gravity. Lastly, we enable root motion for our Animator Component (reference to which is stored in the `anim` variable). That makes the **GrabEdgeClimb** animation work.

13. Next we have to write the `GrabLerp()` function that handles the character's position and **RootTarget**'s position matching:

```
void GrabLerp()
{
    if (grabTarget == null || !adjustPosition)
    {
        return;
    }
    if ((transform.position -
    grabTarget.
```

5
Character Actions and Expressions

This chapter explains the usage of animations for character actions and expressions and covers the following recipes:

- Creating an appear or a disappear animation
- Creating background characters and critters with animation-driven behavior
- Using **Blend Trees** to create randomized actions
- Using `Quaternion.LookRotation()` and `Animator.SetLookAtPosition()` methods to make characters follow an object with their gaze
- Action Points – performing an action in a specified spot
- Synchronizing an animation with objects in the scene
- Using IK for interacting with scene objects
- Animating facial expressions with Blend Shapes

Introduction

In most games, characters perform a variety of actions and expressions. This chapter explains how to use animations to create believable behaviors and interactions.

Creating an appear or a disappear animation

If our game has monsters in it, there is a huge probability that we will need to use an appear or a disappear animation to introduce such characters in the scene. Often times, monsters spawn near our players to ambush them. This is where the appear animations come in handy.

Getting ready

Before we start, you should have a character with at least two animations: a looped **Idle** animation and an **Appear** animation. This animation should start below the ground (or high in the air if your character is a flying one). It should end with the **Idle** pose. See the following image for reference:

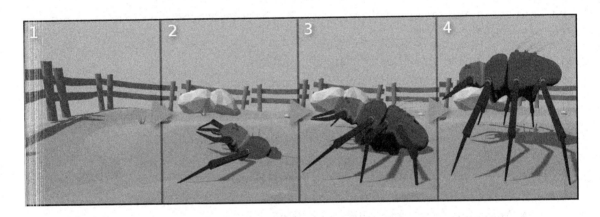

Appear animation key frames (the animation is done "in place")

You can download the provided example; open the project in Unity and go to the Chapter 05 Character actions and expressions\Recipe 01 Creating an appear or disappear animation folder. You will find a scene called Example. Scene there. When you play it, a Spider character will be spawned (instantiated) and it will play the **Appear** animation. In the Rigs directory, you can find the Spider.fbx asset with the required animations.

How to do it...

To create an appear animation, follow these steps:

1. Import your animated character with **Idle** and **Appear** animations.
2. Make sure to check the **Idle** animation's **Loop Time** option.
3. Place the imported character in the scene.
4. Create a new Animator Controller and call it `Appear` (or you can edit an existing controller).
5. Drag and drop your **Appear** animation into the controller and make sure it is the default state. If not, right-click on it and choose the **Set As Layer Default State** option.
6. Drag and drop your **Idle** animation into the controller.
7. Create one transition:
    * **Appear | Idle** with no conditions: **Has Exit Time** should be set to true and **Transition Duration** set to 0.2 seconds.
8. Assign the Animator Controller to the character standing on the scene (to its Animator component).
9. To better see the **Appear** animation in action, create a prefab from the character. To do so, drag and drop it from the **Hierarchy** to any folder in the **Project** View.
10. Delete the character from the **Hierarchy** and write a script to spawn (instantiate) the character in runtime. In this recipe, we use the `Spawner.cs` script from the example Unity project's `Shared Scripts` directory.
11. This script spawns a prefab (a list of prefabs) in the same position and with the same rotation as the **Spawner** game object (the object the `Spawner.cs` script is attached to).

How it works...

We use a very simple mechanism here—when Unity instantiates an animated game object, it always plays the game object's default animation state. So, when we set our **Appear** animation to be the default state, it is played when the character is spawned (instantiated). This way we can create interesting animations to make the characters appear near our players. In this example, our character crawls out from the ground.

There's more...

To make the effect complete, you should also add a spawn VFX to the character. You can find an example of that: a particle system prefab called **RocksEffect** in the `Prefabs` directory in the provided Unity project. This is an "unearthing" effect. We spawn it with the same `Spawner.cs` script. Additionally, this prefab has an `AutoDestroy.cs` script that destroys the spawned effect after a few seconds.

Creating background characters and critters with animation-driven behavior

In this recipe, we are going to create animated characters that will serve as decorations in the game. Such characters' behavior is driven only by animations; thus, we can have quite a large number of them in the game.

Getting ready

Before we start, we need to have a character with a few animations. In this example, we are using a bird. It has **Idle**, **StartFlying**, **FlyingInCircles**, and **Land** animations. The **Idle** animation is looped and played when our birds sits on the ground. The **StartFlying** animation is a transition between **Idle** and **FlyingInCircles**, which is a looped animation of the bird flying around. The last animation, the **Land** animation, is a transition between **FlyingInCircles** and **Idle**. We don't use root motion for those animations because we want the birds to always land in the same position (we don't want to check where the ground is, it's just a decoration).

You can also download the provided example Unity project and go to the `Chapter 05 Character actions and expressions\Recipe 02 Creating background characters and critters with animation driven behavior` directory. You will find a scene called `Example.scene` there, with some birds sitting around. If you press the space bar, the birds will start flying. If you press it again, they will land. In the `Rigs` directory, you can find the `Bird.fbx` character with all required animations.

How to do it...

To create lightweight background characters with animation-driven behaviors, follow these steps:

1. Import your character (a bird with **Idle**, **StartFlying**, **FlyingInCircles**, and **Land** animations) to Unity.
2. Create a new Animator Controller.
3. Drag and drop the **Idle**, **StartFlying**, **FlyingInCircles**, and **Land** animations into the controller.
4. Create a `bool` **Fly** parameter. We will use it later to make the birds start flying.
5. Create four transitions:
    * **Idle | Start Flying** with the conditions: **Fly** parameter should be set to true, **Has Exit Time** set to false, and **Transition Duration** set to 0.2 seconds.
    * **StartFlying | FlyingInCircles** with no conditions: **Has Exit Time** should be set to true and **Transition Duration** set to 0.2 seconds.
    * **FlyingInCircles | Land** with one condition: **Fly** parameter should be set to false, **Has Exit Time** set to true, and **Transition Duration** set to 0.2 seconds. We need to set **Has Exit Time** to true in this case because our **Land** animation starts from the last frame of the **FlyingInCircles** animation.
    * **Land | Idle** with no conditions: **Has Exit Time** set to true and **Transition Duration** set to 0.2 seconds.
6. Place our character in the scene and assign the controller to its Animator component.
7. Add a `Bird` tag to the character. We will use the tag in the following script.
8. Create a new script and call it `FlockDecoration.cs`.
9. In this script, we first find all the game objects with the `Bird` tag and store them in the `GameObject[] birds` array. We do it in the `Start()` function. In the `Update()` function, when the player presses the space bar, we set the `bool` **Fly** parameter in our controller to its inverted value (if it was true, we set it to false, and vice versa). We do it for every bird stored in the `birds` array:

```
for (int i = 0; i < birds.Length; i++)

{

        Animator anim = birds[i].GetComponent<Animator>();
        anim.SetBool("Fly", !anim.GetBool("Fly"));
```

}

10. Assign the script to an empty game object in the scene. Play the game and press the space bar to see the effect. You can also duplicate the **Bird** game object several times.

How it works...

This recipe uses the Animator Controller to create states for the character. Our bird can sit on the ground and fly. We also have transition animations between those two looped states to make the bird start flying or land. With this simple setup, we can create birds that will react to the player. They can, for instance, start flying when player is near and land if player walks away. The purpose of this recipe is to show that we can create interesting behavior with just the animations alone (and one script to call the animations). Animated game objects that have no scripts and no rigid bodies attached are quite lightweight in Unity. That allows us to use them as interesting decorations.

There's more...

In the `FlockDecoration.cs` script, we also try to desynchronize the animations of our birds. We do it in the `Start()` function for every bird by setting the `speed` variable in its `Animator` to a random number:

```
for (int i = 0; i < birds.Length; i++)
{
    Animator anim = birds[i].GetComponent<Animator>();
    anim.speed = Random.Range(0.8f, 1.3f);
}
```

That makes the birds play their animations with randomized playback speed. We could randomize it further by creating multiple versions of **FlyInCircles** and **Idle** animations. Then we would have to randomly choose currently played animation (see the next recipe for details).

In the **Import** settings of our FBX file, in the **Rig** tab, we also checked the **Optimize Game Objects** option. This makes our rig hierarchy (bones) invisible in the **Hierarchy** and reduces the number of game objects Unity has to handle.

Using Blend Trees to create randomized actions

In this recipe, we will create a simple randomized action using a Blend Tree.

Getting ready

Before we start, we need to have a character with at least two different animations for the randomization to work. In this example, we are using a character with the **Walk**, **Idle**, **Hurray**, **Wave**, and **PickUp** animations. The **Walk** and **Idle** animations are used as helpers. The three others are being randomized. You can also use the example project; go to the `Chapter 05 Character actions and expressions\Recipe 03 Using blend trees to create randomized actions` directory. You can find the `Example.scene` scene there, with two characters. You can start the game to see the effect. Both characters should play different animation after walking. You may need to start the game several times because we have only three animations to pick from, so there is a 9 percent chance that both characters will play the same animation. In the `Rigs` directory, you can find the required animations.

Characters with randomized animations

How to do it...

To use randomized animations, follow these steps:

1. Import your character with the animations to pick from. In our case, they are **Hurray**, **Wave**, and **PickUp**. We also use **Idle** and **Walk** animations (the Walk animation is used before the randomized action and the Idle animation is used after).
2. Create a new Animator Controller (or edit an existing one).
3. Create a new `float` parameter in the controller and call it `Random`.
4. Create a new **Blend Tree** in the controller and name it `RandomAction`.
5. In the **Blend Tree** settings, add **Motion Fields** for your randomized animations. In our example, we have three **Motion Fields** (for **Hurray**, **Wave**, and **PickUp**).
6. Assign your animations to the **Motion Fields**.
7. Choose the **Random** parameter as the **Parameter** of the **Blend Tree**.
8. Uncheck the **Automate Thresholds** option.
9. Set the **Thresholds** to integer numbers, starting from 0. In our example, they are 0, 1, and 2.
10. Exit **Blend Tree** settings.
11. Create transitions to and from the **Blend Tree**, if needed. In our example, we have following transitions:
    - **Walk | RandomAction** with no conditions: **Has Exit Time** should be set to true and **Transition Duration** set to 0.2 seconds. Our scene starts with the characters playing one cycle of the **Walk** animation and then transitioning to the **RandomAction** Blend Tree.
    - **RandomAction | Idle** with no conditions: **Has Exit Time** should be set to true and **Transition Duration** set to 0.2 seconds. Our scene ends with the characters transitioning from **RandomAction** to **Idle** animation.
12. Place the character in the scene.
13. Assign the controller to the character's Animator component.
14. Create a new script and call it `RandomAction.cs`.
15. In this script's `Start()` function, we create an integer random value and set it as the value of our `float` **Random** parameter in the controller:

```
Animator anim = GetComponent<Animator>();
int randomValue = Random.Range(0, numActions);
anim.SetFloat("Random", (float)randomValue);
```

16. In the preceding script, `numActions` is a `public int` variable that stores the total number of randomized actions in our **Blend Tree** (3 in our example).
17. Assign the script to the character and play the game to see the effect. You may need to start the game multiple times or copy the character several times.

How it works...

The trick here is to set the **Random** parameter in the controller before we transition to the **Blend Tree**. This way we don't see the sudden change in the animations (the animation is already chosen before we start playing it).

We are still using the `float` type parameter in the **Blend Tree** because we cannot use integers in **Blend Trees** in Unity.

There's more...

There are situations where you need to have multiple randomized animations played one after another, for instance, when your character is standing in place and performing some random actions. To be able to set the parameter responsible for randomizing the animations, you may need to transition through a neutral **Idle** pose. In that state, you can set the parameter value safely. See the following image:

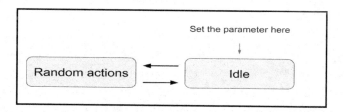

Setting the parameter in the safe Idle state

Additionally, if your random actions blend together nicely (maybe they are different versions of the **Idle** animation), you can allow the parameter to change when you are already in the **Blend Tree**. To do so, make sure to use the `SetFloat()` function with the `dampTime` parameter set to an appropriate value (0.5 should be okay, but you will need to experiment).

Using Quaternion.LookRotation() and Animator.SetLookAtPosition() methods to make characters follow an object with their gaze

Sometimes you need a character to look at an object in the game, for instance, at the camera. To do so, we can use two methods: `Quaternion.LookRotation()` and `Animator.SetLookAtPosition()`. We will cover both in this recipe (the second one is covered in the *There's more...* section).

Getting ready

To follow this recipe, you need a character with one **Idle** animation. You can also go to the `Chapter 05 Character actions and expressions\Recipe 04 Using LookRotation and SetLookAtPosition methods to make characters follow an object with their gaze` directory. Open the `Example.scene` scene there. You will find the **HumanoidLookAt** and **HumanoidIKLookAt** game objects there. The first one uses a generic `LookAt()` method and the second one uses the `Animator.SetLookAtPosition()` function. To see the effect, play the game, switch to the **Scene** View, and move the **Target** game object around (a red shiny sphere).

Characters looking at the Target game object

How to do it...

To make characters follow an object with their gaze, follow these steps:

1. Import the character into Unity and place it in a scene.
2. Make sure to create an Animator Controller with at least one animation, or use an existing one.
3. To use the first `Quaternion.LookRotation()` method, create a new script and call it `CharacterLookAt.cs`.
4. In that script, we use the void `LateUpdate()` function to alter bone rotation after all animations are evaluated. In that function, we first check if a `public float weight` variable is less than or equal to 0. If so, we don't do anything (we turn off the **look at** behavior):

   ```
   if (weight <= 0f)
   {
       return;
   }
   ```

5. If that is not true, we calculate our desired `lookDirection`. This is a vector in which our character should look. We calculate it by subtracting our `public Transform bone` position from the `public Transform target` position. This vector is then damped in time using the `SmoothDamp()` function. This prevents it from sudden changes. We use a `public float dampTime` variable to determine the time in which we smooth the vector out. The `dampVelocity` vector is class member variable required by the `SmoothDamp()` function to store the changes in the `lookDirection` vector between frames:

   ```
   lookDirection = Vector3.SmoothDamp(lookDirection,
   target.position - bone.position, ref dampVelocity,
   dampTime);
   ```

6. Next we check if the angle between our desired `lookDirection` vector and the character's `transform.forward` vector is greater than our `public float maxAngle` value. If so, we calculate the `finalLookVector`. This is our character's `transform.forward` vector, which is rotated toward the desired `lookDirection` vector by the `maxAngle` degrees. This way we create a *cone of vision* for our character and prevent it from breaking the neck joint. We need to use the `Mathf Deg2Rad` constant to change our `maxAngle` degrees to radians because the `Vector3.RotateTowards()` function uses radians instead of degrees. If the angle between `lookDirection` and `transform.forward` is less than or equal to `maxAngle`, we don't alter the `lookDirection`:

```
if (Vector3.Angle(lookDirection, transform.forward) >
maxAngle)
{
    finalLookVector =
    Vector3.RotateTowards(transform.forward,
    lookDirection, Mathf.Deg2Rad*maxAngle, 0.5f);
}
else
{
    finalLookVector = lookDirection;
}
```

7. Finally, we calculate the `Quaternion` rotation value by using the `Quaternion.LookRotation()` method and multiplying its result by a `public Vector3 additinalRotation` value. First we need to turn this `Vector3` into a `Quaternion` by using the `Quaternion.Euler()` function. Multiplying two quaternions is simply adding an additional rotation. We need to use the `additionalRotation` vector because, in most cases, the head bone's forward axis doesn't match the face of our character. By applying an additional rotation of +90 or -90 degrees in one of the axes (*X*, *Y*, or *Z*), we can make the script work for every rig. After calculating the rotation, we linearly interpolate the current `bone.rotation` value to our calculated `rotation` using the `weight` value. This way we can turn the **look at** on and off easily:

```
rotation = Quaternion.LookRotation(finalLookVector) *
Quaternion.Euler(additionalRotation);
bone.rotation = Quaternion.Lerp(bone.rotation, rotation,
weight);
```

8. Save the script and add it to the character.
9. Drag and drop the head bone of the character to the **Bone** field in the script's **Inspector**.
10. Drag and drop the **look at** target transform to the **Target** field in the script's **Inspector**.
11. You may need to adjust the **Additional Rotation** field. Experiment in **Play Mode** with +90 or -90 values in different axes to find a matching value. Modifying one axis at a time should be enough.
12. Move the target transform in **Play Mode** to see the effect (you can do it in the **Scene** View).

How it works...

In this recipe, we are using a `Quaternion.LookRotation()` method that creates a rotation, which works the same way as we would use the `Transform.LookAt()` function. It is applied to the head bone's transform. Our character's rig and all its bones are standard transforms in Unity. We can modify their rotation or position as we would with other game objects, but we need to do it in the `LateUpdate()` function because all the animations have to be evaluated first. We cannot modify any of the bones' transforms in the `Update()` function because all our modifications would be overwritten by the animations.

The `Quaternion.LookRotation()` function creates a rotation that makes a transform forward axis point to the desired direction. In most cases, the head bone's forward axis doesn't match the face of the character; thus, we need to apply an additional rotation. To do so, we use the `public Vector3 additionalRotation` variable.

There's more...

For humanoid characters, we can use the IK approach. To do so, follow these steps:

1. Make sure to check the IK Pass option in the Animator Controller's layer properties.
2. Create a new script and call it `CharacterLookAtIK.cs`.
3. Create a void `OnAnimatorIK(int layerIndex)` function in that script. This function is called in the **IK Pass** after all animations are evaluated.
4. In that script, we use the `SetLookAtPosition()` and `SetLookAtWeight()` functions on the Animator component. We use a `public Transform target` variable to set the **look at** position and a `public float weight` variable to set the weight of the **look at**. We also use the `Vector3.SmoothDamp()` method to damp any sudden changes in the position of our target:

    ```
    targetPosition = Vector3.SmoothDamp(targetPosition,
    target.position, ref dampVelocity, dampTime);
    anim.SetLookAtPosition(targetPosition);
    anim.SetLookAtWeight(weight);
    ```

5. Save the script and assign it to the character.
6. Assign the **Target** game object to the **Target** field in the script's **Inspector**. Make sure to set the **Weight** field to 1.

7. Play the game and move the **Target** game object to see the result (you can do it in the **Scene** View).

8. To turn the **look at** on and off smoothly, interpolate the `weight` value in time using the `Mathf.Lerp()` function.

Action Points – performing an action in a specified spot

Action Points are a common concept used for characters in games that have to perform a certain action in a certain spot. You will find a lot of them in RPG games where NPCs populate towns and perform different actions creating an illusion of a living community. We are going to address a simple case of an Action Point in this recipe.

Getting ready

We are going to use a character with three animations: **Walk**, **Idle**, and **Action**. We are also going to use the `SetSpeedFromAgent.cs` script from the *Using Blend Trees to blend walk and run animations* recipe in `Chapter 5`, *Character Movement*. You can also open the provided example Unity project and go to the `Chapter 05 Character actions and expressions\Recipe 05 Action points performing an action in a specified spot` directory. You will find an `Example.scene` scene there. Play the game to see the effect—the Humanoid character will approach an Action Point and perform a pick up animation.

How to do it...

To create a simple Action Point, follow these steps:

1. Import the character to Unity.
2. Put it on the scene and add a **NavMesh** Agent component to it.
3. Bake the **NavMesh** in the scene.
4. Create an Animator Controller and assign it to the character's Animator component.
5. Create a `float` **Speed** parameter and a `Trigger` **Action** parameter in the controller.

6. Drag and drop the **Idle**, **Walk**, and Action animations to the controller. Make sure that the **Idle** animation is the default state.

7. Create four transitions (see the following image):

   - **Idle | Walk** with one condition: **Speed** parameter greater than 0.5. **Has Exit Time** should be set to false and **TransitionDuration** set to around 0.1 seconds.

   - **Walk | Idle** with one condition: **Speed** parameter less than 0.5. **Has Exit Time** should be set to false and **Transition Duration** set to around 0.1 seconds.

   - **Any State | Action** with one condition: **Action** triggers parameter. **Has Exit Time** should be set to false and **Transition Duration** set to around 0.1 seconds.

   - **Action | Idle** with no conditions: **Has Exit Time** should be set to true and **Transition Duration** set to around 0.1 seconds.

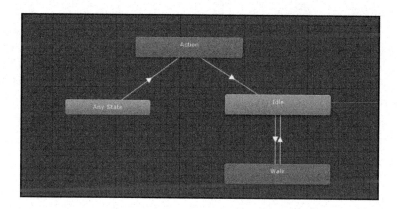

Animator Controller with Action state used by the Action Point

8. Create a new script and call it `ActionPoint.cs`.

9. In that script, we have an `IEnumerator PerformAction()` coroutine that handles the **Action Point** usage (it is started in the `Start()` function). In this coroutine, we first check if our character is close enough to the **Action Point**. If not, we set the **NavMesh Agent's** destination to the **Action Point's** position, wait one frame, and check again:

```
while ((agentTransform.position -
transform.position).sqrMagnitude > actionDistance *
actionDistance)
{
```

```
            agent.SetDestination(transform.position);
            agent.Resume();
            yield return null;
    }
```

10. The `agentTransform` variable holds the reference to the character's transform. The `actionDistance` is the distance from the **Action Point** in which our character should start performing the action.

11. When our character is closer to the **Action Point** than the `actionDistance`, we stop the **NavMesh** Agent and check if we want to match the character's position and/or rotation to our **Action Point** before the character starts playing the action animation. If not, we start playing the animation right away:

```
    agent.Stop();
    if (!matchBeforeAction)
    {
            anim.SetTrigger(actionTrigger);
    }
```

12. Next we check if we want to match character's position and/or rotation with **Action Point's** position/rotation. If so, we use linear interpolation to match the position and/or rotation. If the position and/or rotation of the character are close enough to the **Action Point's** position/rotation, we set the character's position/rotation to be exactly the same as **Action Point's** position/rotation:

```
    while (matchRotation == true || matchRotation == true)
    {
        yield return null;
        if (matchPosition && (agentTransform.position -
        transform.position).sqrMagnitude > 0.01f)
        {
            agentTransform.position =
            Vector3.Lerp(agentTransform.position,
            transform.position, Time.deltaTime *
            lerpSpeed);
        }
        else
        {
            matchPosition = false;
            agentTransform.position =
            transform.position;
        }
        if (matchRotation &&
        Vector3.Angle(agentTransform.forward,
        transform.forward) > 1f)
        {
```

```
        agentTransform.rotation =
        Quaternion.Lerp(agentTransform.rotation,
        transform.rotation, Time.deltaTime *
        lerpSpeed);
    }
    else
    {
        agentTransform.rotation =
        transform.rotation;
        matchRotation = false;
    }
}
```

13. Lastly, we check if we want to play the animation after the character's position and/or rotation was matched with the Action Point. If so, we play the animation now (as the character position and/or rotation was adjusted):

```
if (matchBeforeAction)
{
    anim.SetTrigger(actionTrigger);
}
```

14. Save the script.
15. Create a new empty game object, call it **Action Point**, and place it in the scene, where the character should perform the action.
16. Attach the script to the **Action Point** game object. Drag and drop the character to the **Agent** field of the script's component.
17. You may need to adjust the **Action Distance** value of the script. You can also set the **Match Position, Match Rotation**, and **Match Before Action** options to achieve different results.
18. Play the game to see the effect.

How it works...

The ActionPoint.cs script's role is to tell the character where to go and what animation to play. The PerformAction() coroutine also adjusts the character's position and rotation to match the position and rotation of the **Action Point**. We use the simple Lerp() function here for both the position and the rotation. In most cases, it's enough.

There's more...

You may also use the `MatchTarget()` function to interpolate the character's position and rotation and match it with the **Action Point**. We were using this technique in the *Adding animation to off-mesh links* recipe in `Chapter 4`, *Character Movement*. In such cases, it would be best to have a special approach animation in which the character approaches the **Action Point**.

You may also want to use the randomized actions concept for creating **Action Points** with random actions. The concept is described in the *Using Blend Trees to create randomized actions* recipe. Instead of creating random actions, you can also prepare a `public enum Action` variable containing all your actions as enumerations and a `pu` variable to store the `Action` in the **Actionblic Action actionPointAction variable to store the Action in the Action Point**. Then you need to set the **RandomAction** parameter (as described in the mentioned recipe) to the `(float) actionPointAction` value. This will allow you to use **Blend Trees** for performing specified actions (instead of random ones).

Also, in many cases, you will need to divide your actions into three steps:

- **Pre-Action**: This animation can be used to approach the **Action Point** or as a "state transition" animation. For instance, when we want our character to sit on a chair it is good to have a **Pre-Action** animation of the character sitting (transition from **Idle** to **Sitting** states).
- **Looped-Action**: A looped animation suitable for this Action Point. In our sitting example, that would be a looped sitting animation. It can also be a series of animations (our character can, for instance, sit and eat or sit and drink).
- **Post-Action**: This is an animation that transitions from the **Looped-Action** animation to the **Idle** animation. In our example, it would be a character getting up from the chair.

Synchronizing an animation with objects in the scene

In this recipe, we will synchronize a character's animation with an object placed in the scene. This is again a common mechanism used in games.

Getting ready

To follow this recipe, you need two animated game objects: a character and an interactive object. In our example, we use a wheel lever that the character can rotate. We use only two animations, **WheelStart** and **WheelLoop**, for both the **Character** and the **Wheel** objects. The animations have the same number of frames and are synchronized in a 3D package already. You can also open the provided example Unity project and go to the `Chapter 05 Character actions and expressions\Recipe 06 Synchronizing an animation with objects in the scene` directory. You will find an `Example.scene` there. Play the game and press the space bar to see the **Character** and the **Wheel** play a synchronized animation. You will find all the necessary animations in the `Rigs` directory.

Character and Wheel objects playing synchronized animations

How to do it...

To make the two objects play synchronized animations, follow these steps:

1. Import the **Character** and **Wheel** objects into Unity.
2. Set the **Loop Time** option in the **WheelLoop** animations for both the **Wheel** and the **Character**.
3. Place the **Character** and the **Wheel** in the scene and match their position according to what was set in the 3D package.
4. Create an **Animator Controller** for the Character.
5. Insert the **WheelStart** and **WheelLoop** animations into the controller. Make sure the **WheelStart** animation is the default state.

6. Create a **PlayAnim** bool parameter in the controller.

7. Create two transitions:
   - **WheelStart | WheelLoop** with one condition: **PlayAnim** parameter set to true parameter. **Has Exit Time** should be set to false and **Transition Duration** set to around 0.1 seconds.
   - **WheelLoop | WheelStart** with one conditions: **PlayAnim** parameter set to false. **Has Exit Time** should be set to true and **Transition Duration** set to around 0.1 seconds.

8. Assign the controller to the **Character** game object's **Animator** component.

9. Create an **Animator Override Controller**. Derive it from the **Character's** controller. Assign it to the **Wheel** game object's **Animator** component.

10. Change the animations in the override controller to the **Wheel's** animations.

11. Write a new script and call it `PlayAndStop.cs`. In that script's `Update()` function, we check if the player pressed the space bar. If so, we set the **PlayAnim** `bool` parameter to its inverted value in both the **Character's** and **Wheel's** animator controllers:

```
if (Input.GetKeyDown(KeyCode.Space))
{
    play = !play;
    characterAnimator.SetBool("PlayAnim", play);
    objectAnimator.SetBool("PlayAnim", play);
}
```

12. In the preceding script, `play` is a helper member variable, `characterAnimator` is a reference to the **Character** game object's Animator component, and `objectAnimator` is the reference to the **Wheel** game object's Animator component.

13. Assign the script to the **Character** game object.

14. Drag and drop the **Character** game object to the **Character Animator** field in the script and the **Wheel** game object to the **Object Animator** field.

15. Play the game and press the space bar to see the effect.

How it works...

Animations that have the same number of frames and the same playback speed are synchronized in Unity. All we need to care about is to start them in the same frame. That's why we have the **WheelStart** animations. We also need to take care of the transitions—if the transitions length differs in both **Animator Controllers**, the animations can be out of sync.

There's more...

You can combine this and the previous recipe to create **Action Points** with synchronized object animation. Make sure to have the **Pre-Action** animation before a looped action. This way it will be easier to trigger the animations in the same time (for instance, from an **Animation Event** inside the **Pre-Action** animation).

You may also need to turn off **Rigidbody** physics and the **NavMesh** Agent component for your character to make it stand in the right position before playing the animation. We did it in the *Using triggers to grab an edge while jumping* recipe in `Chapter 4`, *Character Movement*.

Using IK for interacting with scene objects

Sometimes our characters need to interact with objects in the scene. Most likely we will need to have a solution for picking up items from the ground or other objects. This recipe shows a simple solution for that.

Getting ready

In this recipe, we are using only two animations: **Idle** and **Pickup**. The second one makes the character pick something from the ground. You can go to the `Chapter 05 Character actions and expressions\Recipe 07 Using IK for interacting with scene objects` directory. You will find an `Example.scene` there. Open it, play the game, and press the space bar to see the character trying to pick up an object from the ground. You can move the object and play the game again. The character will still try to reach the object.

Character trying to pick an object from the ground

How to do it...

To use IK to interac with scene objects, follow these steps:

1. Import the character to Unity. Make sure to have the **Idle** and **Pickup** animations and set the rig to **Humanoid**.
2. Create an Animator Controller and assign it to the character.
3. Make sure to check the **IK Pass** option in the layer properties of the controller.
4. Drag and drop the **Idle** and **Pickup** animations into the controller. Make sure **Idle** is the default state.
5. Create a `Trigger` parameter and call it `Pickup`. Also create a `float` parameter and call it **PickupIK**.
6. Create two transitions:
   - **Idle | Pickup** with one condition: **Pickup** `Trigger` parameter. **Exit Time** should be set to false and **Transition Duration** set to around 0.1 seconds.
   - **Pickup | Idle** with no conditions. **Has Exit Time** should be set to true and **Transition Duration** set to around 0.1 seconds.
7. Go to the character's **Import** settings in the **Animations** tab.
8. Create a new **Animation Curve** and name it `PickupIK` (the name has to match the `float` **PickupIK** parameter name).
9. Create a smooth curve with the minimum value of 0 and the maximum of 1. The maximum value should match the moment when the character reaches for the object. See the following image for reference:

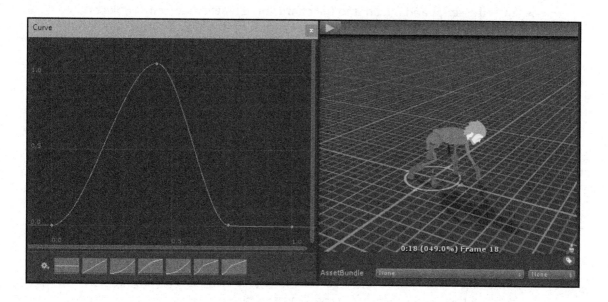

PickupIK Animation Curve. The maximum value (1) matches the frame when character picks up the object

10. Apply the import settings.

11. Create a new script and call it `PickUpIK.cs`. In that script, we have a `void OnAnimatorIK(int layerIndex)` function. This function is called every frame in the **IK Pass** after all animations have been evaluated. In that function, we get the value of the **PickupIK** `float` parameter from the controller (which equals the value of the **Animation Curve**). Then we set this value as the weight for the left-hand IK. We also set the left-hand IK position to match a `public Transform ikTarget` member variable in which we store the reference to the object we want to pick up:

```
ikWeight = anim.GetFloat("PickupIK");
anim.SetIKPosition(AvatarIKGoal.LeftHand,
ikTarget.position);
anim.SetIKPositionWeight(AvatarIKGoal.LeftHand, ikWeight)
```

12. In the `Update()` function of the script, we check if the player pressed the space bar and played the **Pickup** animation.

13. Save the script and attach it to the character. Create a new game object that we want to pick up. Call it **PickupObject** and drag it to the **Ik Target** field in the script's **Inspector**.

14. Play the game and press the space bar to see the effect. You may move the **PickupObject** in the **Scene** View and press the space bar again. Our character will still try to reach it (it may fail due to the limited range of its arms).

How it works...

This recipe works for Humanoid characters only. It uses the Unity's built-in inverse kinematics solver. The key elements of this recipe are as follows:

- **Animation Curve**: We use an Animation Curve to smoothly set the weight for the IK solver during the Pickup animation playback.
- **SetIKPosition()**: This function sets the target position for a given body part. We are using a `public Transform ikTarget` variable in the script and pass it to the function. You can get the target in runtime.
- **SetIKPositionWeight()**: This function sets the weight of the IK solver. A weight value of 1 means that IK is in full control of a given body part and a value of 0 means that the animation is in full control.
- **IK Pass**: To be able to use inverse kinematics for Humanoid characters, we need to enable the **IK Pass** option in the controller's layer properties.

See also

If you want to play with IK solutions a little more, definitely check out the Final IK package published by *RootMotion* in the `Asset` store. It is a very robust full-body IK solution for Unity.

Animating facial expressions with Blend Shapes

If you want to animate a character talking or changing its facial expression, it is best to use Blend Shapes. This recipe covers creating facial expressions with Blend Shapes exported from a 3D package.

Getting ready

We need several **Blend Shapes** that store our facial expressions. In this recipe, we will use **Smile, Angry, BlinkLeft, BlinkRight**, and **BrowsDown** shapes. Create them in your 3D package. If you are using Blender, **Blend Shapes** are called Shape Keys. In other softwares, they may be called Morph Targets.

You can also use the provided example Unity project and go to the Chapter 05 Character actions and expressions\Recipe 08 Animating facial expressions with blend shapes directory. You will find an Example.scene there. Open it, play the game, and adjust the sliders on the UI to see the effect. You can find the character with all the Blend Shapes in the Rigs directory.

How to do it...

To use **Blend Shapes** for facial expressions, follow these steps:

1. Import your character to Unity. Place it on the scene.
2. Create an empty game object in the same place as our character. Call the object **FaceAnims**.
3. Make the character a child of the **FaceAnims** game object.
4. With the **FaceAnims** game object selected, open the **Animation** View (go to **Window | Animation**).
5. Create a new Animation Clip and call it Angry.
6. Click on the Add Property button and choose **Character | Mesh | SkinnedMesh Renderer | Blend Shape.Angry**, where **Character** is the name of your character game object, **Mesh** is the name of your character game object containing the **Skinned Mesh Renderer** component, and **Angry** is the name of the Blend Shape exported from the 3D package.
7. Click on the plus icon next to the **Blend Shape.Angry** option to add the property.
8. Go to the **Curves** tab. Select both key frames and right-click on one of them. Choose the **Edit Keys** option and enter 100 in the **Value** field.
9. This way we've created an **Angry** animation with the **Angry Blend Shape** set to 100 (maximum value).
10. Repeat the steps 5 to 9 for **Smile, BlinkLeft, BlinkRight**, and **BrowsDown** Blend Shapes. Remember to call the animations according to the Blend Shapes names (it makes it easier to recognize animations).
11. An Animator Controller was automatically created for the **FaceAnims** game object. Open it.

12. Delete all the states in the controller and add a new **Blend Tree**.

13. Double-click on the **Blend Tree** to enter its settings.

14. Set the **Blend Tree** type to **Direct**. It allows the blending of multiple animations together.

15. Create five **Motion Fields** in the **Blend Tree** and assign the **Angry**, **Smile**, **BlinkLeft**, **BlinkRight**, and **BrowsDown** animations to them.

16. Create five `float` parameters in the controller, one for each animation. Name them accordingly and assign them to the **Motion Fields** (**Smile** parameter to **Smile** animation, **Angry** parameter to **Angry** animation, and so on).

17. Write a new script and call it `BlendMultiple.cs`. Create five public float member variables in the script and name them according to the **Blend Shape** names (`public float Smile`, `public float Angry`, and so on).

18. In the `Update()` function, we set the values of the controller parameters to the values of the variables. This way when we change the variable's values, the parameters in the controller also change and our character plays facial expressions:

```
anim.SetFloat("Angry", Angry);
anim.SetFloat("Smile", Smile);
anim.SetFloat("BlinkLeft", BlinkLeft);
anim.SetFloat("BlinkRight", BlinkRight);
anim.SetFloat("BrowsDown", BrowsDown);
```

19. Attach the script to the **FaceAnims** game object. Play the game and change the scripts float variables in runtime to see the effect (you can use the **Scene** View).

A mix of different Blend Shapes gives an interesting facial expression

How it works...

This recipe has a few key elements that make it work:

- **Blend Shapes**: You need to export the Blend Shapes from your 3D package. Blend Shapes store different version of the same mesh. The mesh has to have the same number of vertices. When creating new Blend Shapes, you can only move the vertices around (you cannot add or delete vertices).
- **FaceAnims game object**: Our character is a child of a new game object, **FaceAnims**. This allows us to be able to animate facial expressions. As our character has its own Animator component and its own animations, we cannot modify it with the **Animation** View. Adding a parent game object solves the problem.
- **Direct Blend Tree**: We use a **Blend Tree** set to **Direct**. This allows us to blend multiple animations at once. This is suitable for Blend Shapes and facial expressions.

There's more...

You don't have to create Animation Clips for Blend Shapes. Instead, you can manipulate them directly from code. Use the `SetBlendShapeWeight()` function on the **Skinned Mesh Renderer** component. You will need to know the index of the **Blend Shape** in the **Blend Shapes** array (you can check it in the Inspector, in the **Skinned Mesh Renderer** component of the character). We've prepared a small script that sets the weight. It is attached to the **DirectBlendShapes** game object. You can also find it in the `Scripts` directory of this recipe.

Creating animations for **Blend Shapes** gives more flexibility. You can also animate the Blend Shapes' weight with the **Animation** View. This way you can create dialog animations and believable animated facial expressions.

6
Handling Combat

This chapter explains usage of animations in combat and covers the following topics:

- Using Sub-State Machines in Animator Controller
- Using Animation Events to trigger script functions
- Using transitions from Any State to play hit reactions
- Using root motion to create a dodge move
- Checking what Animator state is currently active to disable or enable player actions
- Using Animation Events to draw a weapon
- Using Avatar Masks and animator controller layers to walk and aim
- Using the `LookAt()` method to aim
- Using Blend Trees to aim
- Detecting the hit location on a character

Introduction

Every game is different and every game handles combat mechanics in its own way. Despite that, there is a common set of concepts that are useful in almost every case. In this chapter, we will cover the tools essential for melee and ranged combat.

Using Sub-State Machines in Animator Controller

This recipe shows how to use Sub-State Machines. This concept helps to organize the flow in Animator Controller.

Getting ready

To start, you need to have a character with a few animations. In this example, we are using a character with **NormalIdle**, **NormalMove**, **CombatIdle**, and **CombatMove** animations. These animations will be then grouped in two **Sub-State Machines**: **Combat** and **Normal**.

You can also open the provided example Unity project and go to the `Chapter 06 Handling combat\Recipe 01 Using sub state machines in animator controller` directory. In the `Rigs` directory you, will find all the necessary animations. In the `Controllers` directory, you can find the finished controller with two Sub-State Machines. You can find the **Humanoid** character in the `Example.unity` scene. If you press the space bar, our character will switch from **Normal** to **Combat Sub-State Machine**.

How to do it...

To create a Sub-State Machine in a controller, follow these steps:

1. Create and open a new Animator Controller.
2. Right-click on the empty space and choose **Create Sub-State Machine**. A new Sub-State Machine will be created. Name it `Normal`.
3. Create another Sub-State Machine and name it `Combat`.
4. Create one `bool` parameter: **CombatState**.
5. Create two transitions:
    - **Combat | Normal** with no conditions.
    - **Normal | Combat** with no conditions.
6. Double-click on the **Normal** Sub-State Machine.
7. Create a `float` **Speed** parameter.
8. Drag and drop the **NormalIdle** and **NormalMove** animations to the controller (make sure you are in the **Normal** Sub-State Machine).

9. Create two transitions:
   - **NormalIdle | NormalMove** with one condition: **Speed** parameter greater than 0.5. **Has Exit Time** should be set to `false` and **Transition Duration** should be set to around 0.2 seconds.
   - **NormalMove | NormalIdle** with one condition: **Speed** parameter less than 0.5. **Has Exit Time** should be set to `false` and **Transition Duration** should be set to around 0.2 seconds.

10. Create two transitions—one from **NormalIdle** to **Exit** state and another one from **NormalMove** to **Exit** state—both with one condition: **CombatState** parameter set to `true`. **Time Duration** should be set to around 0.2 seconds and **Has Exit Time** should be set to `false`.

11. Double-click on the empty space in the controller to get out of the **NormalSub-State Machine**.

12. Double-click on the **Combat** Sub-State Machine and repeat steps 9 and 10 with **CombatIdle** and **CombatMove** animations this time.

13. Close the **Animator Controller** and assign it to your character.

14. Write a script to be able to set the **Speed** value and the **CombatState** `bool` parameter. Name it `SetCombatAndSpeed.cs`.

15. In this script's `Update()` function, we check if player pressed the space bar. If so, we invert the **CombatSate** parameter value. We also check if player pressed the up arrow. If so, we set the **Speed** parameter to make the character play movement animations:

```
if (Input.GetKeyDown(KeyCode.Space))

{

    combat = !combat;

    anim.SetBool("CombatState", combat);

}
if (Input.GetKey(KeyCode.UpArrow))
{
    anim.SetFloat("Speed", 1f);
}
else
{
    anim.SetFloat("Speed", 0f);
}
```

16. Assign the script to the character, launch the game, and press the space bar to see the character change Sub-State Machines.

How it works...

The concept of Sub-State Machines makes it easier to organize the controller. You can think of them as of nested controllers. You can have Sub-State Machines inside other Sub-State Machines. Clever organization of your controllers prevents spaghetti graphs.

To exit a Sub-State Machine you have to transition to the **Exit** state. You can have multiple such transitions the same way you can have multiple transitions between Sub-State Machines. Use transition conditions to determine where your graph should transition to.

There's more...

You can also transition from Sub-State Machines to specific states in any other Sub-State Machine. To do so, make a transition to the state named **(Up) Base Layer** (the name can vary depending on the Sub-State Machine you are currently in and the names of your layers). If you do this transition, a menu will appear and let you choose the state you want to transition to; see the following screenshot for reference:

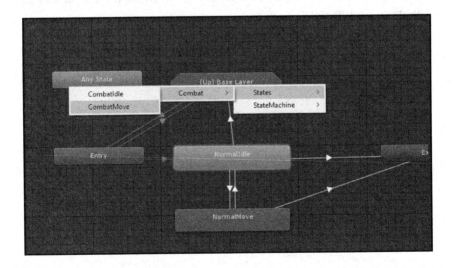

Transition to a specific state in another Sub-State Machine

Using Animation Events to trigger script functions

We used Animation Events sporadically in earlier recipes because they are so handy, and it was simply difficult to until to this moment. Most present games use Animation Events very extensively, especially for handling combat. Creating believable melee encounters would be a lot harder without this handy tool.

Getting ready

Before we start, we need to have a character with an attack animation. In the example files, we named the animation **HumanAttack**. We also need an enemy (we use a **Spider** character in this example) with **Idle** and **Death** animations. You can also download the provided example Unity project and go to the `Chapter 06 Handling combat\Recipe 02 Using animation events to trigger script functions` directory. You will find a scene called `Example.unity` there, with **Humanoid** and **Spider** characters. In the `Rigs` directory, you can find the `Humanoid.fbx` character with all required animations. When you play the game, the **Humanoid** character will attack the **Spider** several times and deal damage to it.

How to do it...

To use Animation Events to trigger script functions, follow these steps:

1. Import your character with the **HumanAttack** animation to Unity.
2. Go to the **Animation** import settings tab in the **Inspector** window.
3. Select the **HumanAttack** animation.
4. Navigate down to the **Events** section and unfold it.
5. Use the **Preview** window to scrub through the animation to the moment of the hit in the attack.

6. Add an **Animation Event** by pressing the **Add Event** button, as shown in the following screenshot:

Adding Animation Events

7. The **Edit Animation Event** window will appear. Type Attack in the **Function** text field. To make the event work, we need to have a function with the same name in a script assigned to our character.

8. We will create a simple fight scene, so we need a script for the enemy. Create a new script and call it Enemy.cs. In this script, we have the public float hitPoints variable to store current health of our enemy. We also have two public virtual void functions: Hit(float damage) and Die(). The Hit(float damage) function subtracts damage from our current hitPoints and calls the Die() function when hitPoin ts drop to 0. The Die() function plays the death animation by setting the bool **Dead** parameter in the controller. These functions are virtual because we want to derive from this script in later recipes to add new functionality:

```
public void Hit(float damage)
{
    hitPoints -= damage;
    if (hitPoints <= 0)
    {
        Die();
    }
}
public void Die()
{
    anim.SetBool("Dead", true);
}
```

9. Create one transition:

10. In it, create the `bool` **Dead** parameter. Drag and drop the **Idle** and **Death** animations to the controller. Make **Idle** the default state.

11. Create a new Animator Controller for our **Spider** character.
    - **Idle | Death** with the condition: **Dead** parameter set to true, **Has Exit Time** set to `false`, and **Transition Duration** set to 0.2 seconds.
    - Place the **Spider** character in the scene. Add a **Rigidbody** component, a **Sphere Collider** component, and our `Enemy.cs` script component to it. Set the **Rigidbody** component to **Is Kinematic**.

12. Assign the controller to **Spider**'s Animator component.

13. Create another Animator Controller for our **Humanoid** character.

14. Place a looped **HumanAttack** animation in that controller and assign it to the **Humanoid** character.

15. Place the **Humanoid** character near the **Spider** in the scene.

16. Create a new script and call it `MeleeAttack.cs`. In this script, we use our `public void Attack()` function. This is the function called from the animation event. We have a list of all enemies in range. We iterate through that list and call the `Hit()` function on every enemy from that list. We also have a `publicfloat damage` variable to store the character's damage value and send it in the `Hit()` function:

```
public void Attack () {

    for (int i = 0; i < enemiesInRange.Count; i++)

    {
        enemiesInRange[i].Hit(damage);
    }
}
```

17. Assign the script to the **Humanoid** character.

18. We need one more script to get the targets in range. Create a new script and call it `TargetTrigger.cs`. In the `void OnTriggerEnter(Collider other)` function of this script, we check if the object entering the trigger has an `Enemy.cs` component. If so, we add it to the `enemiesInRange` in the `MeleeAttack.cs` component:

```
Enemy e = other.gameObject.GetComponent<Enemy>();
if (e != null)
{
    if (!attackScript.enemiesInRange.Contains(e))
    {
```

```
            attackScript.enemiesInRange.Add(e);
        }
    }
```

19. In the `void OnTriggerExit(Collider other)` function, we remove the enemy from the `enemiesInRange` list:

```
Enemy e = other.gameObject.GetComponent<Enemy>();
if (e != null)
{
    if (attackScript.enemiesInRange.Contains(e))
    {
        attackScript.enemiesInRange.Remove(e);
    }
}
```

20. In the preceding script, `attackScript` is the reference to the `MeleeAttack.cs` script component.

21. Create an empty game object and name it `TargetTrigger`. Add a **Box Collider** component to it and set the collider to **Is Trigger**. Assign our `TargetTrigger.cs` script to it.

22. Make the **TargetTrigger** game object the child of our **Humanoid** character and shape the **Box Collider** for checking melee hit range. See the following screenshot:

Melee attack range trigger

23. Play the game to see the effect.

How it works...

Animation Events call public functions from the scripts assigned to the game object playing the animation. To make it work, the **Function** field of the Animation Event needs to have the same name as the function we want to call from the script.

Events are extremely useful because they allow us to synchronize function calls with animations. The best moment to check if player hits the target is when we see a visual hit in the animation—a fist is in its extreme position in a punch, or a sword is in its extreme position in a swing. Without Animation Events, we would have to always manually delay function calls to achieve similar results.

There's more...

Animation Events can also have an `int`, `float`, `string`, or an object type parameter. To use these parameters, we have to implement them in our functions called by the event. These parameters can be useful for playing special effects or sounds (you can find more information about it in the *Using Animation Events to trigger sound and visual effects* recipe in `Chapter 7`, *Special Effects*.

Using transitions from Any State to play hit reactions

Often, there are situations when we would like to transition to an animation from any other one. The most common example is the hit reaction. Our characters can be hit while standing, walking, or even attacking. Creating and managing all those transitions would be cumbersome and difficult. In Unity, we can use a special **Any State** in the controllers to achieve transitions from any given animation.

Getting ready

We are going to use the characters from the previous recipe and add one animation to the **Spider** character: **HitReaction**. You can also use the example project and go to the `Chapter 06 Handling combat\Recipe 03 Using transitions from any state to play hit reactions` directory. You can find the `Example.unity` scene there, with two characters: **Humanoid** and **Spider**. When you play the game, **Spider** will react to hits. In the `Rigs` directory of the previous recipe, you can find the required animations.

How to do it...

To use Any State transitions, follow these steps:

1. Follow the previous recipe to import the characters and place them on the scene.
2. Create a new **Animator Controller** for the **Spider** (you can also edit the existing one).
3. Create a new `bool` parameter in the controller and call it **Dead**.
4. Create a new `Trigger` parameter in the controller and call it **Hit**.
5. Drag and drop the **Idle**, **Death**, and **HitReaction** animations of the **Spider** into the controller. The **Idle** animation should be our default state.
6. Find the blue **Any State** node in the controller. See the following screenshot for reference:

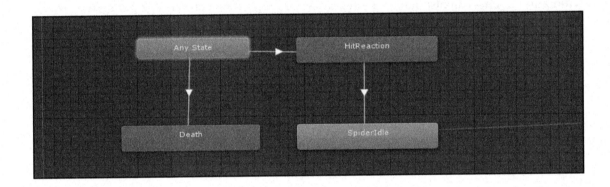

Transitions from Any State

7. Right-click on it and create the following transitions:
   - **Any State | HitReaction** with one condition: **Hit** `Trigger` parameter. **Has Exit Time** should be set to `false`, **Can Transition To Self** set to true, and **Transition Duration** set to 0.2 seconds.
   - **Any State | Death** with one condition: **Dead** `bool` parameter set to `true`. **Has Exit Time** should be set to `false`, **Can Transition To Self** set to false, and **Transition Duration** set to 0.2 seconds.
   - **HitReaction | Idle**: For this one, you need to right-click on the **HitReaction** state first. It should have no conditions, **Has Exit Time** set to `true`, and **Transition Duration** set to 0.2 seconds.

8. Assign the controller to the **Spider's Animator** component.
9. Create a new script and call it `EnemyWithHits.cs`.

10. Derive this script from the `Enemy.cs` script instead of `MonoBehaviour`. You can find the `Enemy.cs` script in the previous recipe.

11. To make our hit reactions work, we need to `override` the `Hit()` and `Die()` functions. In the first one, we check if our character's `isAlive` flag. If our **Spider** is dead already, we don't attempt to play hit reactions. If it is alive, we play the hit reaction by setting the **Hit** `Trigger` parameter in the controller. Next we call the `base` implementation of the `Hit()` function:

```
public override void Hit(int damage)

{

    if (!isAlive)
    {
        return;
    }
    anim.SetTrigger("Hit");
    base.Hit(damage);
}
```

12. In the `Die()` function, we set the `isAlive` flag to false and call the base implementation of the `Die()` function:

```
public override void Die()
{
    isAlive = false;
    base.Die();
}
```

13. Assign the script to the **Spider** character and play the game to see the effect.

How it works...

Any State is a powerful tool for organizing animation graphs. If we know we need to access an animation state from any other state, we can create a transition from Any State node, instead of creating a web of transitions from all the necessary states.

This special state's transitions have one additional parameter: **Can Transition to Self**. If set to `false` it blocks transitions to the same state.

Any State transitions are most useful for hit reactions and death animations.

Using root motion to create a dodge move

We can achieve a lot of gameplay actions in combat using just animations. A great example of such an action is the dodge move.

Getting ready

To follow this recipe, we need a character with **SpiderIdle** and **Dodge** animations (we will be using our **Spider** character in this example). The dodge animation should be created with root motion. Please check the example in the following screenshot:

Spider dodge with root motion translation

You can also go to the `Chapter 06 Handling combat\Recipe 04 Using root motion to create a dodge move` directory. Open the `Example.unity` scene there. You will find the same **Humanoid** and **Spider** characters we had in previous recipes. They have the same animations and scripts as in the *Using transitions from Any State to play hit reactions* recipe. The **Spider** has one additional animation: **Dodge**. If you hit the space bar in **Play Mode**, the **Spider** will attempt to dodge the sword swing. You can find all the necessary animations in the `Chapter 06 Handling combat\Recipe 02 Using animation events to trigger script functions\Rigs` directory.

How to do it...

To make a character dodge, follow these steps:

1. Import the character into Unity and place it in a scene.
2. If you want the character to get damage and play hit reactions, follow the previous recipe.
3. Create a new Animator Controller or edit the one from the previous recipe.
4. Drag and drop the **Dodge** animation into the controller.
5. Create a **Dodge** `Trigger` parameter in the controller.
6. Create two transitions:
   - **SpiderIdle | Dodge** with one condition: **Dodge** `Trigger` parameter. **Has Exit Time** should be set to false and **Transition Duration** set to 0.2 seconds.
   - **Dodge | SpiderIdle** with no conditions: **Has Exit Time** should be set to true and **Transition Duration** set to 0.2 seconds.
7. Add a **Rigidbody** component to the **Spider** character and freeze its rotations.
8. Add a collider to the **Spider** character (we are using **Sphere Collider** for our **Spider**). You may also need to create a zero friction **Physical Material** and add it to the collider. It allows the animation to control Rigid Body movement without any additional friction.
9. Set the **Animator** component's **Update Mode** to **Animate Physics** in our **Spider**.
10. Attach the controller to the **Animator** component of our **Spider**.
11. Create a new script and call it `Dodge.cs`. In this script's `Update()` function, we simply set the **Dodge** `Trigger` in the controller when player presses the space bar:

```
if (Input.GetKeyDown(KeyCode.Space))
```

```
{
    anim.SetTrigger("Dodge");
}
```

12. As always, the `anim` variable stores the reference to the **Animator** component and is set in the `Start()` function.
13. Attach the script to the **Spider** character.
14. Play the game and press the space bar to see the **Spider** play the dodge animation. It should be able to get out of the **Humanoid** character's attack range and avoid being hit.

How it works...

This recipe uses a very simple, yet powerful concept. The only additional thing we do here is triggering the **Dodge** animation. This animation uses root motion and translates our **Spider** character. Our **Humanoid** character uses the **Attack Animation Event** and the **TargetTrigger** to check if an enemy is in its attack range (see the *Using Animation Events to trigger script functions* recipe for details). If our **Spider** leaves the **TargetTrigger** before the **Attack** event occurs, it will avoid being hit.

There's more...

The Dodge animation will also work for other hit detection mechanisms. For instance, you can manually check the range and attack angle in the **Attack** event using the `Vector3.Distance()` and `Vector3.Angle()` methods. You can also use a **Rigidbody** component on the sword and check its collisions with the `void OnCollisionEnter(Collision collision)` method. In both cases, our **Dodge** move will work just fine. It will also work for bullets that use collisions to determine hits (for example, arrows).

You can use the same concept for other actions: dashes, combos, and some crazy melee attacks that use root translation and/or rotation (for instance, jump attacks). Root motion is a very powerful tool for combat design. Try experimenting with your own animation ideas to create interesting moves and actions.

Checking what Animator state is currently active to disable or enable player actions

There are situations when we need to block or allow certain actions depending on the currently played animation. This recipe describes how to easily check what animation is currently being played.

Getting ready

We are going to use the same **Spider** character from the previous recipe. It has **SpiderIdle**, **Dodge**, **HitReaction**, and **Death** animations. You can open the provided example project and go to the `Chapter 06 Handling combat\Recipe 05 Checking what animator state is currently active to disable or enable player actions` directory. There is a **Spider** character in the `Example.unity` scene. When you press the *H* key, it will start a healing action, only when in **SpiderIdle** state. You can find all the necessary animations in the `Chapter 06 Handling combat\Recipe 02 Using animation events to trigger script functions\Rigs` directory.

How to do it...

To check which Animator state is currently active, follow these steps:

1. Import the character to Unity.
2. Create an Animator Controller for it or use an existing one.
3. If you want your character to react to hits, follow the *Using transitions from Any State to play hit reactions* recipe.
4. In this recipe, we are going to use the healing action as an example. Create a new script and call it `Healing.cs`. In this script's `Update()` function, first we check if player pressed the *H* key. Then we check if our character is playing in the proper **Animator** state and saved in the `public stringhealingAllowedState` variable. We also check if a healing action is not active because we don't want to stack healing actions. If all these conditions are met, we start a healing coroutine:

```
if (Input.GetKeyDown(KeyCode.H))
{
    if (anim.GetCurrentAnimatorStateInfo(0).IsName(
healingAllowedState))
    {
        if (!isHealing)
```

```
        {
            StartCoroutine("Heal");
        }
    }
}
```

5. The `IEnumarator Heal()` coroutine is responsible for increasing our Spider's `hitPoints` in time:

```
isHealing = true;
Enemy enemyScript = GetComponent<Enemy>();

while (enemyScript.hitPoints <
(float)enemyScript.initialHitPoints)
{
    enemyScript.hitPoints += healingSpeed * Time.deltaTime;
    yield return null;
}

enemyScript.hitPoints = enemyScript.initialHitPoints;
isHealing = false;
```

6. Assign the script to the **Spider** character.
7. Play the game and press the *H* key to start the healing action. Our character needs to be in the **SpiderIdle** state (the `public string healinAllowedState` is set to `Base Layer.SpiderIdle` in the **Inspector**).

How it works...

To check the **Animator** state our character is currently in, we first use the `GetCurrentAnimatorStateInfo(int layerIndex)` function to get the state the character's Animator is in. We need to call this function on the Animator component; thus, we need to have a variable storing a reference to it (`anim` in our example). Then we call the `IsName(string name)` function on the state we got from the `GetCurrentAnimatorStateInfo(int layerIndex)` function. The `IsName(string name)` function compares the Animator state name to the `name` we put as the parameter.

We need to specify the full name of the state. This name needs to be in this format: `<Layer Name>.<State Name>`. For instance, our **SpiderIdle** state is in the **Base Layer**, so we need to put `Base Layer.SpiderIdle` as the name parameter in the `IsName()` function.

There's more...

Sometimes we need to check not only the current state of the **Animator** but also a specified moment in it. Let's assume we have a 2-second long jump attack animation. Our character starts the jump in the first second of the animation, and then it jumps and lands on the ground with a strike at the end of the animation. We may want to allow players to break the animation when the character is still on the ground (for instance, with a dodge animation). To do so, we may use **Animation Curves** to set an **AllowBreak** `float` parameter (you can choose a different name) in the controller and check this parameter value while trying to perform actions or transition to other states. **Animation Curves** are described in the *Using animations for better looking transitions* recipe in `Chapter 4`, *Character Movement*.

Using Animation Events to draw a weapon

Another common case in combat mechanics is drawing and sheathing a weapon. In this recipe we will use Animation Events along with a Draw animation to make our character draw and sheath a sword.

Getting ready

To follow this recipe, we need to have a **Warrior** character with two animations: **Idle** and **Draw**. The first one is a standard, looped **Idle** animation. The second one is an animation in which our character reaches for their weapon in a sheath attached to the character's belt. We are not using a sheath model here to make the recipe more simple and condensed. You can open the provided example project and go to the `Chapter 06 Handling combat\Recipe 06 Using animation events to draw a weapon` directory. There is a **Warrior** character in the `Example.unity` scene. When you press the space bar, it will draw or sheath a sword. You can find all the necessary animations in the `Rigs` directory.

How to do it...

To make a character draw or sheath a weapon, follow these steps:

1. Import the **Warrior** character with the **Idle** and **Draw** animations into Unity.
2. Import a **Sword** prop to Unity.
3. Go to the **Import Settings | Animation** tab. Select the **Draw** animation and navigate to the **Events** section.

4. Add a **Draw** event in the frame where the character's hand reaches the sword in the sheath.

5. Create an **Animator Controller** with the **Idle** and **Draw** animations.

6. Create a **Draw** `Trigger` parameter in the controller.

7. Create two transitions:
   - **Idle | Draw** with one condition:**Draw** `Trigger` parameter. **Has Exit Time** should be set to `false` and **Transition Duration** set to around 0.2 seconds.
   - **Draw | Idle** with no conditions: **Has Exit Time** should be set to `true` and **Transition Duration** set to around 0.2 seconds.

8. Place the **Warrior** character in the scene.

9. Assign the controller to the **Warrior** game object's **Animator** component.

10. Place the **Sword** prop in the scene. Move it near the character's hips and pose it as it needs to be when it lays in the sheath.

11. When you are happy with the **Sword's** position, create an empty child object in it. Name it **SheathMarker** and drag it onto the hip bone of the character to parent it to **Warrior's** hips. This way the **SheathMarker** will store our **Sword's** initial position and rotation relative to our character's hips. You should also parent the Sword to **SheathMarker**. See the following screenshot for reference:

Sheath Marker (red) stores sword's desired position and rotation

12. Move the **Sword** to the **Warrior**'s hand. Pose the sword as desired. Create another empty child object in the **Sword** and name it **HandMarker**. Drag and drop the **HandMarker** game object onto the right-hand bone in the character's rig to parent it to the **Warrior's** hand. See the following screenshot for reference:

Hand Marker (orange) stores sword's desired position and rotation in the hand

13. Write a new script and call it `DrawWeapon.cs`. In this script's `Update()` function, we check if player pressed the space bar. If so, we first set the **Draw** `Trigger` parameter in the controller to play the animation:

```
if (Input.GetKeyDown(KeyCode.Space))
{
    anim.SetTrigger("Draw");
}
```

14. We also interpolate the **Sword's** position and rotation to its parent game object's position and rotation (**Hand Marker** or **Sheath Marker**):

```
if (weapon.parent != null)
{
    if ((weapon.position -
weapon.parent.position).sqrMagnitude > 0.0001f)
    {
        weapon.position =
        Vector3.Lerp(weapon.position,
        weapon.parent.position, Time.deltaTime *
        lerpSpeed);
        weapon.rotation =
        Quaternion.Lerp(weapon.rotation,
        weapon.parent.rotation, Time.deltaTime *
```

```
                    lerpSpeed);
            }
    }
```

15. In the preceding script, the `weapon` variable holds the reference to **Sword's Transform** component. The `public float lerpSpeed` variable is set in the **Inspector**.

16. This script has also a `public voidDraw()` function, which is called by an **Animation Event** set in the **Draw** animation. In this function, we check if the sword is already in hand with the `public bool weaponInHand` variable. We need to set this variable's initial value in the **Inspector**, depending on the initial **Sword** position (in hand or in sheath). The `Draw()` function only changes the **Sword** parent and sets the `weaponInHand` flag:

```
if (weaponInHand)
{
    weaponInHand = false;
    weapon.parent = sheathMarker;
}
else
{
    weaponInHand = true;
    weapon.parent = handMarker;
}
```

17. Attach the script to the character. Drag and drop the **Sheath Marker** game object to the **Sheath Marker** field in the script, the **Sword** game object to the **Weapon** field, and the **Hand Marker** to the **Hand Marker** field. Set the **Weapon In Hand** checkbox to match the **Sword's** initial position.

18. Play the game and press the space bar to see the effect.

How it works...

We use the **Animation Event** in the **Draw** animation to find the moment where our character reaches for the weapon attached to the character's belt. In this event, we change the parent of the weapon to attach it to the hand or to the belt (depending on whether our character is drawing or sheathing the weapon). We additionally use the `Lerp()` method to adjust or match the position and rotation of our weapon with appropriate slots in the character (the **Hand Marker** and the **Sheath Marker**). This way our **Draw** animation doesn't have to perfectly match with the desired positions of the weapon. It makes it easier to use the same animation for a wider range of different weapons.

Using Avatar Masks and animator controller layers to walk and aim

This recipe shows how to use Avatar Masks and Layers in the Animator Controller to play animations on certain body parts. In combat, it can be useful for playing aim animations on the upper body and movement animations on the lower body.

Getting ready

In this recipe, we are using **WalkForward, WalkLeft, WalkRight,** and **Idle** animations, and a looped **AimForward** animation. The first four animations are covered in the *Using root motion to steer a character* recipe in `Chapter 4`, *Character Movement*. The last one is a simple looped aim animation where our character aims a crossbow straight ahead. You can go to the `Chapter 07 Special effects\Recipe 07 Using sprite sheets to animate particles` directory. You will find an `Example.unity` scene there. Open it and play the game. You can move the character with the *WSAD* keys and rotate the camera with the mouse. You can find the **AimForward** animation in the `Rigs` directory and all the other required animations in the `Chapter 04 Character movement\Recipe 03 Using root motion to steer a character` directory. We also need a **Crossbow** prop, which you can find in the `Props` folder.

How to do it...

To use Avatar Masks and Layers, follow these steps:

1. Import the character and the **Crossbow** prop to Unity. Make sure to have all the required animations.
2. Create an Animator Controller and assign it to the character.
3. Follow the *Using root motion to steer a character* recipe in `Chapter 4`, *Character Movement*, to make the character move.
4. Open the Animator Controller and find the **Layers** tab.

5. Click on the plus button near the **Layers** tab to create a new **Layer** and name it **Aim**. See the following screenshot for reference:

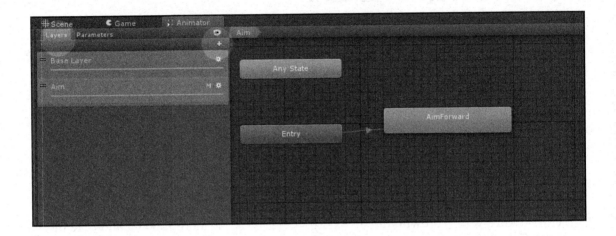

Layers tab

6. Drag and drop the **AimForward** animation to it.
7. Click on the small gear icon in the **Layer**. The **Layer Properties** window will appear.
8. Find the **Weight** slider and drag it all the way up to 1.
9. Right-click on **Project View** and choose **Create | Avatar Mask** to create a new **Avatar Mask**. Name it **AimMask**.
10. Click on it and unfold the **Humanoid** foldout.

11. Unselect the legs of the character. See the following screenshot for reference:

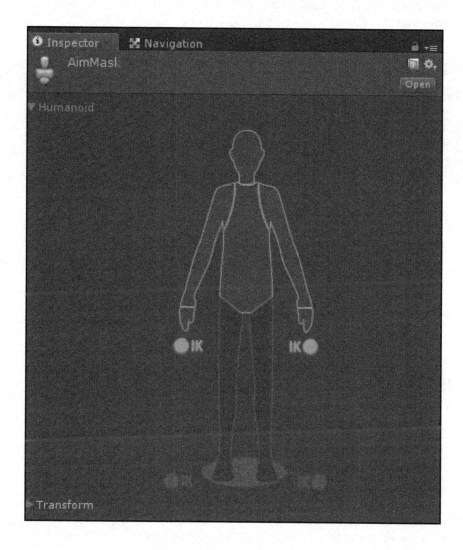

Avatar Mask with only the upper body turned on

12. Go back to the **Animator Controller**, open the **Layer Properties** of the **Aim Layer**, and assign the **AimMask** to the **Mask** field. See the following screenshot for reference:

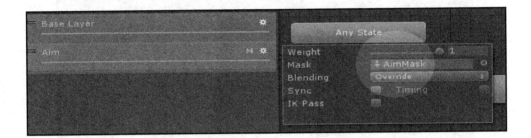

Avatar Mask assigned to the Aim Layer

13. Assign the `RootMotionSteering.cs` script to the character to make the character walk. You can find it in the *Using root motion to steer a character* recipe (`Chapter 04 Character movement\Recipe 03 Using root motion to steer a character\Scripts`).

14. Play the game to see the effect.

How it works...

This recipe has a few key elements that make it work:

- **Layers**: Animator Controller Layers are useful for overriding animations. The **Blending** drop-down menu in the **Layer Properties** defines the type of animation blending. We can override the animations or use additive blending (this will be covered in the next chapter).

- **Layer Weight**: When blending **Layers**, Unity takes the **Weight** parameter into account. A weight of 1 means 100 percent override. You can set the Weight in runtime by using the `animator.SetLayerWeight(int index, float weight)` function (`animator` is a variable that holds the reference to the Animator component).

- **Avatar Masks**: We can create an Avatar Mask asset and specify the body parts on which we want to play an animation. Then we can use this **Avatar Mask** in our **Layers** to override only certain body parts' animations. This way we can play the **AimForward** animation on the upper body and not on the legs and root. This makes the character move while playing the **AimForward** animation.

There's more...

You can also select the Sync option in the **Layer Properties**. It will inherit the structure of another, chosen layer, but you will be able to change all the animations. This option may be useful for implementing different types of animations for different character states (normal/wounded for example).

We are also using a `CameraLook.cs` script in this recipe. The script can be found in the `Shared Scripts` folder of the provided Unity project. This script works with basic camera rig. The rig is built from three game objects:

- **CameraRig**: This game object follows the Target transform specified in the `CameraLook.cs` script component. It also rotates in the global *Y* axis responding to player's horizontal mouse input.
- **CameraPivot**: This game object rotates in its local *X* axis to tilt the camera up and down. It responds to the vertical mouse input.
- **Main Camera**: This is the standard game camera. It is moved away from the **CameraPivot** game object in local *Z* axis. This way we have a crane behavior for the camera. It orbits around the **CameraPivot** game object.

Using the LookAt() method to aim

In this recipe, we will use a simple but effective implementation of aiming mechanics.

Getting ready

We are going to use the same assets as in the previous recipe. Additionally, we are going to use the `CharacterLookAt.cs` created in the *Using Quaternion.LookRotation() and Animator.SetLookAtPosition() methods to make characters follow an object with their gaze* recipe in `Chapter 5`, *Character Actions and Expressions*.

You can also use the provided example Unity project and go to the `Chapter 06 Handling combat\Recipe 08 Using the LookAt method to aim` directory. You will find an `Example.unity` scene there, with a **Humanoid** character. Play the game to see the aiming effect.

How to do it...

To use the `LookAt()` method for aiming, follow these steps:

1. Import your character to Unity and place it on the **Scene**.
2. Follow the previous recipe to make a character walk and aim.
3. Attach the `CharacterLookAt.cs` script to the character.
4. Create a new **Sphere** object and name it `AimTarget`.
5. Assign the chest bone to the `CharacterLookAt.cs` component's **Bone** field.
6. Assign the **AimTarget** to the **Target** field of the `CharacterLookAt.cs` component.
7. Make the **AimTarget** a child of the **Main Camera** game object. We are using the same `CameraLook.cs` script in this recipe. You can find the script in the `Shared Scripts` folder in the example Unity project provided.
8. Offset the **AimTarget** position in its local Z axis around 20 units.
9. Play the game to see the effect. Our character will try to aim at the **AimTarget**. You may need to adjust the **Additional Rotation** vector in the `CharacterLookAt.cs` component. In our example, it is set to 15 in X and 20 in Y.

How it works...

We are using the same principle as in the *Using LookRotation() and SetLookAtPosition() methods to make characters follow an object with their gaze* recipe. Our script rotates the chest bone in such a way that the character appears to aim at the target. We use the **Additional Rotation** vector in the `CharacterLookAt.cs` script to adjust the rotation (chest is not facing straight forward in most animations). This way of aiming is good for games in which characters walk relative to the camera (it is suitable for TPP games with an over-the-shoulder camera). It fails when characters have to rotate more than 50-60 degrees. The next recipe solves this problem.

There's more...

`LookAt()` aiming is best used with robots and machines. It can be very useful for implementing turrets. You can find a **Turret** game object in the scene. It is built of three objects:

- **Turret**: This is the base of the Turret.
- **TurretPivot**: This game object only rotates horizontally (in the *Y* axis). This is a child object of the **Turret**.
- **Gun**: This object always points at the target. It is a child object of the **TurretPivot**. The **TurretPivot** rotates horizontally, so the **Gun** looks like it only rotates vertically.

The Turret game object has a `TurretAim.cs` script attached. In this script's `Update()` function, we first damp the `public Transform target` position and save the value in the `Vector3 dampedTargetPosition` variable. Then we use this variable to calculate the `aimVector` and we use the `aimVector` to calculate the `horizontalAimVector` (we simply remove the *Y* component from it). Lastly, we calculate new rotations for the **TurretPivot** and **Gun** game objects (stored in `public Transform` variables) using our `aimVector` and `horizontalAimVector`:

```
dampedTargetPosition =
Vector3.SmoothDamp(dampedTargetPosition,
aimTarget.position, ref refDampSpeed, dampTime);

aimVector = dampedTargetPosition - turretGun.position;

horizontalAimVector = aimVector;
horizontalAimVector.y = 0f;

turretPivot.rotation =
Quaternion.LookRotation(horizontalAimVector);
turretGun.rotation = Quaternion.LookRotation(aimVector);
```

Using Blend Trees to aim

In this recipe, we will use a more sophisticated method of aiming. This method is based on using several aim animations combined into a Blend Tree.

Getting ready

We are going to use the same assets as in the previous recipe, but instead of using the `CharacterLookAt.cs` script, we will use additional animations: **AimForward**, **AimForwardUp** (aim 45 degrees up), **AimForwardDown** (45 degrees down), **AimLeft** (45 degrees left), **AimLeftUp** (45 degrees left and 45 degrees up), **Aim LeftDown** (45 degrees left and 45 degrees down), **AimRight** (45 degrees right), **AimRightDown** (45 degrees right and 45 degrees down), **AimRightUp** (45 degrees right and 45 degrees up). See the following screenshot for reference:

Nine directional aim animations

You can also use the provided example Unity project and go to the `Chapter 06 Handling combat\Recipe 09 Using blend trees to aim` directory. You will find an `Example.unity` scene there, with a **Humanoid** character. Play the game to see the effect. You can find all the necessary animations in the `Rigs` directory.

How to do it...

To use the **Blend Trees** methods for aiming, follow these steps:

1. Import your character with all the necessary animations to Unity and place it on the **Scene**.
2. Follow the *Using Avatar Masks and animator controller layers to walk and aim* recipe to make the character walk and aim.
3. Open the controller and go to the **Aim Layer**.
4. Delete the **AimForward** state and create a new **Blend Tree**.
5. Create two float parameters: **AimVer** and **AimHor**.

6. Set the **Blend Type** to **Freeform Cartesian**.

7. Set the first parameter of the **Blend Tree** to **AimHor** and the second one to **AimVer**.

8. Create nine **Motion Fields** in the **Blend Tree** and assign all the aim animations to them.

9. Set the **Motion Fields** as follows (also see the following screenshot for reference):

  - **AimLeftDownPos X** set to -45, **Pos Y** set to -45
  - **AimLeftPos X** set to -45, **Pos Y** set to 0
  - **AimLeftUpPos X** set to -45, **Pos Y** set to 45
  - **AimForwardDownPos X** set to 0, **Pos Y** set to -45
  - **AimForwardPos X** set to 0, **Pos Y** set to 0
  - **AimForwardUpPos X** set to 0, **Pos Y** set to 45
  - **AimRightDownPos X** set to 45, **Pos Y** set to -45
  - **AimRightPos X** set to 45, **Pos Y** set to 0
  - **AimRightUpPos X** set to 45, **Pos Y** set to 45

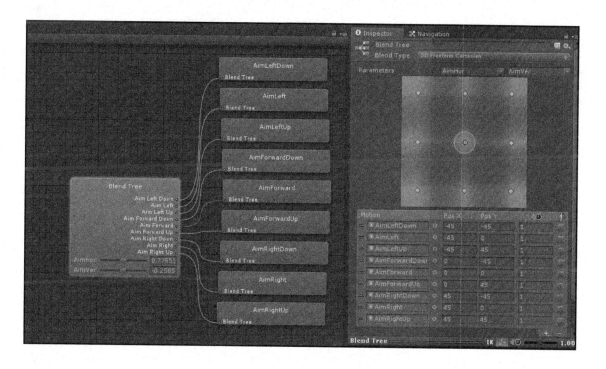

Aim Blend Tree settings

10. Create a new **Sphere** object and name it **AimTarget**.

11. Make **AimTarget** a child of the **Main Camera** game object. We are using the same `CameraLook.cs` script in this recipe. You can find the script in the `Shared Scripts` folder in the provided example Unity project.

12. Offset the **AimTarget** position in its local Z axis by around 20 units.

13. Create a new script and call it `AimWithBlendTree.cs`. In the `Update()` function of this script, we first calculate the `aimVector`. This is a vector from a helper `aimNode` transform to the `target` transform. Then we use this vector to calculate a `horAimVector`, a horizontal vector for aiming. Then we use the `horAimVector` to calculate the `aimHor` angle. We use the `Vector3.Angle()` method to find the angle between the `horAimVector` and `transform.forward` axis and `Mathf.Sign()` with `Vector3.Dot()` to determine the sign of the angle. We calculate the `aimVer` angle in a similar way, but we use the `horAimVector` instead of the `transform.forward` axis. Lastly, we assign the **AimVer** and **AimHor** parameters in the controller:

```
aimVector = target.position - aimNode.position;

horAimVector = aimVector;
horAimVector.y = 0f;

aimHor = Vector3.Angle(horAimVector, transform.forward) *
Mathf.Sign(Vector3.Dot(horAimVector, transform.right));

aimVer = Vector3.Angle(horAimVector, aimVector) *
Mathf.Sign(Vector3.Dot(aimVector, Vector3.up));

anim.SetFloat("AimHor", aimHor, aimSmooth, Time.deltaTime);
anim.SetFloat("AimVer", aimVer, aimSmooth, Time.deltaTime);
```

14. Assign the script to the character. Drag and drop the **AimTarget** transform to the **Target** field of the script.

15. Create an empty game object and name it **AimNode**. Place it roughly where the chest of the character is and make it a child of the character's transform.

16. Assign the **AimNode** transform to the **Aim Node** field of the script. You can use the **AimNode** to adjust the `aimVector` calculation.

17. Play the game to see the effect.

How it works...

We are using a similar principle as used in the *Using root motion to create flying characters* recipe in `Chapter 4, Character Movement`. Our script calculates the angles between our target and our character's forward axis. Then it assigns those angles as parameters in the controller. The Blend Tree uses those parameters to blend between nine directional aim animations.

There's more...

You can further develop this recipe with additional animations to handle more extreme angles. You can even have animations targeting +180 and -180 degrees in horizontal angles. This would make your character aim in every possible direction.

Detecting the hit location on a character

Another animation-related topic in combat is the hit location detection. This recipe shows how to easily detect hits to different body parts.

Getting ready

We are going to use a simple character with just one looped **Idle** animation in this recipe. You can also use the provided example Unity project and go to the `Chapter 06 Handling combat\Recipe 10 Detecting the hit location on a character` directory. You will find an `Example.unity` scene there, with a **Humanoid** character. Play the game to see the effect.

How to do it...

To be able to detect hits for different body parts, follow these steps:

1. Import your character with all the necessary animations to Unity. Place it on the scene.

2. Create a new **Layer** and name it **BodyParts**. To do so, go to the **Layers** menu and choose the **Edit Layers** option, as shown in the following screenshot:

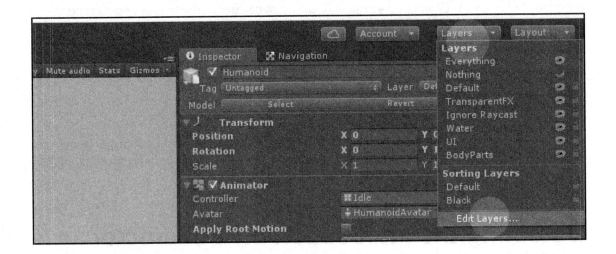

Adding a new Layer

3. Create a new script and name it `BodyPart.cs`. Create only one `public string` `bodyPartName` variable in this script. We will use it as a dummy script for our body parts. You will be able to implement custom effects of given body part hits in this script layer.

4. Create an empty game object and name it `Head`.

5. Assign the `BodyPart.cs` script to the **Head** game object. Type `Head` in the **Body Part Name** field of the `BodyPart.cs` component.

6. Assign a **Capsule Collider** component to the **Head** game object.

7. Set the **Head Layer** to **BodyParts**.

8. Add a **Rigidbody** component to the **Head** game object and set it to **Is Kinematic**.

9. Go to the **Edit | Project Settings | Physics** menu. Unselect the collisions between **BodyParts <-> BodyParts** Layers and **BodyParts <-> Default** Layers, as shown in the following screenshot :

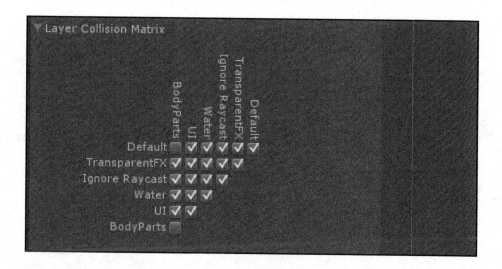

Collision matrix for BodyParts layer

10. Find the head bone in the character rig's hierarchy. Drag and drop the **Head** game object onto the head bone to parent it.

11. Zero out the **Head** transform's rotation and position.

12. Adjust the **Capsule Collider's** settings to roughly encapsulate the character's head shape.

13. Copy the **Head** game object and name it **Chest**. Type **Chest** in the **Body Part Name** of the `BodyPart.cs` component.

14. Drag and drop the **Chest** game object onto the chest bone in the character rig's hierarchy.

15. Zero out the **Chest's** position and rotation.

16. Adjust the **Chest's Capsule Collider** properties to roughly match the shape of the character's chest.

17. Repeat the steps 13 to 16 for all the body parts. In this example, we've created **Head**, **Chest**, **ArmL** (and a copy of it for the forearm), **ArmR** (and a copy of it for the forearm), **LegL** (and a copy of it for the shin), **LegR** (and a copy of it for the shin), and **Groin**. See the following screenshot for reference:

Body parts encapsulated by colliders

18. All the body parts will move along with the character. They do not collide with one another or with the **Default** layer. It prevents the character's physics from behaving in strange ways. You may also need to turn the collisions off for other layers in your game.

19. We are going to detect the body part hit with a simple script attached to the camera. Create a new script and name it Shoot.cs. In this script's Update() function, we constantly cast a ray from the camera's forward axis. We use the Physics.Raycast() implementation with the **LayerMask** parameter. This allows us to hit only those colliders that have the appropriate layer. If we hit such collider, we check if it has the BodyPart.cs component attached. If so, we set an on-screen UI text to the name of the body part we've hit:

```
Transform cameraTransform = Camera.main.transform;

if (Physics.Raycast(cameraTransform.position,
cameraTransform.forward, out hit, maxDistance,
bodyPartsLayer))
```

```
    {
        BodyPart p =
        hit.collider.gameObject.GetComponent<BodyPart>();
        if (p != null)
        {
            bodyPartText.text = "Hit body part: " +
            p.bodyPartName;
        }
        else
        {
            bodyPartText.text = "No body part was hit";
        }
    }
    else
    {
        bodyPartText.text = "No body part was hit";
    }
```

20. Attach the script to the camera.
21. Create a **UI Text** in the scene and attach it to the `BodyPart.cs` component's **Body Part Text** field.
22. Set the **Body Parts Layer** layer mask in the `BodyPart.cs` component to **BodyParts**.
23. Attach any free look script to the camera; you can also use the `CameraLook.cs` script from the `Shared Scripts` folder.
24. Play the game to see the effect.

How it works...

We are using the Unity's **Hierarchy** to attach colliders to the bones in the character's rig. This way we can check collisions with those body parts and react to them via scripts. To make this recipe simple, we only display the hit body part's name on the UI, but you can easily implement complex reactions to certain body part hits. For instance, you could implement additional damage for head shots or even a sophisticated wound system.

There's more...

We've covered hit detection using the `Physics.Raycast()` method, which is good for targeting body parts or fast moving projectiles. But you can just as easily implement body part detection in melee combat. All you need to do is to implement the `void OnCollisionEnter(Collision collision)` method in either the `BodyPart.cs` script or a new script attached to the weapon (it needs to have a **Collider** and a **Rigid Body** component set to **Is Kinematic**). You would then have to check if the entering collision object has a proper script or tag attached to determine whether you hit a body part.

7
Special Effects

and covers the following recipes:

This chapter explains how to achieve interesting effects with animations and covers the
following recipes: Using Animation Events to trigger sound and visual effects

- Creating camera shakes with the **Animation** View and the Animator Controller
- Using the **Animation** View to animate public script variables
- Using additive Mecanim layers to add extra motion to a character
- Using Blend Shapes to morph an object into another one
- Using wind emitters to create motion for foliage and particle systems
- Using sprite sheets to animate particles
- Animating properties of a particle system with the **Animation** View
- Using waveform of a sound clip to animate objects in the scene
- Creating a day and night cycle with the **Animation** View

Introduction

We've learned a lot in the previous chapters. This chapter is all about encouraging you to
experiment with Unity's animation system. During the next 10 recipes, we will create
interesting effects and use animations in new, creative ways. This chapter also covers
additional built—in Unity features that can be used to animate our scenes.

Using Animation Events to trigger sound and visual effects

This recipe shows a simple, generic way of playing different sound and visual effects with Animation Events.

Getting ready

To start, you need to have a character with one looped animation: **Jump**. We also need a sound effect and a particle system. We will need a transparent `DustParticle.png` texture for the particle system. It should resemble a small dust cloud. You can open the provided example Unity project and go to the `Chapter 07 Special effects\Recipe 01 Using animation events to trigger sound and visual effects` directory. In the `Rigs` directory, you will find all the needed animations, and in the `Resources` folder, you will find all other necessary assets. When you play the game, you will see a character playing the **Jump** animation. It will also play a sound effect and a particle effect when landing.

How to do it...

To play sound and visual effects with Animation Events, follow these steps:

1. Import the character with the **Jump** animation.
2. In the **Import Settings**, **Animation** tab, select the **Jump** animation.
3. Make it loop.
4. Go to the **Events** section.
5. Scrub through the timeline in the **Preview** section and click on the **Add Event** button. The **Edit Animation Event** window will appear, as shown in the following screenshot:

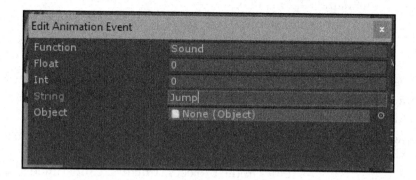

Edit Animation Event window

6. Type Sound in the **Function** field and Jump in the **String** field. This will call a **Sound** function in a script attached to the character and pass the **Jump** word as a string parameter to it.

7. Create another Animation Event. Set the **Function** field to **Effect** and the **String** field to **Dust**.

8. Apply the **Import Settings**.

9. Create an Animator Controller for the character with just the **Jump** animation in it.

10. Place the character in the scene.

11. Attach the controller to the Animator component of the character.

12. Attach an **Audio Source** component to the character.

13. Uncheck the **Play On Awake** option.

14. Create an empty game object and name it **Dust**.

15. Add a **Particle System** component to it. This will be our dust effect.

16. Set the **Particle System's** parameters as follows:
    - **Duration** to 1 second
    - **Start Life Time** to 0.5 seconds
    - **Start Speed** to 0.4
    - **Start Size** to random between two constants: 1 and 2
    - **Start Color** to a light brown
    - **Emission I Rate** to 0
    - **Emission I Bursts** to one burst with Time set to 0, **Min** and **Max** set to 5
    - **Shape I Shape** to Sphere

- **Shape** | **Radius** to 0.2
- **Color Over Lifetime**—Create a gradient for the alpha channel. In the 0% mark and 100% mark, it should be set to 0. In the 10% and 90% mark, it should be set to 255.

17. Create a new **Material** and set the shader to **Particles** | **Alpha Blended**.

18. Drag and drop a transparent texture of a `DustParticle.png` into the **Texture** field of the **Material**.

19. Drag and drop the **Material** into the **Renderer** | **Material** slot of our **DustParticle System**.

20. Create a `Resources` folder in the project's structure. Unity can load assets from the `Resources` folder in runtime, without the need to reference them as prefabs.

21. Drag and drop the `Jump.ogg` sound and the **Dust** game object into the `Resources` folder.

22. Write a new script and name it `TriggerEffects.cs`.

23. This script has two public void functions. Both are called from the **Jump** animation as Animation Events. In the first function, we load an Audio Clip from the `Resources` folder. We set the `Audio Clip` name in the Animation Event itself as the string parameter (it was set to **Jump**). When we successfully load the `Audio Clip`, we play it using the Audio Source component, reference to which we store in the `source` variable. We also randomize the pitch of the Audio Source to have a little variation when playing the `Jump.ogg` sound:

```
public void Sound (string soundResourceName) {

    AudioClip clip = (AudioClip)
    Resources.Load(soundResourceName);

    if (clip != null)
    {
        source.pitch = Random.Range(0.9f, 1.2f);
        source.PlayOneShot(clip);
    }
}
```

24. In the second function, we try to load a prefab with the name specified as the function's parameter. We also set this name in the Animation Event (it was set to **Dust**). If we manage to load the prefab, we instantiate it, creating the dust effect under our character's feet:

```
public void Effect (string effectResourceName) {
    GameObject effectResource =
```

```
(GameObject)Resources.Load(effectResourceName);
if (effectResource != null)
{
    GameObject.Instantiate(effectResource,
    transform.position, Quaternion.identity);
}
}
```

25. Assign the script to our character and play the game to see the effect.

How it works...

We are using one important feature of Animation Events in this recipe: the possibility to pass a `string`, `int`, or `float` parameter to our script's functions. This way we can create one function for playing all the sound effects associated with our character and pass the clips' names as `string` parameters from the Animation Events. The same concept is used for spawning the **Dust** effect.

The `Resources` folder is needed to get any resources (prefab, texture, audio clip, and so on) with the `Resources.Load(string path)` function. This method is convenient for loading assets using their names.

There's more...

Our **Dust** effect has the `AutoDestroy.cs` script attached to make it disappear after a certain time. You can find that script in the `Shared Scripts` folder in the provided example Unity project.

Creating camera shakes with the Animation View and the Animator Controller

In this recipe, we will use a simple, but very effective method for creating camera shakes. Those effects are often used to emphasize impacts or explosions in our games.

Getting ready

You don't need anything special for this recipe. We will create everything from scratch in Unity. You can also download the provided example Unity project and go to the `Chapter 07 Special effects\Recipe 02 Creating camera shakes with the animation window and the animator controller` directory. When you open the `Example.unity` scene and play the game, you can press the space bar to see a simple camera shake effect.

How to do it...

To create a camera shake effect, follow these steps:

1. Create an empty game object in the **Scene View** and name it **CameraRig**.
2. Parent the **Main Camera** to the **CameraRig**.
3. Select the **Main Camera** and add an **Animator** component to it.
4. Open the **Animation View**.
5. Create a new **Animation Clip** and call it **CamNormal**. The camera should have no motion in this clip. Add keys for both the camera's position and rotation.
6. Create another **Animation Clip** and call it **CameraShake**. Animate the camera's rotation and position to create a shake effect. The animation should have about 0.5 seconds.
7. Open the automatically created **Main Camera** controller.
8. Add a **Shake** `Trigger` parameter.
9. Create two transitions:
    - **CamNormal | CameraShake** with the condition: **Shake** `Trigger` parameter. **Has Exit Time** should be set to false and **Transition Duration** set to 0.2 seconds.
    - **CameraShake| CamNormal** with no conditions: **Has Exit Time** should be set to true and **Transition Duration** set to 0.2 seconds.
10. Write a new script and call it `CamShake.cs`.
11. In this script's `Update()` function, we check if player pressed the space bar. If so, we trigger the **Shake** `Trigger` in our controller:

```
if (Input.GetKeyDown(KeyCode.Space))

{

    anim.SetTrigger("Shake");
```

```
    }
```

12. As always, the `anim` variable holds the reference to the Animator component and is set in the `Start()` function with the `GetComponent<Animator>()` method.

13. Assign the script to the **Main Camera**.

14. Play the game and press the space bar to see the effect.

How it works...

In this recipe, we've animated the camera's position and rotation relative to the **CameraRig** object. This way we can still move the **CameraRig** (or attach it to a character). Our **CameraShake** animation only affects the local position and rotation of the camera. In the script, we simply call the **Shake** `Trigger` to play the **CameraShake** animation once.

There's more...

You can create more sophisticated camera shake effects with **BlendTrees**. To do so, prepare several shake animations with different strength and blend them in a **Blend Tree** using a **Strength** `float` parameter. This way, you will be able to set the shake's strength, depending on different situations in the game (the distance from an explosion for instance).

Using the Animation View to animate public script variables

In Unity, we can animate public script variables. Most standard types are supported. We can use this to achieve interesting effects that are not possible to achieve directly. For instance, we can animate fog color and density, which is not directly accessible through the Animation View.

Getting ready

In this recipe, everything will be created from scratch, so you don't need to prepare any special assets. You can also use the example project and go to the `Chapter 07 Special effects\Recipe 03 Using the animation window to animate public script variables` directory. You can find the `Example.unity` scene there. If you open it and press the space bar, you can observe the fog changing color and density.

It is achieved by animating the public variables of a script.

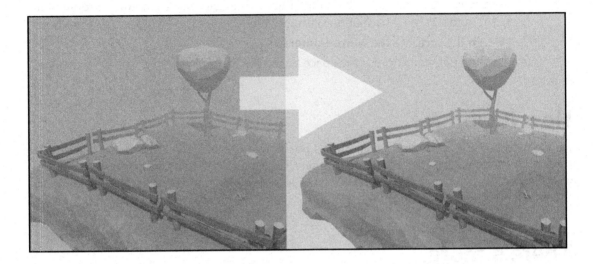

Animated fog

How to do it...

To animate public script variables, follow these steps:

1. Create a new script and call it `FogAnimator.cs`.
2. Create two public variables in this script: `public float fogDensity` and `public Color fogColor`.
3. In this script's `Update()` function, we call the **ChangeFog** `Trigger` in the controller when player presses the space bar. We also set the `RenderSettings.fogColor` and `RenderSettings.fogDensity` parameters using our public variables. We also adjust the **Main Camera**'s background color to match the fog color:

```
if (Input.GetKeyDown(KeyCode.Space))
{
    anim.SetTrigger("ChangeFog");
}
RenderSettings.fogColor = fogColor;
RenderSettings.fogDensity = fogDensity;

Camera.main.backgroundColor = fogColor;
```

4. Create a new game object and name it `FogAnimator`.
5. Attach the `FogAnimator.cs` script to it.
6. Select the **FogAnimator** game object and add an Animator component to it.
7. Open the **Animation** View.
8. Create a new Animation Clip.
9. Make sure the record button is pressed.
10. Create an animation for `public float fogDensity` and `public Color fogColor` parameters by changing their values.
11. You can create any number of animations and connect them in the automatically created Animator Controller with transitions based on the **ChangeFog** `Trigger` (you need to add this parameter to the controller first).
12. The following is an example controller:

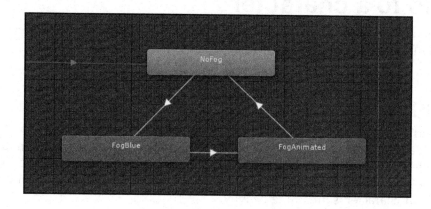

Example controller for different fog animations

13. Remember that you don't need to create animations of the fog changing its color or density. You can rely on blending between animations in the controller. All you need to have is one key for the density and one for the color in each animation. In this example, all **Transition Durations** are set to 1 second and every transition's **Has Exit Time** parameter is set to false.
14. Make sure fog is enabled in the **Lighting** settings.
15. Play the game and press the space bar to see the effect.

How it works...

Normally, we can't animate the fog's color or density using the **Animation** View. But we can do it easily with a script that sets the `RenderSettings.fogColor` and `RenderSettings.fogDensity` parameters every frame. We use animations to change the script's public variables values in time. This way we've created a workaround for animating fog in Unity.

We've just scratched the surface of what's possible with animating public script variables. Try experimenting to achieve awesome effects.

Using additive Mecanim layers to add extra motion to a character

In previous recipes, we were using Mecanim layers in override mode. We can set a layer to be additive. This can add additional movement to our base layer animations.

Getting ready

We will need a character with three animations: **Idle**, **TiredReference**, and **Tired**. The **Idle** animation is a normal, stationary idle. The **TiredReference** animation has no motion and is used as a reference pose for calculating additive motion from the **Tired** animation. The **TiredReference** animation can be the first frame of the **Tired** animation. In the **Tired** animation, our character is breathing heavily.

You can also go to the `Chapter 07 Special effects\Recipe 04 Using additive mecanim layers to add extra motion to a character` directory. Open the `Example.unity` scene there. You will find the same **Humanoid** character there. If you play the game and press the space bar, our character will start breathing heavily while still playing the **Idle** animation. You can find all the needed animations in the `Rigs` directory.

How to do it...

To use additive layers, follow these steps:

1. Import the character into Unity and place it in a scene.
2. Go to the **Animation** tab in the **Import Settings**.

3. Find the **TiredReference** animation and check the **Additive Reference Pose** option (you can also use the normal **Tired** animation and specify the frame in the **Pose Frame** field).

4. Loop the **Idle** and **Tired** animations.

5. Create a new Animator Controller.

6. Drag and drop the **Idle** animation into the controller and make it the **Default** state.

7. Find the **Layers** tab in upper left corner of the **Animator** window.

8. Select it and click on the plus button below to add a new layer.

9. Name the newly created layer **Tired**.

10. Click on the **Gear** icon and set the **Blending** to **Additive**, as shown in the following screenshot:

Additive layer settings

11. Drag and drop the **Tired** animation to the newly created layer.

12. Assign the controller to our character.

13. Create a new script and call it `Tired.cs`. In this script's `Update()` function, we set the weight of the **Tired** layer when player presses the space bar. The **Tired** layer has the index of 1. We use a helper variable `weightTarget` to set the new `weight` to 0 or 1, depending on its current value. This allows us to switch the additive layer on and off every time player presses the space bar. Finally, we interpolate the `weight` value in time to make the transition more smooth and we set the `weight` of our additive layer with the `SetLayerWeight()` function:

```
if (Input.GetKeyDown(KeyCode.Space))
{
    if (weightTarget < 0.5f)
    {
        weightTarget = 1f;
    }
    else if (weightTarget > 0.5f)
    {
        weightTarget = 0f;
    }
}
weight = Mathf.Lerp(weight, weightTarget, Time.deltaTime *
tiredLerpSpeed);

anim.SetLayerWeight(1, weight);
```

14. Attach the script to the **Humanoid** character.

15. Play the game and press the space bar to see the additive animation effect.

How it works...

Additive animations are calculated using the reference pose. Movements relative to this pose are then added to other animations. This way we can not only override the base layer with other layers but also modify the base movements by adding secondary motion.

Try experimenting with different additive animations. You can, for instance, make your character bend, aim, or change its overall body pose.

Using Blend Shapes to morph an object into another one

Previously, we used Blend Shapes to create face expressions. Blend Shapes are also an excellent tool for special effects. In this recipe, we will morph one object into another.

Getting ready

To follow this recipe, we need to prepare an object with Blend Shapes. We've created a really simple example in Blender—a subdivided cube with one shape key that looks like a sphere. See the following screenshot for reference:

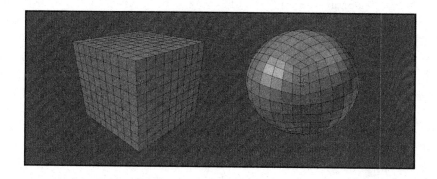

A cube with a Blend Shape that turns it into a sphere

You can also go to the Chapter 07 Special effects\Recipe 05 Using blendshapes to morph an object into another one directory. Open the Example.unity scene there. You will see a number of cubes there. If you hit the space bar in play mode, the cubes will morph into spheres. You can find the Cuboid.fbx asset with the required **Blend Shapes** in the Model directory.

How to do it...

To use **Blend Shapes** to morph objects, follow these steps:

1. Import the model with at least one **Blend Shape** to Unity. You may need to go to the **Import Settings**, **Model** tab, and choose **Import BlendShapes**.
2. Place the model in the **Scene**.

3. Create a new script and call it `ChangeShape.cs`. This script is similar to the one from the previous recipe. In the `Update()` function, we change the weight of the first Blend Shape when player presses the space bar. Again, we use a helper variable `weightTarget` to set the new `weight` to 0 or 100, depending on its current value. Blend Shapes have weights from 0 to 100 instead of 1. Finally, we interpolate the `weight` value in time to make the transition smoother. We use the `SetBlendShapeWeight()` function on the `skinnedRenderer` object. This variable is set in the `Start()` function with the `GetComponent<SkinnedMeshRenderer>()` function:

```
if (Input.GetKeyDown(KeyCode.Space))
{
    if (weightTarget < 50f)
    {
        weightTarget = 100f;
    }
    else if (weightTarget > 50f)
    {
        weightTarget = 0f;
    }
}
weight = Mathf.Lerp(weight, weightTarget, Time.deltaTime *
blendShapeLerpSpeed);
skinnedRenderer.SetBlendShapeWeight(0, weight);
```

4. Attach the script to the model on the scene.
5. Play the game and press the space bar to see the model morph.

How it works...

stores vertices position of a mesh. We have to create them in a 3D package. Unity imports Blend Shapes and we can modify their weights in runtime using the `SetBlendShapeWeight()` function on the **Skinned Mesh Renderer** component. We can also use animations as shown in the, *Animating facial expressions with Blend Shapes* recipe in `Chapter 5`, *Characters Actions and Expressions*.

Blend Shapes have trouble with storing **Normals**. If we import **Normals** from our model, it may look weird after morphing. Sometimes, setting the **Normals** option to **Calculate** in the **Import Settings** can helps with the problem. If we choose this option, Unity will calculate **Normals** based on the angle between faces of our model. This allowed us to morph a hard surface cube into a smooth sphere in this example.

Using wind emitters to create motion for foliage and particle systems

Unity supports wind emitters with which we can create realistic effects for foliage and particles. Using them is really simple.

Getting ready

To follow this recipe, you need to have a particle system and a tree created with Unity's built—in **Tree Creator**. You can open the provided example project and go to the `Chapter 07 Special effects\Recipe 06 Using wind emitters to create motion for foliage and particle systems` directory. In the `Example.unity` scene there, you can find a tree and a simple particle system (falling leaves). Play the game to see the tree and particles moving with the wind.

Tree with a falling leaves particle system. Both animated with a WindZone

How to do it...

To use Unity's wind, follow these steps:

1. Place the tree and the particle system in the scene.
2. Create a new **WindZone**. To do so, go to the **GameObject | 3D Object | Wind Zone** option.

3. The tree will move when you play the game, but the particle system needs to be adjusted.

4. To make the particle system react to wind, open its properties and check the **External Forces** option.

5. Click on it to unfold it. You can edit the **Multiplier** field to increase or decrease the influence of the wind.

6. If you're not sure whether your particles react to wind, set their **Start Speed** to 0.

7. Play the game to see the effect.

How it works...

Wind Zones are a built—in Unity feature, useful for animating foliage and particle systems. There are two types of Wind Zone:

- **Directional**: This is a global wind for the whole scene (still you can have several of them). It blows in one direction.
- **Spherical**: This type has a **Radius** in which it influences particles and trees. It's useful for helicopters and explosions.

Wind Zones are described by a series of parameters defining the strength of the wind:

- **Main**: This is the main wind force. It changes softly over time.
- **Turbulence**: This produces a rapidly changing force and is useful for creating storms.
- **Pulse Magnitude**: This describes how much the wind changes over time.
- **Pulse Frequency**: This describes the frequency of the wind changes.

Remember that you can animate the Wind Zone's parameters with the **Animation** View. This gives you a great amount of control over how the wind should change in time. For instance, you can create a strong, spherical wind for explosions with an animation of the **Main** and **Turbulence** parameters quickly fading out. You can also animate the Wind Zone rotation and/or position (applicable only to the Spherical type) to change the effect.

Using sprite sheets to animate particles

We can add sprite sheet animation to Unity's particles to make them more interesting. This concept is especially useful for various explosions and magical effects.

Getting ready

To follow this recipe, we need an animation exported as a sprite sheet. If you want to know how to create a sprite sheet animation, you can read the *Exporting a 2D sprite animation from a 3D package* recipe in `Chapter 3`, *2D and User Interface Animation*, where you can find an example sprite animation.

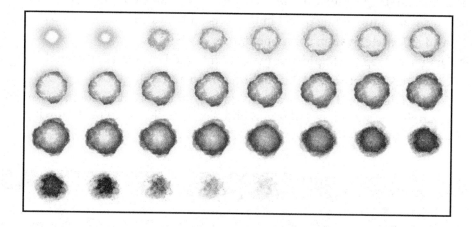

Example sprite sheet animation

You can also open the provided example project and go to the `Chapter 07 Special effects\Recipe 07 Using sprite sheets to animate particles` directory. If you open the `Example.unity` scene there and play the game, you will see a particle system with explosions using sprite sheet animation. You can find the necessary sprite sheet in the `Rigs` directory.

How to do it...

To use sprite sheets for particles animation, follow these steps:

1. Import the sprite sheet texture into Unity. Its size should be a power of 2. The animation should be rendered from left to right and from top to bottom in equal tiles (128 × 128, 256 × 256, or similar).

2. Set it as a normal **Texture** (not a Sprite) and check the **Alpha Is Transparency** option.

3. Create a new **Material** and name it `Explosion`.

4. Set the **Shader** to **Particles** | **Alpha Blended** (you can also use Additive or Additive Soft).

5. Drag and drop the texture into the **Particle Texture** slot in the **Material**.

6. Create an empty game object in the scene and name it `AnimatedExplosion`.

7. Add a **Particle System** component to it.

8. Drag and drop the **Explosion** material into the **Renderer** | **Material** slot.

9. Check the **Texture Sheet Animation** option and unfold it.

10. Set the **Tile**'s **X** and **Y** fields according to your exported sprite sheet. In our example, the sheet has **8** tiles in **X** and **4** in **Y**, as shown in the following screenshot:

Texture Sheet Animation settings

11. Adjust the **Start Lifetime** of the particles to match the frame rate of your exported sprite sheet animation. If your exported animation lasts 1 second, then the **Start Lifetime** of a particle should be also equal to 1 second.

12. Adjust the other settings of the particle system to your liking. In this example, those settings are as follows:
    - **Start Lifetime**: 1
    - **Looping**: True
    - **Start Speed**: 0
    - **Start Size**: 5

- **Emission** | **Rate**: 1
- **Shape** | **Shape**: Sphere
- **Shape** | **Radius**: 4

13. Play the game or simulate the particle system to see the effect.

How it works...

Unity's particle system can play sprite sheet animation for each of its particles. To do so, the **Texture Sheet** Animation option has to be checked. This option has several important settings:

- **Tiles**: The **X** and **Y** fields specify how many tiles in **X** and **Y** the texture sheet has. Animation is played from left to right and from top to bottom.
- **Animation**: We can use the whole sheet or a single row. If the **Single Row** option is selected, we can use a random row of the Sprite Sheet or specify a single row for our animation. This way we can have multiple animations in one sprite sheet. It also gives us the possibility to have multiple animations per particle system, instead of playing the same one for every particle (Random Row has to be checked to achieve this).
- **Frame Over Time**: This is a curve describing which frame should be played over time. Remember that, by default, the whole sprite sheet is always played during the whole lifetime of a particle.
- **Cycles**: Here we can specify how many cycles of the animation should be played in one lifetime of a particle.

Animating properties of a particle system with the Animation View

This recipe shows how to use the Animation View to animate a particle system's properties. Not all of them can be directly accessed with the **Animation** View, but we will use the same trick as with the fog in the *Using the Animation View to animate public script variables* recipe.

Getting ready

This recipe is created from scratch in Unity; you don't need any special assets. You should have a particle system ready before we start. You can go to the Chapter 07 Special effects\Recipe 08 Animating properties of a particle system with the animation window directory. You will find an Example.unity scene there. Open it and play the game to a particle system with animated properties.

How to do it...

To animate particle system properties, follow these steps:

1. Create an empty game object and name it **AnimatedParticleSystem**.
2. Add a **Particle System** component to it.
3. Create the particle system to your liking. We have a very simple particle system with particles flying in straight line in this example.
4. Add an **Animator** component to the **AnimatedParticleSystem** game object.
5. Create an animation of the **Emission | Rate** parameter. It is only possible to directly animate **Emission Module** and **Shape Module** of a particle system.
6. To animate other properties, create a new script and call it ParticleAnims.cs. In this script, we have two public variables: public float gravityModifier and public Color color. We use those variables to set the gravityModifier and the startColor properties of the particle system in the Update() function. The reference to the Particle System component is set in the Start() function and stored in the particles variable:

```
void Update () {
    particles.gravityModifier = gravityModifier;
    particles.startColor = color;
}
```

7. Assign the script to the **AnimatedParticleSystem** game object.
8. Open the **Animation** View again and animate the **Color** and **Gravity Modifier** public fields of the script. This way we can create a workaround to animate the particle system's properties unreachable from the **Animation** View.
9. Play the game to see the effect.

How it works...

This recipe uses the same concept as described in the *Using the Animation View to animate public script variables* recipe. This time we use the public script variable animation to animate a particle system's properties, normally unreachable from the **Animation** View. Unity has the animate *everything* philosophy, so I think we may expect that all the particle system's properties will be available to animate directly in the **Animation** View in the future.

Using waveform of a sound clip to animate objects in the scene

In this recipe, we will use a waveform of a sound effect to create motion based on the average volume of the fragment of the waveform.

Getting ready

To follow this recipe, we need a sound effect. You can use the provided example Unity project and go to the Chapter 07 Special effects\Recipe 09 Using waveform of a sound clip to animate objects in the scene directory. If you open the Example.unity scene there and play the game, you will be able to see a few cubes react to the playing audio clip.

How to do it...

To use sound waveforms for animation, follow these steps:

1. Import the sound into Unity.
2. Create an empty game object and name it AudioSource.
3. Add an Audio Source component to it, and make the sound **Loop** and **Play On Awake**. Drag and drop your sound into the **AudioClip** field.
4. Create a **Cube** game object (go to **Game Object | 3D Object | Cube**).
5. Create a new script and call it ScaleWithWaveForm.cs. In this script, we have one public AudioSource audioSource variable, one public float lerpSpeed variable, one float[] samples array, and a float currentSample variable to store the average volume of the samples. In this script's Start() function, we set the size of the samples array to 1024 (it needs

to be a power of 2). This is the number of samples we will read from the Audio Source. We also start a IEnumerator SampleAudio() coroutine:

```
public AudioSource audioSource;
public float lerpSpeed = 100f;
float[] samples;
float currentSample;

void Start()
{
    samples = new float[1024];
    StartCoroutine("SampleAudio");
}
```

6. This coroutine uses the audioSource.GetOutputData() function to get and store the output audio samples in the samples array. Then we sum all the squared samples and calculate an average volume (the **RMS**). Lastly, we use this value to scale the Cube game object. Additionally, we interpolate the scale changes in time to make it smoother. The currentSample value is multiplied by 10 to make the changes more visible (**RMS** ranges from 0 to 1):

```
IEnumerator SampleAudio()
{
    while (true)
    {
        audioSource.GetOutputData(samples, 0);
        currentSample = 0f;
        for (int i = 0; i < samples.Length; i++)
        {
            currentSample += (samples[i] *
            samples[i]);
        }
        currentSample = Mathf.Sqrt(currentSample /
        samples.Length);
        transform.localScale =
        Vector3.Lerp(transform.localScale,
        Vector3.one * currentSample*100f,
        Time.deltaTime*4f);
        yield return null;
    }
}
```

7. Assign the script to the **Cube** game object.
8. Drag and drop the **AudioSource** game object into the **Audio Source** field of the script.
9. Play the game to see the effect.

How it works...

The key component of this recipe is the `AudioSource.GetOutputData(float[]` `samples, int channel)` function. It grabs a number of samples from the currently playing audio. The number of samples is specified by the length of the `float[] samples` array. This length has to be a power of 2. We get the samples every frame in the `IEnumerator SampleAudio()` coroutine. We average the values of squared samples to calculate an RMS of the audio (an average volume of a number of samples). The more samples we average, the smoother the changes of the RMS. For most sounds, 1024 is a good number. We use the calculated RMS to scale the **Cube** game object.

See also

You can perform more complex signal analysis of the waveform to create more interesting effects. For instance, if you want to create an equalizer showing different frequencies of the sound, you need to use the fast Fourier transform. You can find a lot of interesting information about it in the Unity forums.

Creating a day and night cycle with the Animation View

In this recipe, we will create a simple day and night cycle animation using the Animation View.

Getting ready

We are going to create this recipe from scratch in Unity, so we don't need any additional assets. You can also use the provided example Unity project and go to the `Chapter 07 Special effects\Recipe 10 Creating a day and night cycle with the animation window` directory. You will find an `Example.unity` scene there.

Open it and play the game to see the effect.

Simple day and night cycle

How to do it...

To create a day and night cycle with the Animation View, follow these steps:

1. Create an empty game object and call it `DayAndNight`.
2. Create another empty game object, call it `SunAndMoonPivot`, and parent it to the **DayAndNight** game object.
3. Create two more game objects, **SunPivot** and **MoonPivot**, and parent them to **SunAndMoonPivot**.
4. Then create the **Sun** and **Moon** objects and parent the first one to **SunPivot** and the second one to **MoonPivot**.
5. Lastly, create two **Directional Lights** and two **Spheres** and parent one of each to the **Sun** object and the remaining two to the **Moon** object.
6. The hierarchy should look like the following:
    1. **DayAndNight | SunAndMoonPivot**
    2. **SunAndMoonPivot | SunPivot**
    3. **SunAndMoonPivot | MoonPivot**
    4. **SunPivot | Sun**
    5. **MoonPivot | Moon**
    6. **Sun | Directional Light**

7. **Sun | SunSphere**
8. **Moon | Directional Light**
9. **Moon | MoonSphere**

7. Create two materials: **Moon** and **Sun**. Choose the **Unlit | Color** shader for them and adjust the colors to your liking (you can also use the Standard Shader with an Emission color).
8. Apply the materials to the **SunSphere** and **MoonSphere** objects.
9. Move the **Sun** and the **Moon** away from the center. You can also use the **SunPivot** and **MoonPivot** to rotate the **Sun** and the **Moon**. See the following screenshot for reference:

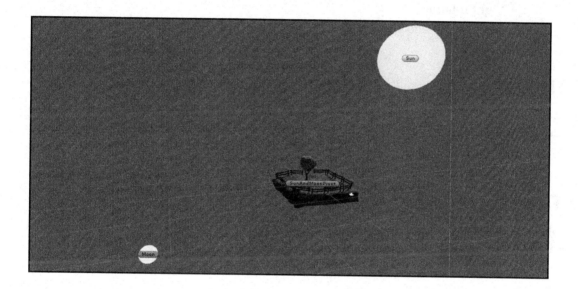

Sun and Moon placement

10. Select the **DayAndNight** game object and add an **Animator** component to it.
11. Create a new script and call it `CameraColor.cs`. This script has one `public Color cameraColor` variable. In the `Update()` function of this script, we set the `backgroundColor` of the main camera to the `cameraColor` variable's value:

```
void Update () {
    Camera.main.backgroundColor = cameraColor;
}
```

12. Assign the script to the **DayAndNight** game object.

13. With the **DayAndNight** game object selected, open the **Animation** View.

14. Create an animation of the **Sun** and **Moon** moving on the horizon. Rotate the **SunAndMoonPivot** to make the job easier.

15. Animate the **Directional Light** colors and their **Intensity** and **Shadow Strength**. In the day, only the **Sun's Directional Light** should cast shadows, and in the night, only the **Moon's Directional Light** should cast shadows.

16. If you are using the camera's background color as the background color of the scene, animate it using the `public Color cameraColor` of the script attached to **SunAndMoonPivot** game object. If you're using Unity's parametric skybox, make sure to choose your **Sun's Directional Light** as the **Sun** in the **Lighting** settings. This will make the skybox change with the respect of **Sun's Directional Light** rotation.

17. Run the game to see the effect.

How it works...

In this recipe, we use the **Hierarchy** to animate rotation of **Sun** and **Moon**. We also animate the **Intensity**, **Color**, and **Shadow Strength** of **Directional Lights** attached to those game objects. This way, we can create an illusion of a day and night cycle.

There's more...

To control the speed of the day and night cycle animation, you can modify the `anim.speed` parameter in runtime from scripts. The `anim` variable is a reference to the **Animator** component attached to the **DayAndNight** game object.

8
Animating Cutscenes

This chapter explains how to create and play cutscenes in games and covers the following recipes:

- Using the **Animation** View to animate the camera

- Changing cameras with animation

- Synchronizing animation of multiple objects

- Importing a whole cutscene from a 3D package

- Synchronizing subtitles

- Using root motion to play cutscenes in gameplay

Introduction

In this chapter we will handle cutscenes. These are short animated sequences used mostly to unveil new story events. You can create a lot of them directly in Unity, or import animations from your favorite 3D package (we will be using Blender 3D as an example).

Using the Animation View to animate the camera

In this recipe, we will create camera animation using Unity's built-in **Animation** View:

Simple vertigo effect created with the Animation View

Getting ready

We don't need anything fancy for this recipe as we will create it from scratch in Unity. You may need some decorations in the scene though. You can also open the provided example Unity project and go to the `Chapter 08 Animating Cutscenes\Recipe 01 Using the animation view to animate the camera` directory. You can find an animated **Camera (1)** game object in the `Example.unity` scene there. If you play the game, the camera will play an animation.

How to do it...

To create camera animation with the **Animation** View, follow these steps:

1. Select the camera you want to animate (you can also add a new camera to the scene).
2. Open the **Animation** View (go to **Window | Animation**).

3. Create a new Animation Clip and call it `CameraAnimation`.
4. Make sure the record button is pressed.
5. Move and rotate the camera to create the desired animation. If the camera is not parented to any game object, the animation will be done in world space.
6. If you want to use this animation as a cutscene, create a prefab from the camera.
7. Play the game to see the effect.

How it works...

Cameras can be animated the same way as other game objects. We can animate their **Transforms,** but additionally, we can also animate the **Camera** component. This way we can create interesting effects with the **Field of View** parameter (for instance, the simple vertigo effect shown in the example project).

There's more...

If you create a prefab out of an animated camera, you can instantiate it to play a cutscene. Remember to set the cutscene camera's **Depth** to be greater than the in-game camera's. This way, simply instantiating the cutscene camera prefab will automatically play the cutscene. All you need to do is to destroy the instantiated game object after the animation ends. You can do so with an Animation Event associated with a function that will destroy the object (you need to use a script for that).

You should also remember to disable the **Audio Listener** component in the in-game camera when you instantiate the cutscene camera. After the cutscene is finished, make sure to re-enable the **Audio Listener** component again.

Changing cameras with animation

Not only can we animate cameras using the Animation View, but we can also change the shots in time.

Getting ready

This recipe will also be created from scratch in Unity. You can download the example Unity project provided and go to `Chapter 08 Animating Cutscenes\Recipe 02 Changing cameras with animation` directory. You can find a **Camera Changer** game object in the `Example.unity` scene there, with three cameras as children. If you play the game, the cameras will change.

How to do it...

To change cameras using animation, follow these steps:

1. Create an empty game object in the **Scene** View and name it `CameraChanger`.
2. Rename the **Main Camera** to **Camera (1)** and copy it two times. You should have **Camera (1)**, **Camera (2)**, and **Camera (3)** game objects.
3. Parent all three cameras to the **CameraChanger**.
4. Place the cameras as you wish.
5. Set the **Depth** of the cameras in increasing order. Every new shot should have a greater **Depth** value.
6. Select the **CameraChanger** game object and open the **Animation** View.
7. Create a new **Animation Clip** and call it **CameraChange**.
8. Make sure the record button is pressed.
9. Select all cameras and disable their game objects. Then select the first camera and enable its game object. New keys should be created in the first frame of the animation. The first camera should be active and the remaining two should be inactive (you can check this by clicking on a key). You may need to set the cameras to active to create the keys and then set them to inactive (Unity sometimes doesn't create a key if you deactivate an object and only creates the key if you click to enable it):

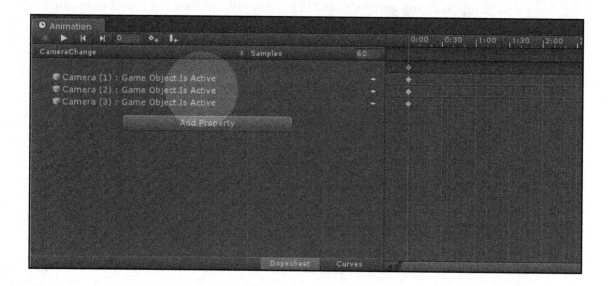

Keys containing cameras' state (active/inactive)

10. Adjust the timeline and activate the second camera. You don't need to deactivate the first one, but you should have only one Audio Listener component enabled.

11. Adjust the timeline again and activate the third camera.

12. Close the **Animation** View.

13. Play the animation or run the game to see the effect.

How it works...

This recipe has a few important elements:

- **Cameras as children**: All cameras are children of the **CameraChanger** game object. This way, we can add the Animator component to the **CameraChanger** and animate all its children cameras using one Animation Clip.

- **Camera's Depth**: The depth parameter describes the "layer" of the camera. Cameras with greater Depth are rendered on top of cameras with lesser Depth. This way, we can change the cameras without the need to worry about not rendering anything.

- **Enabling/disabling game objects**: We can enable or disable game objects using animation. All we need to do is to click on the enable checkbox, as shown in the following screenshot. As always, parameters that are animated (have keys in the animation) are marked in red:

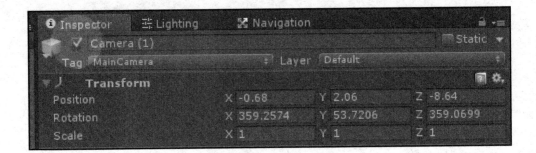

Enable / disable game object checkbox with a key frame

Synchronizing animation of multiple objects

In a cutscene, we have to synchronize animation of multiple objects in time. This recipe shows how to do it.

Getting ready

To follow this recipe, you will need an animated character and an animated object. You can download the provided example Unity project and go to the `Chapter 08 Animating Cutscenes\Recipe 03 Synchronizing animation of multiple objects` directory. You can find the `Example.unity` scene there. If you play the game, you will see a character kicking a soccer ball. Both objects are animated and synchronized. You can find the needed animations in the `Animations` directory:

Synchronized animation of the ball and a the character kicking it

How to do it...

To synchronize animation of multiple objects, follow these steps:

1. Open both objects in your 3D package (we are using Blender in this example).
2. Synchronize both objects' animations in the 3D package. In our example, the animation has about 160 frames. Both objects have the same length of animation:

Ball and character animation synchronized in a 3D package

3. In this example, the ball has no skeletal animation; we only animate its **Transform**.

4. Make sure to have key frames for both the ball and the character in the first and last frames of the animation. This way, the animations will have equal length after importing them to Unity.

5. After synchronizing the animation in a 3D package, save it to two files: one with only the ball object and its animation, and one only with the character and its animation. Unity can import multiple transform animations, but has problems with importing multiple skeletal animations (for example, you will not be able to set the rig to **Humanoid**).

6. Export both files separately to FBX format and make sure to include the **Default Take**. In Blender, use the 6.1 version of FBX.

7. Import both files to Unity.

8. If you want to use a **Humanoid** character, make sure to set all the **Based Upon** options to **Original** in the **Animation Import Settings**.

9. Create an Animator Controller for the ball and another one for the character with the soccer kick animation.

10. Place the ball and the character in the same location on the scene. Attach the Animator Controllers to them.

11. Play the game to see the effect.

How it works...

The best way to synchronize cutscene animations is to make sure that they have the same length and are synchronized in a 3D package. If we import them in Unity and start the playback in the same moment, they will stay synchronized.

Remember that you need to export the characters as separate files if you want to use the **Humanoid** rigs.

There's more...

You can also synchronize animations using Animation Events. In our example, we could create the ball animation from the moment it is kicked by the character and transition to it using an Animation Event in the character's kick animation. Although this is possible, it is more cumbersome than synchronizing the whole cutscene in a 3D package.

Importing a whole cutscene from a 3D package

The best way of creating cutscenes in Unity is to import whole animations from a 3D package. We did a similar thing in the previous recipe (we synchronized the animations in a 3D package before importing them to Unity). Here we are going to create a full cutscene with camera animations.

Getting ready

For this recipe, we need the same character as in the previous recipe, with a *kicking the ball* animation. Additionally, we've added three simple cubes to the animation. Those cubes are animated and represent cameras. We used cubes instead of empty objects or cameras because Unity sometimes has trouble with importing the motion of objects that are not rigs nor have mesh renderers:

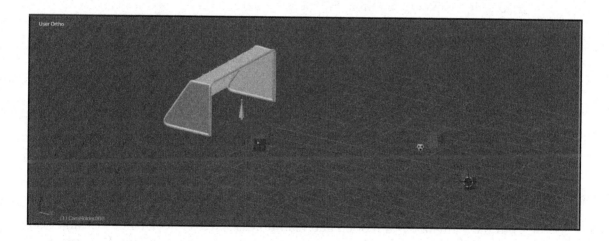

Cutscene objects in Blender. Red cubes hold camera positions

You can also go to the `Chapter 08 Animating Cutscenes\Recipe 04 Importing a whole cutscene from a 3D package` directory. You can find the `Example.unity` scene there. If you play the game, you will see a character kicking a soccer ball. The cameras will animate and change as the animation progresses. You can find all the needed animations in the `Animations` directory.

How to do it...

To import a whole cutscene from a 3D package, follow these steps:

1. Create the cutscene in a 3D package. Remember that all the objects' animations should have the same length. They should have keys on the first and last frame.

2. If you plan to use **Humanoid** rigs, save every character as a separate file before importing it to Unity.

3. Import the cutscene to Unity (and all the characters, if needed). All objects that use **Generic** rigs can be exported together as one file. In such cases, a **Generic** rig will be created for the whole cutscene.

4. If you are using Blender and want to export the cutscene to FBX format, use the 6.1 version and make sure to check the **Default Take** option.

5. Go to the **Animation** tab in **Import Settings**.

6. The **Default Take** holds the whole cutscene animation. You may see additional clips in the Animation tab (especially if you are using skeletal animation). Don't use them. You can remove them from the Import Settings and change the **Default Take** clip name to something more descriptive.

7. If you are using **Humanoid** rigs for the characters, import them one by one from the separate files.

8. Create an **Animator Controller** for the cutscene and one for every character (if you are using the **Humanoid** rig).

9. Place the cutscene animation in the controllers.

10. Place all the objects in the same place on the scene.

11. If you want to animate cameras, create one camera for every shot of your cutscene.

12. Parent the cameras to the animated camera holder objects from the cutscene. You may need to adjust camera rotations.

13. Our cameras are children of the camera holder objects (and the cutscene object). But the animation is imported and read-only. So, we cannot change the cameras the same way we did in the *Changing cameras with animation* recipe. We need a script on the root object of the cutscene (the one with the Animator component). Create a new script and call it `CutsceneCameraChanger.cs`. In this script, we have a list of all the cutscene cameras and a `public void ChangeCamera()` animation event that changes the camera based on the given `int` `newCameraIndex` parameter. It disables all other cameras from the list:

```
public void ChangeCamera (int newCameraIndex)
{
```

```
for (int i = 0; i < cutsceneCameras.Length; i++)
{
    cutsceneCameras[i].gameObject.
            SetActive(false);
}
    cutsceneCameras[newCameraIndex].gameObject.
            SetActive(true);
}
```

14. Assign the script to the root object of the cutscene.
15. Open the **Animation Import Settings** for the cutscene.
16. Adjust the timeline to the place you want to change the shot.
17. Add Animation Events to enable appropriate cameras and change the shots. Use the int parameter to provide the newCameraIndex for the ChangeCamera function. Remember to set the **Depth** parameters of the cameras to be higher than the gameplay camera.
18. Apply the **Animation Import Settings** and disable the **Mesh Renderer** components for each of the camera holder objects so that they will not be visible in-game.
19. Play the game to see the effect.

How it works...

Unity can import whole cutscenes as single assets. You can animate a cutscene with a lot of objects and characters and then export it to FBX (or simply save the file if you are using Blender). After the import, the **Default Take** holds the whole animation. You cannot change the animation (it is read-only), but you can write scripts to enable/disable cameras using Animation Events. You need to add the events in the Animation Import Settings though.

If you plan to reuse the animation for different characters, you need to export every rig from the cutscene as a separate file. Only then can you set it to **Humanoid**.

You cannot export particle systems from a 3D package. Only transform and skeletal animation is supported. You will need to create VFX in Unity and synchronize them with the cutscene using Animation Events. The same rule applies to sound effects. We were doing this in the *Using Animation Events to trigger sound and visual effects* recipe in Chapter 7, *Special Effects*.

There's more...

According to Unity's roadmap, a Director tool is planned sometime in the 5.x schedule. It may make authoring cutscenes in Unity easier. But, for animators used to their favorite 3D packages, importing whole cutscenes can still be the preferred option.

Synchronizing subtitles

In this recipe, we create subtitles and synchronize them with the animation:

Subtitles synchronized with animation

Getting ready

In this recipe, we will use the same cutscene as in the previous one. You can also open the example Unity project and go to the `Chapter 08 Animating Cutscenes\Recipe 05 Synchronizing subtitles` directory. If you open the `Example.unity` scene there and play the game, you will see changing subtitles synchronized with the animation.

How to do it...

To synchronize subtitles with a cutscene, follow these steps:

1. Import the cutscene the same way as in the previous recipe.
2. Create a new **Image** (go to **Game Object | UI | Image**).
3. Name it **SubtitlesContainer**.
4. Create a new Text game object and parent it to the **SubtitlesContainer**. To do so, right-click on the **SubtitlesContainer** and choose **UI | Text**.
5. Change the color of the **SubtitlesContainer**'s **Image** component to semitransparent black. Change the color of the **Text** component to white. Adjust the position and size of the objects as desired.
6. Place the model in the **Scene**.
7. Create a new script and call it `Subtitles.cs`. This script has a `string subtitlesText` variable in which we will store the text displayed in the subtitles. It also has public references to the **SubtitlesContainer** and **Text** game objects: `public GameObject subtitlesContainer` and `public Text textComponent`. This script has one `public void SetSubtitles(string text)` function. It is called from an Animation Event and is used to set the `subtitlesText` variable's value:

```
public void SetSubtitles(string text)
{
    subtitlesText = text;
}
```

8. In the `Update()` function of this script, we check if the `subtitlesText` variable contains any text. If so, we enable the **SubtitlesContainer** game object and set the **Text** game object to display our subtitles. If `subtitlesText` is an empty string, we disable the **SubtitlesContainer**:

```
if (string.IsNullOrEmpty(subtitlesText)
&& subtitlesContainer.activeSelf)
{
    subtitlesContainer.SetActive(false);
}
else if (!string.IsNullOrEmpty(subtitlesText)
&& !subtitlesContainer.activeSelf)
{
    subtitlesContainer.SetActive(true);
}
else
{
```

```
textComponent.text = subtitlesText;
}
```

9. Attach the script to the cutscene game object (the one that has the Animator component and animates all the props).

10. Open the **Animation Import Settings** for the cutscene animation.

11. You can scrub through the timeline and add Animation Events.

12. Add an Animation Event and name the function as **SetSubtitles**. Enter the text you want to display as subtitles in the `String` parameter, as shown in the following screenshot:

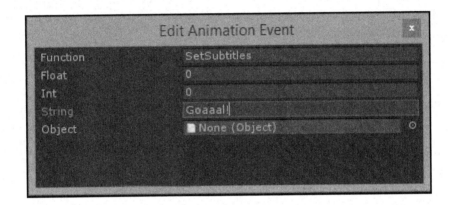

SetSubtitles Animation Event with the "Goooal!" text

13. If you want the subtitles to disappear, add a **SetSubitles** Animation Event and leave the `String` parameter empty.

14. Apply the **Animation Import Settings**.

15. Play the game to see the effect.

How it works...

In this recipe, we use **Animation Events** to synchronize subtitles with the cutscene. The principle is the same as in the *Using Animation Events to trigger sound and visual effects* recipe in `Chapter` 7, *Special Effects*. The `Subtitles.cs` script also handles showing and hiding the subtitles, depending on the value of the `subtitlesText` variable set by the `public voidSetSubitltes(string text)` function that we call with the Animation Events.

If you want to localize your subtitles, use string localization keys instead of text. The `Subtitles.cs` script will then have to search for the text in your localization base using those keys.

Using root motion to play cutscenes in gameplay

We can also play cutscenes in gameplay without changing the camera, and using smooth transitions to move in and out of a cutscene. This recipe shows an example of that.

Getting ready

In this recipe, we will use the same cutscene as in the previous recipe. You can also open the example Unity project and go to the `Chapter 08 Animating Cutscenes\Recipe 06 Using root motion to play cutscenes during gameplay` directory. If you open the `Example.unity` scene there and play the game, you will be able to move the character. Approach the red sphere marker and press the space bar to play the cutscene:

Cutscene played during gameplay

How to do it...

To play cutscenes during gameplay, follow these steps:

1. Import your cutscene. Make sure to import the character animation as a separate file.

2. Go to the cutscene asset's **Import Settings, Animation** tab.

3. Rename the **Default Take** animation to `Cutscene`.

4. Create a new Animation Clip, choose the **Default Take** as the source, and set the **Start** frame to 0 and the **End** frame to 1. Call this animation **CutsceneIdle** and make it loop.

5. Place the cutscene game object (in our example this is the **Ball** game object) and the character in the scene.

6. Follow the *Using root motion to steer a character* recipe from `Chapter 4`, *Character Movement*. This way, you will have a moving character you can control.

7. Create an Animator Controller for the cutscene.

8. Make the **CutsceneIdle** the default animation.

9. Drag and drop the **Cutscene** animation.

10. Create a `Trigger` parameter and name it `Cutscene`.

11. Make a transition from **CutsceneIdle** to **Cutscene** animation using the **Cutscene** `Trigger` parameter. Set the **Has Exit Time** to false and the **Transition Duration** to 0.1 seconds.

12. Assign the `Player` tag to the character.

13. Add the cutscene animation to the character's Animator Controller. In our example, the animation is called **SoccerKick**.

14. Add a **Cutscene** `Trigger` parameter to the character's controller.

15. Create a transition from **Any State** to **SoccerKick** with the **Cutscene** `Trigger` as the condition. **Has Exit Time** should be set to false and **Transition Duration** set to around 0.5 seconds.

16. Add another transition from **SoccerKick** to **Idle**, with no conditions, and **Has Exit Time** set to true. **Transition Duration** should also be set to around 0.5 seconds.

17. Create a new C# script and call it `CutsceneTrigger.cs`. In this script, we have the `void OnTriggerEnter()` and `void OnTriggerExit()` functions. Their main task is to set the `bool inTrigger` flag. The `OnTriggerEnter()` function also stores the reference to the player's game object:

```
void OnTriggerEnter (Collider other) {
    if (other.gameObject.CompareTag("Player"))
    {
```

```
        player = other.gameObject;
        inTrigger = true;
    }
}
void OnTriggerExit(Collider other)
{
    if (other.gameObject.CompareTag("Player"))
    {
        inTrigger = false;
    }
}
```

18. We check the `inTrigger` flag's value in the `Update()` function. If it is set to true, the player can press the space bar to start the cutscene. This starts a coroutine to match the character's position and rotation with the trigger's position and rotation. This position and rotation is the one our character should have when the cutscene starts. We also enable or disable a hint, the reference to which we store in the `public GameObject onScreenInfo` variable. When the player starts the cutscene, we turn off the **Box Collider** component to disable the trigger:

```
if (inTrigger)
{
    onScreenInfo.SetActive(true);

    if (Input.GetKeyDown(KeyCode.Space))
    {
        GetComponent<BoxCollider>().enabled = false;
        inTrigger = false;
        StartCoroutine("StartCutscene");
    }
}
else
{
    onScreenInfo.SetActive(false);
}
```

19. In the `IEnumerator StartCutscene()` coroutine, we first set the **Rigidbody** component of the character to **Kinematic**. This way, we turn off the physics simulation. Then we interpolate the player's position and rotation so that it matches the position and rotation of the trigger. If it is close enough, we set the **Cutscene** `Trigger` in the player's and cutscene's Animator component to play the animation simultaneously on both objects:

```
IEnumerator StartCutscene()
{
    player.GetComponent<Rigidbody>().isKinematic =    true;
```

```
   bool positionAdjusted = false;
   bool rotationAdjusted = false;
    while(true)
    {
    yield return null;
        if ((player.transform.position -
        transform.position).magnitude <= 0.01f)
        {
            positionAdjusted = true;
        }
        else
        {
        player.transform.position =
        Vector3.Lerp(player.transform.position,
        transform.position, positionAdjustmentSpeed
        * Time.deltaTime);
        }
        if (Vector3.Angle(player.transform.forward,
        transform.forward) <= 1f)
        {
            rotationAdjusted = true;
        }
        else
        {
        player.transform.rotation =
        Quaternion.Lerp(player.transform.rotation,
        transform.rotation, positionAdjustmentSpeed
        * Time.deltaTime);
        }
        if (positionAdjusted && rotationAdjusted)
        {
            break;
        }
    }
player.GetComponent<Animator>
().SetTrigger(animationTrigger);
cutsceneAnimator.SetTrigger(animationTrigger);
}
```

20. Create a new empty game object and name it CutsceneTrigger. Add a **Box Collider** component to it and set it to **Is Trigger**.

21. Place it in the exact spot at which the character has to be in the cutscene. Rotate it the same way the character needs to be rotated. You may use an empty object in the cutscene (exported from the 3D package) to make it easier.

22. Assign the `CutsceneTrigger.cs` script to the **CutsceneTrigger** game object.
23. Create a hint **UI Text** and assign it to the **On Screen Info** field of the **Cutscene Trigger** component.
24. Assign the cutscene game object's **Animator** component to the **CutsceneAnimator** field of the **Cutscene Trigger** component.
25. Create another C# script and call it `SetKinematic.cs`. In this script, we have just one `public void NotKinematic()` function, in which we set the **Rigidbody** component to non-kinematic:

```
public void NotKinematic()
{
    GetComponent<Rigidbody>().isKinematic = false;
}
```

26. Attach the script to the character.
27. With the character selected, open the **Animation** View.
28. Select the **SoccerKick** animation.
29. Add an **Animation Event** near the end of the animation and choose **NotKinematic()**. This will make the character react to physics again.
30. Play the game, approach the trigger, and press the space bar to see the effect.

How it works...

This recipe uses a similar concept to the one used in the *Action Points – performing an action in a specified spot* recipe from `Chapter 5`, *Characters Actions and Expressions*. Here we've added a one-frame looped CutsceneIdle animation to the animated props (a Ball game object in our example). This makes the objects wait for the cutscene to start. Our character's cutscene animation is exported as a separate file, which enables us to set its rig to **Humanoid** and use it along with other animations.

Our character starts playing the animation in the same moment as the cutscene game object. This makes them synchronized.

Another important thing is that we set the **Rigidbody** component of our character to **Is Kinematic** for the time of the cutscene. This makes the animation control our character with 100 percent weight. No collisions can interrupt our character from playing the animation. After the cutscene is finished, we turn off the **Is Kinematic** option to make our character behave normally.

9
Physics and Animations

This chapter presents Unity's 5 physics engine and what can be achieved with it. It covers the following recipes:

- Using cloth
- Using rigid body joints
- Destructible objects
- Creating a humanoid ragdoll with the ragdoll wizard
- Creating a generic ragdoll with character joints
- Applying force to a ragdoll
- Dismemberment
- Getting up from a ragdoll

Introduction

Unity's physics engine can be used to create interesting effects as well as gameplay mechanics. Previously we were using rigid bodies to move our character and to detect collisions. In this chapter, we will focus on more visually appealing aspects of rigid bodies and physics.

Using cloth

In this recipe, we will create a simple cloth simulation:

Cloth simulation used to create a flag

Getting ready

For this recipe, we need a model of the cloth. It should be a plane divided several times to have enough vertices for the cloth simulation to work. In our example, we use one additional model: the flag pole. You can go to the `Chapter 09 Physics and animations\Recipe 01 Using cloth` directory. You will find a **FlagPole** game object in the `Example.unity` scene there. This object contains the **Flag** and the **FlagPole** objects as children. The **Flag** game object uses the cloth simulation.

How to do it...

To use cloth simulation, follow these steps:

1. Place the **Flag** game object in the scene.
2. Add the **Cloth** component to the **Flag** game object (go to **Component | Physics | Cloth**).

3. Notice that a **Skinned Mesh Renderer** component is automatically added. You may remove the **Mesh Renderer** component from the object.

4. Find the mesh of the **Flag** and drag it to the **Mesh** field in the **Skinned Mesh Renderer** component. If your game object still has the **Mesh Filter** component, you may click on the mesh attached to it and it will be displayed in the **Project View**. This makes it easier to find the mesh we need.

5. If your game object still has the **Mesh Filter** component attached, you can remove it.

6. You may need to add a material to the **Flag** game object. If it lacks the material, drag appropriate materials into the **Materials** section in the **Skinned Mesh Renderer**.

7. Go to the Cloth component settings in the **Inspector** and click on the **Edit Constraints** button, as shown in the following screenshot:

Edit Constraints button

8. The **Cloth Constraints** window will appear, as shown in the following screenshot:

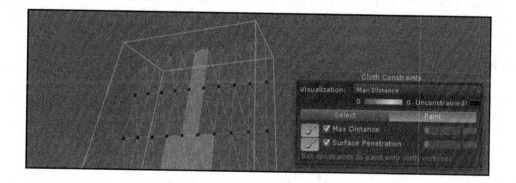

Editing constraints

9. It is used to constrain the cloth movement. To pin a cloth to something, select the **Paint** tab and click on the **Max Distance** checkbox. By left-clicking on a vertex, you can paint it red, which means its movement is fully constrained. You may choose a different color to make the cloth move slightly. Black means no constrains at all.

10. After painting at least one vertex, you may switch to the **Select** tab. In this tab, you can box-select vertices. After selecting a group of vertices, you may check the **Max Distance** checkbox and edit the value for all selected vertices at once.

11. If you cannot select or paint the vertices, rotate the view—you may be looking at your mesh from the backfaces side. Selecting and painting works only on the frontfaces side, unless you check the **Manipulate Backfaces** option in the **Visualization** dropdown.

12. Our Flag's orientation is top to bottom (it is pinned with its top to the pole). So we should select all top vertices and paint them red (set the **Max Distance** to 0). In your case, you may want to pin other vertices.

13. To remove the constrain from any given vertex, select it (you need to be in the **Select** tab) and uncheck the **Max Distance** checkbox. The vertex will turn black, which means it is not constrained any more.

14. To make the **Flag** collide with other game objects, go to the **Capsule Colliders** and **Sphere Colliders** array in the **Cloth** component's settings. You may add **Sphere Colliders** or **Capsule Colliders** located in the scene here. **Cloth** can collide only with those two types of colliders.

15. Play the game to see the effect.

How it works...

Cloth simulation uses vertices of a mesh to simulate cloth-like behavior. The mesh needs to be dense enough to make the simulation look good. The flag used in this example has 100 vertices.

The **Cloth** component has a number of options to use and tweak:

- **Stretching Stiffness**: How stiff the cloth is when stretching.
- **Bending Stiffness**: How stiff the cloth is when bending.
- **Use Tethers**: This helps prevent unconstrained vertices going too far away from the constrained ones
- **Use Gravity**: This applies gravity to cloth vertices.
- **Damping**: This damps the motion of cloth vertices.

- **External Acceleration**: This is a constant acceleration of cloth vertices and can be used to simulate wind.
- **Random Acceleration**: This is similar to the preceding option, but is random. It is useful for simulating wind.
- **World Velocity Scale**: This scales the world velocity of the object to which the cloth is attached to. It is useful for a character's clothing.
- **World Acceleration Scale**: This scales the world acceleration of cloth vertices when the object the cloth is attached to accelerates. It is useful for a character's clothing.
- **Friction**: The friction to apply when cloth vertices collide with something.
- **Collision Mass Scale**: This scales the mass of cloth vertices when they collide with something.
- **Use Continuous Collision**: This is similar to the continuous collision detection of the rigid bodies and improves collision quality but is heavier on performance.
- **Use Virtual Particles**: This adds one virtual particle/vertex per cloth triangle and improves collision quality.
- **Solver Frequency**: Number of solver iterations per second.

: The threshold after which cloth stops being simulated (sleeps). Sleep Threshold: The threshold after which cloth stops being simulated (sleeps).
Capsule Colliders: An array of capsule colliders to collide with.

- **Sphere Colliders**: An array of sphere colliders to collide with.

There's more...

Cloth works best with single-sided flat meshes (subdivided planes). It can also be used on thin subdivided boxes. Avoid using copied planes with inverted face normals (that makes two sheets of cloth that constantly collide with each other).

For best results, you should use some kind of double-sided shader on the single-sided flat mesh. You may use a simple shader provided with the example project; you can find it in the `Textures materials and shaders\Shaders` directory. It doesn't support shadows. You can also find good double-sided shaders in the Asset Store; I can recommend the **Double Sided Standard Mobile Legacy Shaders** package created by Mario Lelas.

Cloth components can be used with any Skinned Mesh Renderer. So you can make parts of your characters be simulated as cloth. The best practice would be to have a second Skinned Mesh Renderer with just the cloth mesh (it will be far easier to constrain such mesh than trying to constrain the whole character).

Using rigid body joints

In this recipe, we will create two objects with physics simulation: a rope and doors. We will use rigid body joints to constrain the movement and rotation of those objects.

Getting ready

For this recipe, we need four models: a **RopePole** (similar to the one from the previous recipe), a skinned **Rope** with a **RopeRig** containing around 10 bones, a **Frame** and two doors, **DoorLeft** and **DoorRight** (resembling those swing doors from a saloon). We also need a character with a rigid body to collide with our objects. You can go to the `Chapter 09 Physics and animations\Recipe 02 Using rigid body joints` directory. You will find all these objects in the `Example.unity` scene. When you play the game, try to walk with our character and collide with the rope and doors to see the effect.

Rope and swing doors

How to do it...

To use rigid body joints, follow these steps:

1. Import our swing doors to Unity. The model should contain three objects: **Frame**, **DoorLeft**, and **DoorRight**.
2. Place the objects in the scene and parent them all to an empty game object, which you may call **SwingDoors**.
3. Add a **Mesh Collider** to the **Frame** game object to prevent our character from going through it.
4. Add a **Box Collider** or a **Mesh Collider** set to **Convex** to the **DoorLeft** game object.
5. Add a **Rigidbody** component to the **DoorLeft** game object.
6. Add a **Hinge Joint** component to **DoorLeft**.
7. Set the **Axis** parameter to 0 X, 1 Y, and 0 Z. This is the axis in which our **Hinge Joint** can rotate.
8. Check the **Use Limits** option and set the **Min** to -120 and **Max** to 120 (exact limits may differ in your particular case). Those values describe the range in which our **Hinge Joint** can rotate from its neutral position.
9. If you want the doors to come back to their original position after they are pushed, check the **Use Spring** option.
10. Set the **Spring** parameter to 1 and **Damper** to 0.5 (you may need to experiment with the exact values).
11. Repeat steps 4-10 for the **DoorRight** game object.
12. Play the game and make any other rigid body collide with the doors to see the effect (you may use your character if it uses rigid body physics to move).

To create a rope using **Hinge Joints**, follow these steps:

1. Import our skinned **Rope** model to Unity. Rope should have enough bones to simulate its behavior (around 10-20 should be enough in most cases). Make sure the bones have identical or similar size and are not parented to each other (it will make the editing much easier).
2. Place the **Rope** model in the scene.
3. Go to the **RopeRig** game object and select all the bones.
4. Add **Capsule Collider**, **Rigidbody**, and **Hinge Joint** components to all the bones in the rig.
5. With all the bones selected, use the Inspector to scale the **Capsule Colliders** to fit the bones sizes.

6. Make sure the **Auto Configure Connected Anchor** option is selected in each bone's **Hinge Joint** settings.

7. For every bone, find its **Hinge Joint** settings. Drag and drop the next bone to the **Connected Body** field of the previous bone. For instance, if you have a rig containing five bones, **Bone1**, **Bone2**, **Bone3**, **Bone4**, **Bone5**. **Bone5** is the top one—drag and drop **Bone5** to the **Connected Body** field in the **Hinge Joint** settings of **Bone4**. Drag and drop **Bone4** to **Connected Body** field in the **Hinge Joint** settings of **Bone3** and so on. Leave the top bone's **Connected Body** field empty—this will constrain its movement in space.

8. You may also need to adjust the **Limits** and **Axis** fields. The rotation axis should point in the same direction in which the bones are pointing. If you select a game object with a **Hinge Joint**, you may see the rotation axis as a small brownish arrow.

9. Disable or remove the **Animator** component from the **Rope** game object.

10. Play the game and collide with the rope to see the effect.

How it works...

In this recipe, we used Hinge Joints—one of the joint types in Unity. Those joints constrain rigid body movement. If we use them on a rig of a Skinned Mesh Renderer, we can introduce physics simulation to it (as we did with the rope). Hinge Joints have a few interesting parameters:

- **Connected Body**: We can connect the object to another rigid body by placing it into this field. Connected objects can form ropes, chains, and other interesting structures.
- **Anchor**: A defined local space position around which the joint can rotate.
- **Axis**: This specifies the axis around which the joint can rotate.
- **Auto Configure Connected Anchor**: If we check this, the Connected Anchor will be configured automatically to match the Connected Body's Anchor.
- **Connected Anchor**: Here we can manually configure the connected body position (we have to disable **Auto Configure Connected Anchor** first).
- **Use Spring**: If this option is checked, the joint will behave as if a spring is attached to it. It will try to get back to its **Target Position** (see further down this list).
- **Spring**: This is the force of the spring.
- **Damper**: This damps the movement caused by the spring force. The object will slow down in time until it completely stops.

- **Target Position**: This is the target angle to which the joint's spring wants to pull the object.
- **Use Motor**: This makes the object spin around its joint **Axis**.
- **Target Velocity**: This is the velocity the object wants to achieve when rotating.
- **Force**: This is the force applied to the object to achieve the **Target Velocity**.
- **Free Spin**: When you enable this option, the object will not try to slow down to match the **Target Velocity**, it will only accelerate.
- **Use Limits**: Enable this option if you want to limit the rotation of the object around its joint **Axis**.
- **Min**: This is the lowest rotation limit.
- **Max**: This is the highest rotation limit.
- **Bounciness**: How much the object will bounce off when it reaches the rotation limit.
- **Contact Distance**: It makes the limits *have some width* to decrease jitter. In this distance from the limits, the joint will have contact with the given limit.
- **Break Force**: This is the force needed to break the joint and is useful if you want to ram your doors.
- **Break Torque**: Similar to the preceding one, this is the torque needed to break the joint.
- **Enable Collision**: This enables collision between rigid bodies connected to the joint.
- **Enable Preprocessing**: his is used to stabilize the situations that are impossible to fulfill.

Destructible objects

In this recipe, we are going to create a simple destructible object.

Getting ready

To follow this recipe, you will need an object with two states: normal and shattered. The shattered object is a cut-to-pieces version of the normal one. Each piece of the fractured object should be a separate game object. See the following screenshot (we are using Blender fracture tools to fracture a simple sphere):

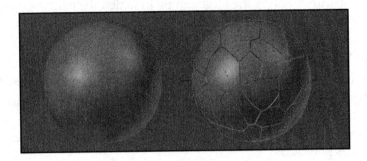

Normal ball and a fractured one: each fractured element is a separate game object

You can also download the provided example Unity project and go to the `Chapter 09 Physics and animations\Recipe 03 Destructible objects` directory. You can find the `Example.unity` scene there. If you play the game, you will see a ball falling down. When it hits the ground, it will be fractured into pieces.

How to do it...

To create a destructible object, follow these steps:

1. Import the normal and shattered objects to Unity. In our example, we have an object called **Ball** and the other one is called **BallFractured**.
2. Drag and drop both objects into the scene.
3. Select all child game objects (pieces) of the **BallFractured** game object. Add the **Rigidbody** and **Mesh Collider** components to them. Set the **Mesh Collider** to **Convex**.
4. Create a prefab from the **BallFractured** game object (containing all the pieces).
5. Select the **Ball** game object and add a **Rigidbody** and a **Sphere Collider** to it (or another type, depending on the shape of your object).
6. Write a new C# script and call it `SpawnFracturedObject.cs`. In this script, we have a `void Fracture()` function that spawns a fractured game object prefab (our **BallFractured**), applies velocity to all its pieces, and destroys the main object (**Ball**):

```
void Fracture()
{
    GetComponent<Collider>().enabled = false;
    GameObject fracturedObject =
    (GameObject)GameObject.Instantiate(fracturedObject
```

```
Prefab, transform.position, transform.rotation);
Rigidbody[] rigidBodies =
fracturedObject.GetComponentsInChildren<Rigidbody>    ();
for (int i = 0; i < rigidBodies.Length; i++)
{
    rigidBodies[i].velocity +=
    lastRigidBodyVelocity;
}
Destroy(gameObject);
}
```

7. The `void Fracture()` function is called when our main object collides with anything:

```
void OnCollisionEnter(Collision col)
{
    Fracture();
}
```

8. The Ball's velocity is saved every frame to the `float lastRigidBodyVelocity` variable (in the `FixedUpdate()` function):

```
void FixedUpdate () {
    lastRigidBodyVelocity = rb.velocity;
}
```

9. Assign the script to the **Ball** game object and drag the **BallFractured** prefab onto the **Fractured Object Prefab** field in the **Inspector**.

10. Play the game to see the effect:

Before and after collision

How it works...

two objects, a normal one and a fractured one built out of a number of pieces. The normal object works as any other game object in our game. The fractured game object is spawned only when we destroy the normal object. We save the normal object's velocity (its rigid body velocity in this example) every frame to be able to add this velocity to our spawned, fractured pieces. This makes them continue movement after the normal object was destroyed.

In this recipe, we created two objects, a normal one and a fractured one built out of a number of pieces. The normal object works as any other game object in our game. The fractured game object is spawned only when we destroy the normal object. We save the normal object's velocity (its rigid body velocity in this example) every frame to be able to add this velocity to our spawned, fractured pieces. This makes them continue movement after the normal object was destroyed. There's more...

You can use this simple technique to create even more complex objects (destructible barrels where each plank is a separate object is a good example). There are also different fracture systems available on the Asset Store (try searching for "fracture," "shatter," or "destructible").

Creating a humanoid ragdoll with the ragdoll wizard

In this recipe, we will turn our character into a ragdoll and learn how to enable the ragdoll and disable it. We will use Unity's built-in Ragdoll Wizard, which is useful for creating humanoid ragdolls:

A character with the ragdoll effect applied

Getting ready

For this recipe, we need an animated character. We can use the one we were using before (for instance, the one from the `Chapter 4`, *Character Movement*). You can also go to the `Chapter 09 Physics and animations\Recipe 04 Creating a humanoid ragdoll with ragdoll wizard` directory. You can find the `Example.unity` scene there. If you play the game and press the space bar, the character will turn into a ragdoll. You can press the space bar again to turn the ragdoll off.

How to do it...

To create a humanoid ragdoll, follow these steps:

1. Place your character in the scene.
2. Go to **Game Object** | **3d Object** | **Ragdoll** to open the **Create Ragdoll** window.
3. Drag and drop the bones from your character rig to the fields in the **Create Ragdoll** window. The fields' names aren't very accurate. **Left Hips** means left thigh, **Left Knee** means left shin, **LeftArm** means the left upper arm, and **LeftElbow** means the lower left arm, as shown in the following screenshot. The same applies to the right side. The rest of the names are self-explanatory:

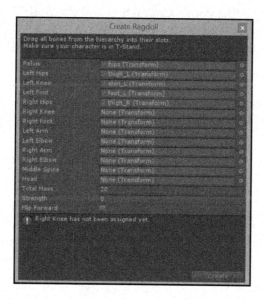

Create Ragdoll window

4. After you assign all the bones, click on the **Create** button. The ragdoll will be created. **Rigidbody**, **Capsule Collider** (or **Box Collider**), and **Character Joint** components will be added to the required bones.

5. You may need to adjust the size of the colliders to better match your character's shape. See the following screenshot:

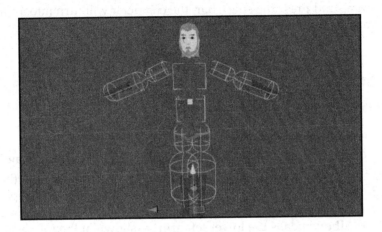

Configured ragdoll

6. Add two layers in the game: **Characters** and **Ragdoll**. To do so, go to **Edit | Project Settings | Tags and Layers**.

7. Set the character's layer to **Characters** and its rig with all its children (the ragdoll) to **Ragdoll**.

8. Go to **Edit | Project Settings | Physics** and disable the collision between the **Characters** and **Ragdoll** layers. This is a good way to prevent our ragdoll colliding with our character's main collider which would cause unwanted behavior (jitter, glitches in movement, and so on).

9. Create a new C# script and name it `HandleRagdoll.cs`. In this script, we have the `public void EnableRagdoll(bool enable, List<Rigidbody> rigidbodies)` function. It iterates through all the rigid bodies attached to any of the children of the `public Transform charactersRig` transform and enables them or disables them depending on the enable flag. It also enables or disables the `mainRigidbody` and the `mainCollider` (attached to the character's root object). Finally, it enables or disables the character's **Animator** component:

```
public void EnableRagdoll(bool enable, List<Rigidbody>
rigidbodies)
{
```

```
for (int i = 0; i < rigidbodies.Count; i++)
{
    rigidbodies[i].isKinematic = !enable;
}
if (mainCollider != null)
{
    mainCollider.enabled = !enable;
}
if (mainRigidbody != null)
{
    mainRigidbody.isKinematic = enable;
}
if (anim != null)
{
    anim.enabled = !enable;
}
}
```

10. We call this function every time player presses the space bar. At the start of the game, we collect all rigid bodies attached to character's rig children objects and store them in a global list. We pass that list to the `EnableRagdoll()` function every time we call it. We also call the `EnableRagdoll()` function at the start of the game with the `enable` parameter set to `false`. This disables the ragdoll.

11. Attach the script to the character and drag its rig to the **Characters Rig** field of the script.

12. Play the game and press the space bar to see the effect.

How it works...

The **Create Ragdoll** window helps with attaching **Character Joint**, **Capsule Collider**, and **Rigidbody** components to humanoid characters' rigs. Those characters don't have to use the HumanoidumanoidHumanoid rig in the same way as the Mecanim feature.

Rigid bodies, colliders, and character joint components create a ragdoll. To turn the ragdoll on, we need to disable the Animator component as animations override the movement of rigid bodies. This is what our script does. It also makes the ragdoll's rigid bodies kinematic when the ragdoll is off, to turn the physics simulation off when it's not needed.

Creating a generic ragdoll with character joints

This time we will create a ragdoll for a non-humanoid character. We cannot use the Ragdoll Wizard in this case, but instead we will make the ragdoll manually.

A generic character ragdoll in action

Getting ready

For this recipe, we need a nonhumanoid character. We use our old fellow **Spider** as an example. The character needs to be rigged. You can also open the example Unity project and go to the Chapter 09 Physics and animations\Recipe 05 Creating a generic ragdoll with character joints directory. If you open the Example.unity scene there and play the game, you will see a falling spider with the ragdoll already turned on. You can find the **Spider** in the Rigs directory.

How to do it...

To create a generic ragdoll, follow these steps:

1. Import the character to Unity and place it in the scene.
2. Select all the bones of the character's rig that will be used in the ragdoll simulation. In our example, we skipped the fangs.
3. Add **Capsule Collider**, **Rigidbody**, and **Character Joint** components to the selected bones.

4. Adjust the shapes of the colliders to match the limbs of the character. You should avoid colliders intersecting with each other. You may need to change a few colliders to **Box Colliders** or **Sphere Colliders** (our Spider's abdomen has **Box Colliders** instead of **Capsule Colliders** and the head has a **Sphere Collider**).

5. Make sure all **Character Joints** have the **Auto Configure ConnectedAnchor** option selected.

6. Choose the root body part of your character (for our **Spider**, it was the abdomen).

7. Remove the **Character Joint** component from that body part to make it work just like a normal rigid body.

8. Connect all other **Character Joints** to their parent game objects (also containing the **Character Joint** components). For instance, if the character has a leg with three segments, **Leg1**, **Leg2**, and **Leg3**, drag the **Leg2** object to **Leg3** object's **Connected Body** field in the **Character Joint** component. Then drag **Leg1** to the **Connected Body** field of **Leg2**. Finally, drag **Leg1** to its root bone's **Connected Body** field (in our case it's the **Abdomen**).

9. Repeat this process for all the bones with **Character Joints**. The hierarchy of the joints should reflect the hierarchy of the rig.

10. Disable the character's **Animator** component and play the game to see the effect. You may need to further adjust **Character Joint** components' properties to achieve the desired effect:

Spider with a defined ragdoll

How it works...

In this recipe, we use the **Character Joint** components to create a ragdoll from scratch. Every such component works with a **Rigidbody** component and a **Collider** component that have to be attached to the same game object. We can create chains of **Character Joint** components by dragging a connected game object to the **Connected Body** field of the joint.

Character Joint components have a set of parameters we can tweak:

- **Connected Body**: This is the parent object to which the joint is connected.
- **Anchor**: This is the point in space the joint rotates around.
- **Axis**: This is the twist axis—the one our bone will twist around. It is visualized with an orange arrow.
- **Auto Configure Connected Anchor**: Enable this if you want Unity to try to autoconfigure the Connected Anchor.
- **Connected Anchor**: If you disable the **Auto Configure Connected Anchor**, you can manually configure it here.
- **Swing Axis**: This is the axis our bone will swing (or bend) around . It is visualized with a green arrow.
- **Low Twist Limit**: This is the lower limit angle for bone twisting.
- **High Twist Limit**: This is the higher limit angle for bone twisting.
- **Swing 1 Limit**: This is the lower limit angle for bone swinging.
- **Swing 2 Limit**: This is the upper limit angle for bone swinging.
- **Break Force**: This is the force needed to break the joint.
- **Break Torque**: This is the torque needed to break the joint.
- **Enable Collision**: If this is checked, collisions between rigid bodies connected to this joint are enabled.
- **Enable Preprocessing**: This is used to stabilize impossible-to-fulfill scenarios.

Applying force to a ragdoll

In this recipe, we are going to apply some additional force to a ragdoll when we turn it on. Normally, when you turn the ragdoll on, it starts from idle; no initial movement is introduced. It looks stiff and unnatural. Applying force to a body part will help to avoid that.

Getting ready

We are going to use the same character as in the *Creating a humanoid ragdoll with the ragdoll wizard* recipe. We will also use the `HandleRagdoll.cs` script from the same recipe to turn the ragdoll on. You can also open the example Unity project and go to the `Chapter 09 Physics and animations\Recipe 06 Applying force to a ragdoll` directory. If you open the `Example.unity` scene there and play the game, you will be able to click on any body part of the character. That will turn the ragdoll on and apply force to this body part, which will make the character look like it was hit or shot in that particular limb:

Force applied directly to the head of the character

How to do it...

To apply force to a ragdoll's body part, follow these steps:

1. Follow the *Creating a humanoid ragdoll with the ragdoll wizard* recipe to have a character with a working ragdoll and the `HandleRagdoll.cs` script (a script to turn the ragdoll on).

2. Create a new C# script and name it `RagdollForceApply.cs`. In this script's `Update()` function, we first check whether the player clicks on the left mouse button. Then we create a ray from the mouse cursor position in the camera's direction and we check if we hit a collider that has one of the layers described by the `publicLayer Mask ragdollBodyPartsLayer` variable. If we manage to hit a collider, we try to get the **Rigidbody** component from it and store it in our `Rigidbody hitBodyPart` variable. If we indeed find the rigid body, we call the `void ApplyForce()` function:

```
if (Input.GetKeyDown(KeyCode.Mouse0))
```

```
    {
        if (Physics.Raycast(Camera.main.ScreenPointToRay
        (Input.mousePosition), out hitInfo, 100f,
        ragdollBodyPartsLayer))
        {
            hitPodyPart = hitInfo.collider.gameObject
            .GetComponent<Rigidbody>();
            if (hitPodyPart != null)
            {
        AddForce();
            }
        }
    }
```

3. The `void ApplyForce()` function turns the ragdoll on using
   the `HandleRagdoll` script. After that, it applies the force in the camera direction
   with the `public float forceMagnitude` strenght:

```
void AddForce()
{
    ragdollHandler.EnableRagdoll(true);
    force = (hitInfo.point -
    Camera.main.transform.position).normalized *
    forceMagnitude;
    hitPodyPart.AddForce(force, ForceMode.Impulse);
}
```

4. We set the reference to the `HandleRagdoll` script in the `Start()` function.
5. Add the script to the character.
6. Make sure the character ragdoll's body parts have the proper Layer set.
7. Set the **Ragdoll Body Parts Layer** mask in the **RagdollForceApply** in
   the **Inspector** to match the layer of the ragdoll's body parts.
8. Play the game and click on any given body part of the character to see the effect.

How it works...

This recipe simply applies a force to a chosen body part of the ragdoll using the
`AddForce()` function called on the limb's **Rigidbody** component. This function requires
a `Vector3 force` parameter that describes the direction and magnitude of the applied
force. We can also specify a `ForceMode` mode parameter to change the mode of the applied
force. Here we've chosen to use the `ForceMode.Impulse` as our force is applied only in one
frame.

The rest of the script handles selecting the body part we want to apply the force to. In this example, we are using the mouse input to cast a ray and try to hit a body part's collider. If we manage to do so, we choose this particular limb as the target that we want to apply the force to.

There's more...

You can also use the concept illustrated in the *Destructible objects* recipe to store the velocity of the character (or of its limbs) and then apply it to the ragdoll's body parts. To do so, you may calculate the linear and angular velocity of any given body part in the `Update()` function, by subtracting the previous position from the current position, and the previous rotation in Euler angles from the current rotation. Then you can apply the calculated values as the `velocity` and `angularVelocity` to that part's **Rigidbody** component when you turn the ragdoll on.

Dismemberment

This recipe shows how to create a dismemberment effect for a rigged character. We are going to create a decapitation as an example. This effect is often used in various combat games (both shooters and melee combat games):

Decapitation—an example of the dismemberment effect

Getting ready

We are going to use the same character as in the *Creating a humanoid ragdoll with the ragdoll wizard* recipe. We will also use the `HandleRagdoll.cs` script from the same recipe to turn the ragdoll on. On top of that, we will need to have two additional meshes: the **Head** model and the **Neck** model. See the following screenshot for reference:

Neck and head models

You can also open the example Unity project and go to the `Chapter 09 Physics and animations\Recipe 07 Dismemberment` directory. If you open the `Example.unity` scene there, play the game and press the space bar so that the poor character will be decapitated. You can find all the additional models in the `Models` directory.

How to do it...

To create a decapitation effect, follow these steps:

1. Follow the *Creating a humanoid ragdoll with the ragdoll wizard* recipe to have a character with a working ragdoll and the `HandleRagdoll.cs` script (a script to turn the ragdoll on).
2. Import the **Neck** and **Head** models and place them in the scene near the character.
3. Create two empty game objects; name the first one **HeadMarker** and the second one **NeckMarker**.
4. Parent the **HeadMarker** to the head bone and the **NeckMarker** to the neck bone. Make sure that the local position of **HeadMarker** and **NeckMarker** is 0.
5. Parent the **Head** object to the **HeadMarker** and the **Neck** object to the **NeckMarker**. Zero out **Head**'s and **Neck**'s local rotation and position.

6. Use the **HeadMarker** and **NeckMarker** to position the **Head** and the **Neck** to match the head and neck of the character as closely as possible. Remember that **Head**'s and **Neck**'s local position and rotation is 0, so when we position them by manipulating **HeadMarker** and **NeckMarker**, it will make is easier for us to spawn the **Head** and **Neck** later.

7. Add a **Sphere Collider** and a **Rigidbody** component to the **Head** game object.

8. Make a prefab from the **Head** game object and another one from the **Neck** game object.

9. Delete **Head** and **Neck** from the scene, but make sure to leave **HeadMarker** and **NeckMarker** still parented to their corresponding bones in the character's rig.

10. Create a new C# script and name it `Dismemberment.cs`. In this script's `Update()` function, we check whether the player presses the space bar and we call the `void Decapitate()` function if the `wasSevered` flag is `false` (you can really only decapitate someone once):

```
if (Input.GetKeyDown(KeyCode.Space) && !wasSevered)
{
    Decapitate();
}
```

11. The `void Decapitate()` function does the rest. First it checks if the `HandleRagdoll.cs` script was found (the reference to it is set in the `Start()` function). If it was found, we enable the ragdoll with it and disable the script. Next we remove the **Character Joint**, **Rigidbody**, and **Collider** components from the head bone (we are going to scale it to 0 because we don't want to bother with this joint anymore). Next we spawn the new, severed **Head** from a prefab stored in the `public GameObject headPrefab` variable. The **Head** is spawned with the **HeadMarker** position and rotation, a reference to which is stored in the `public Transform headMarker` variable. Then we get the **Rigidbody** component of the spawned **Head** and apply a random force and random torque to make it move. We use the `public Vector3` variables to store the `randomForce1, randomForce2, randomTorque1,` and `randomTorque2` values. We have a small helper function `Vector3 RandomVector(Vector3 v1, Vector3 v2)` that takes two vectors and returns a random vector build from those two parameters. Lastly, we scale the head bone to 0 (reference to it is stored in the `public Transform head` variable). Finally, we spawn the **Neck** prefab and parent it to the **NeckMarker**:

```
wasSevered = true;
if (ragdollHandler != null)
```

```
{
    ragdollHandler.EnableRagdoll(true);
    ragdollHandler.enabled = false;
}
Joint headJoint = head.GetComponent<Joint>();
if (headJoint != null)
{
    Destroy(headJoint);
}
Collider headCollider = head.GetComponent<Collider>();
if (headCollider != null)
{
    Destroy(headCollider);
}
Rigidbody headRigidBody = head.GetComponent<Rigidbody>();
if (headRigidBody != null)
{
    Destroy(headRigidBody);
}
GameObject spawnedHead =
(GameObject)GameObject.Instantiate(headPrefab,
headMarker.position, headMarker.rotation);

Rigidbody spawnedHeadRB = spawnedHead.GetComponent<Rigidbody>();
    if (spawnedHeadRB != null)
    {
        spawnedHeadRB.AddForce(RandomVector(randomForce1,
        randomForce2), ForceMode.Impulse);

        spawnedHeadRB.AddTorque(RandomVector(randomTorque,
        randomTorque2),ForceMode.Impulse);
    }
    head.localScale = Vector3.zero;

    GameObject spawnedNeck =
    (GameObject)GameObject.Instantiate(neckPrefab,
    neckMarker.position, neckMarker.rotation);
    spawnedNeck.transform.parent = neckMarker;
```

12. Add the script to the character.
13. Play the game and press the space bar to see the effect.

How it works...

The main feature of this recipe is hiding the character's head. To do so, we simply need to scale the head bone to 0. All vertices assigned to this bone will be then squashed to the same point in space. After we hide the head, we can spawn a second one with a **Rigidbody** component and a **Collider** attached. This way our second head will fall down. To make the effect more spectacular, we're adding a small random force and torque to the newly spawned head. This makes it rotate and fly up after the decapitation.

We also spawn a neck game object to mask the stretched polygons that appear after we scale the head to 0. We use the **HeadMarker** and **NeckMarker** game objects parented to the corresponding bones in the character's rig just because they make it easier to match the position and rotation of the **Head** and **Neck** objects.

There's more...

You can also cut off other limbs with this technique. If you want to use this concept for cutting off arms or legs, consider spawning a rigged severed arm or leg with a ragdoll. Such a ragdoll can contain only two **Rigidbody** components, two **Colliders**, and one **Character Joint** (the elbow or the knee).

Getting up from a ragdoll

This recipe is slightly more advanced but fun to implement. It makes our character use three different rigs: the original animated rig, the rig our character's mesh is skinned with, and a ragdoll. By using these three rigs, we can smoothly blend between ragdoll and animation any time.

Getting ready

Again, we are going to use the same character as in the *Creating a humanoid ragdoll with the ragdoll wizard* recipe. We will need two getting up animations: one from face facing down and one from face facing up positions. Name them **StandUpFaceUp** and **StandUpFaceDown**. We also need at least a looped **Idle** animation.

You can also open the example Unity project and go to the `Chapter 09 Physics and animations\Recipe 08 Getting up from a ragdoll` directory. If you open the `Example.unity` scene there, play the game and press the space bar; the character will fall down using ragdoll. If you press the space bar again, it will blend from a ragdoll to a getting up animation and will be animated again.

How to do it...

To make a character get up from being a ragdoll, follow these steps:

1. Place your character in the scene.
2. Make two copies of it and name the characters **CharacterAnimated**, **CharacterSkinned**, and **CharacterRagdoll**. We will use these names for better clarity.
3. Make all characters stand in the exact same place in the scene.
4. Select the **CharacterRagdoll** and follow the *Creating a humanoid ragdoll with the ragdoll wizard* recipe to make a character a working ragdoll. We are not going to use the `HandleRagdoll.cs` script this time, so you can stop after using the Ragdoll Wizard.
5. Select **CharacterRagdoll** game object's rig and name it `Ragdoll`.
6. Select the **CharacterAnimated** and expand its hierarchy.
7. Remove all objects but the rig of the character. You cannot change the rig's name.
8. Select the **CharacterSkinned** and expand its hierarchy.
9. Rename the **CharacterSkinned** rig to `SkinnedRig`.
10. Select the **SkinnedRig** and the skinned mesh (or meshes if you have more). Drag and drop them onto **CharacterAnimated**. A window warning about prefab connection loss may appear. Click on **Continue**. This will parent the **SkinnedRig** and the mesh skinned to it to the **CharacterAnimated** game object.
11. Select **CharacterRagdoll**, grab the **Ragdoll** rig, and drop it onto the **CharacterAnimated** game object to parent it. Again click on **Continue** if the warning appears.
12. You can delete the **CharacterRagdoll** and **CharacterSkinned** game objects.
13. Create an Animator Controller or open an existing one.
14. In this controller, create two Triggers: **StandUpFaceUp** and **StandUpFaceDown**.

15. Create four transitions:
      - **Any State | StandUpFaceDown** with one
        condition: **StandUpFaceDown** Trigger. **Has Exit Time** should be set to
        false and **Transition Duration** set to 0.
      - **Any State | StandUpFaceUp** with one condition: **StandUpFaceUp**
        Trigger. **Has Exit Time** should be set to false and **Transition Duration**
        set to 0.
      - **StandUpFaceDown | Idle** with no conditions: **Has Exit Time** should
        be set to true and **Transition Duration** set to around 0.2.
      - **StandUpFaceUp | Idle** with no conditions: **Has Exit Time** should be
        set to true and **Transition Duration** set to around 0.2.

16. Assign the controller to the character's Animator component.

17. [Optional] You can find the `ShowRig.cs` script in the `Shared Scripts` folder. If
    you attach it three times to the **CharacterAnimated** game object, you may drag
    and drop its three rigs, one to each `ShowRig` script. You may also assign different
    colors for each rig. If you play the game, you will be able to see the three rigs
    working. In the following screenshot, the red rig is the ragdoll, the yellow one is
    the one that is animated (we cannot change its name, in our example it's
    called **metarig**), and the green one is the one our mesh is skinned to (it's not
    clearly visible because it's hidden inside the mesh).

Ragdoll rig (red), animated rig (yellow), and skinned rig (green)

18. Create a new C# script and name it `RagdollWeight.cs`. This script contains several functions. First, in the `void Init()` function that is called from the `Start()` function, we set references to the bones of our three rigs to be able to blend between them later on. We also get the reference to the **Rigidbody** and Animator components attached to our character. Finally, we turn the ragdoll game object off:

```
void Init()
{
    rb = GetComponent<Rigidbody>();
    anim = GetComponent<Animator>();
    skinnedRigTransforms =
    skinnedRig.GetComponentsInChildren<Transform>();
    ragdollTransforms =
    ragdoll.GetComponentsInChildren<Transform>();
    animatedRigTransforms =
    animatedRig.GetComponentsInChildren<Transform>();
    ragdoll.gameObject.SetActive(false);
}
```

19. In the `voidEnableRagdoll()` function, we first check whether our `float` `blendFactor` is not greater than 0.5 (that would mean we are still in the "ragdoll phase"). If it is less than 0.5, we set all ragdoll bones' positions and rotations to match the `animatedRigTransforms` (we match the pose of the ragdoll to the current character pose). Finally, we set the main **Rigidbody** component to kinematic and enable the ragdoll game object. We also set the `blendFactor` to 1, which means the ragdoll is fully enabled:

```
void EnableRagdoll()
{
    if(blendFactor > 0.5f)
    {
        return;
    }
    for (int i = 0; i < ragdollTransforms.Length; i++)
    {
        ragdollTransforms[i].localPosition =
        animatedRigTransforms[i].localPosition;
        ragdollTransforms[i].localRotation =
        animatedRigTransforms[i].localRotation;
    }
    rb.isKinematic = true;
    ragdoll.gameObject.SetActive(true);
    ragdollOn = true;
    blendFactor = 1f;
}
```

20. In the `voidDisableRagdoll()` function, we check if our character is lying face down or face up and play an appropriate standing up animation. After we trigger the animation, we start the `IEnumeratorBlendFromRagdoll()` coroutine to blend smoothly from the `ragdoll` rig to the `animatedRig`:

```
void DisableRagdoll()
{
    bool faceUp = Vector3.Dot(
    faceDirectionHelper.forward, Vector3.up) > 0f;
    if (faceUp)
    {
        anim.SetTrigger("StandUpFaceUp");
    }
    else
    {
        anim.SetTrigger("StandUpFaceDown");
    }

    StartCoroutine("BlendFromRagdoll");
}
```

21. The `IEnumerator BlendFromRagdoll()` coroutine decreases the `blendFactor` in time and checks if it's still greater than 0. If it is less than or equal to 0, we set it to be exactly 0, enable the main **Rigidbody** component again, and disable the ragdoll:

```
IEnumerator BlendFromRagdoll()
{
    while (blendFactor > 0f)
    {
        blendFactor -= Time.deltaTime * blendSpeed;
        yield return null;
    }
    blendFactor = 0f;
    rb.isKinematic = false;
    blendFactor = 0f;
    ragdollOn = false;
    ragdoll.gameObject.SetActive(false);
}
```

22. In the `FixedUpdate()` function, if the ragdoll is on, we move our character's **Rigidbody** to the position of the ragdoll's hips. We additionally check the ground position to make sure our main **Rigidbody** stands on the ground and doesn't levitate. We also rotate the **Rigidbody** so that the character looks in the hips -> head direction. We intentionally omit the Y component of the `Vector3desiredLookVector` to prevent our character's capsule from tilting. Moving our character's **Rigidbody** to the position of the ragdolls hips makes the blending from ragdoll to animation easier:

```
void FixedUpdate()
{
    if (!ragdollOn)
    {
        return;
    }
    desiredLookVector = head.position - hips.position;
    desiredLookVector.y = 0f;
    desiredLookVector = desiredLookVector.normalized;
    lookVector = Vector3.Slerp(transform.forward,
    desiredLookVector, Time.deltaTime);

    if (Physics.Raycast(hips.position, Vector3.down,
    out groundHit, groundCheckDistance,
    groundCheckMask))
    {
        finalPosition = groundHit.point;
    }
    else
    {
        finalPosition = hips.position;
    }
    rb.MovePosition(finalPosition);
    rb.MoveRotation(Quaternion.LookRotation(lookVector
    ));
}
```

23. In the `Update()` function, we check whether the player pressed the space bar. If so, we enable or disable the ragdoll depending on whether it is enabled or disabled at the moment:

```
void Update()
{
    if (Input.GetKeyDown(KeyCode.Space))
    {
        if (ragdollOn)
        {
```

```
            DisableRagdoll();
        }
        else
        {
            EnableRagdoll();
        }
    }
}
```

24. In the `LateUpdate()` function, we constantly interpolate the `localPosition` and `localRotation` of all the bones of the `skinnedRig` (the one our character's mesh is using). The position and rotation of the bones is interpolated between the position and rotation of the `ragdoll` and the `animatedRig`. We use the `blendFactor` variable for the interpolation:

```
void LateUpdate()
{
    for (int i=0; i<skinnedRigTransforms.Length; i++)
    {
        skinnedRigTransforms[i].localPosition =
        Vector3.Lerp(
        animatedRigTransforms[i].localPosition,
        ragdollTransforms[i].localPosition,
        blendFactor);

        skinnedRigTransforms[i].localRotation =
        Quaternion.Lerp(
        animatedRigTransforms[i].localRotation,
        ragdollTransforms[i].localRotation,
        blendFactor);
    }
}
```

25. Add the preceding script to the character.

26. Drag and drop the animated rig (in our example it's called **metarig**) to the **Animated Rig** field, the **Ragdoll** to the **Ragdoll** field, and the **SkinnedRig** to the **Skinned Rig** field. Choose the chest bone as the **Face Direction Helper** (if it doesn't work, you may create an empty object parented to the chest bone—the goal here is to have the forward axis of this helper object point down when the character lays face down, and up when it lays face up). Set the **Ground Check Mask** to contain your level layers. Assign the hips bone to the **Hips** field and the head bone to the **Head** field (you may choose different bones that properly describe your character's rotation when the ragdoll is on).

27. Play the game and press the space bar to see the effect.

How it works...

The concept behind this recipe is based on having three rigs: one that holds the animations, one that is a simple ragdoll, and one to which the mesh is skinned. To make it work in Unity, we need to copy our character three times. One of the copies is used to create the ragdoll, the second is the animated rig and we need to remove the mesh from it, and the last one is the mesh with the rig but has no **Animator** component. All these objects finally get parented to the animated rig's parent (the **CharacterAnimated** game object). This way, our character is still a single game object and can be driven with root motion. The final hierarchy looks like the following:

- **CharacterAnimated**
- **metarig (the original name of the rig of this character)**
- **SkinnedRig**
- **SkinnedMesh**
- **Ragdoll**

With such a setup, we can get all the transforms from the metarig (the rig that is actually animated), the **SkinnedRig** (the rig to which the mesh is skinned), and the ragdoll. Since our character's mesh is using the **SkinnedRig** (we cannot see the two remaining rigs in the game), we can dynamically set its transforms' location and rotation. This way we can use the Vector3.Lerp() and Quaternion.Lerp() functions to interpolate the **SkinnedRig** transforms' between the **Ragdoll**'s and **metarig**'s (the animated rig's) transforms.

The standing up animations are prepared in such a way that the hips of the character are roughly at the 0,0,0 point. We move the main **Rigidbody** of the character to the point where the hips of the ragdoll are. This way, when we blend to the standing up animation, our character's animated rig (an animation) matches the position of the ragdoll. The rest is handled by blending the pose from the ragdoll to the current animation.

There's more...

You can also use this concept on non-humanoid characters.

10
Miscellaneous

This chapter contains a number of extra recipes:

- Using math to animate an object
- Using the `Lerp()` function to animate an object
- Using the `Rotate()` function to animate an object
- Preparing motion capture files for humanoid characters
- Adding behaviors to Mecanim states

Introduction

This chapter contains additional recipes with useful tricks and solutions.

Using math to animate an object

We can use mathematical formulas to create interesting-looking animations. We are going to use this concept to make an endless curve animation with the `Mathf.Sin()` and `Mathf.Cos()` functions.

Getting ready

We don't need anything special for this recipe. We are going to create it from scratch in Unity. You may also download the provided example project. Open the Chapter 10 Miscellaneous\Recipe 01 Using math to animate an object directory and load the Example.unity scene there. If you run the game, you will see the finished effectâ©©a curve animated with the Mathf.Sin() and Mathf.Cos() functions:

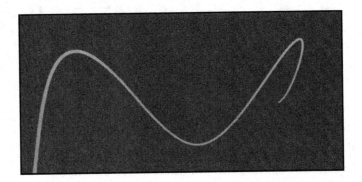

Final effectâ□□curve animated with the Mathf.Sin() and Mathf.Cos() functions

How to do it...

To use math for animating a curve, follow these steps:

1. Create an empty game object.
2. Add a **Line Renderer** component to it.
3. Create a new material of your liking and assign it to the **Line Renderer**.
4. Make sure the **Use World Space** option in the **Line renderer** component is not selected (we will use local coordinates in this example as it makes it slightly easier to position the **Line Renderer** in the camera).
5. Change the **Start Width** and **End Width** of the **Line Renderer** to 0.2 to make the line thinner.
6. Create a new C# script and name it MathAnim.cs. In this script's Start() function, we set the number of points of the Line Renderer using the SetVertices() method:

```
positions = new Vector3[linePoints];
lRenderer = GetComponent<LineRenderer>();
```

```
if (lRenderer != null)
{
    lRenderer.SetVertexCount(linePoints);
}
```

7. Then, in the `Update()` function, we call the `void SetLinePositions()` function and we move the game object so that the line center is at the (0, 0, 0) point:

```
transform.position = new Vector3(-0.5f
                    * lineLenght, 0f, 0f);
SetLinePositions();
```

8. In the `void SetLinePositions()` function, use the `Mathf.Sin()` and `Mathf.Cos()` functions to calculate the point's Y and Z positions. We set the line points positions with the `SetPositions()` function. We also use a simple timer to introduce time into our formula. We have two timers: `timerY` and `timerZ`. The first one works for the Y position values and the second one for Z position values. We also have the `public float` variables for controlling `frequencyY`, `frequencyZ`, `amplitudeY`, and `amplitudeZ`. The X positions of the line points are set in equal distances so that the total length of the line is equal the `public float lineLength` variable's value:

```
if (lRenderer == null)
{
    return;
}

timerY += Time.deltaTime * speedY;
timerZ += Time.deltaTime * speedZ;

for (int i = 0; i < positions.Length; i++)
{
    positions[i].x = lineLenght * (float)i /
                (float)positions.Length;
    positions[i].y = amplitudeY * Mathf.Sin(frequencyY
            * ((2f*Mathf.PI * (float)i /
            (float)positions.Length) + timerY));
    positions[i].z = amplitudeZ * Mathf.Cos(frequencyZ
            * ((2f * Mathf.PI * (float)i /
            (float)positions.Length) + timerZ));
}
lRenderer.SetPositions(positions);
```

9. Attach the script to our game object.

10. Play the game to see the effect.

How it works...

We have plenty of mathematical formulas that we can use from the `Mathf` library. Using some of them can give interesting results for animation. We are using the `Mathf.Sin()` and `Mathf.Cos()` functions in this example. They are periodic, which gives us an infinite loop motion.

Using the Lerp() function to animate an object

We were using the `Lerp()` method previously, but it is important to know that we can use it in two different ways. This recipe covers both of these uses.

Getting ready

We are going to create this recipe from scratch and we don't need any special assets. You can download the example project and go to the `Chapter 10 Miscellaneous\Recipe 02 Using the Lerp function to animate an object` directory. Open the `Example.unity` scene there and play the game. You will see two objects: **RedDot** and **BlueDot** (both are children of the **Canvas** object). The first one uses the standard `Lerp()` method and interpolates its position from a minimum to a maximum value in time. The second one uses the `Lerp()` method in a different way and continuously follows the mouse pointer.

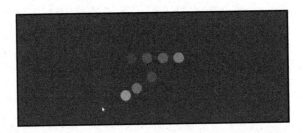

RedDot interpolates its position between min and max and BlueDot follows the cursor

How to do it...

To use the `Lerp()` function for animating objects, follow these steps:

1. First we need to create some objects to work with. Create a new **Image** (go to **Game Object** | **UI** | **Image**). Name it `RedDot` (you can add a circle sprite to it or leave it as it is). Change its color to red.

2. Set the **RedDot** position to (0,0,0) and its **Anchor Preset** to middle center, as shown in the following screenshot:

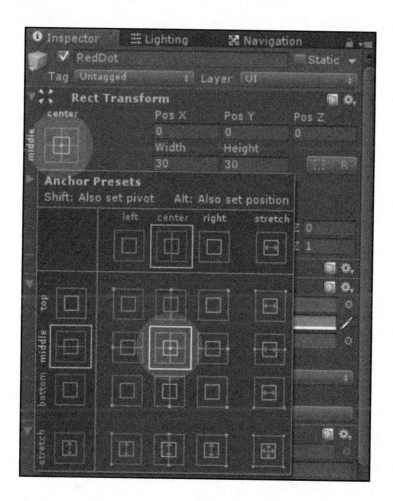

RedDot's Anchor Preset

3. Create another **Image** and name it **BlueDot**. Change its color to blue.

4. Change its **Anchor Preset** to bottom left.

5. Create a new C# script and name it `LerpNormal.cs`. In this script's `Update()` function, we interpolate a `float posX` variable's value from the `public float minPos` to `public float maxPos` value. We use a `float timer` that increases to the value of 1 in time. If its value reaches 1, it starts to decrease to 0. If it reaches 0, it starts to increase again. Finally, we set the `localPosition` of **RedDot** `rectTransform` using our interpolated `posX` value. The `posY` and `posZ` values are set in the `Start()` function and are constant:

```
if (timer > 1f)
{
    lerpDir = -1f;
}
else if (timer < 0f)
{
    lerpDir = 1f;
}

timer += lerpDir*Time.deltaTime * speed;

posX = Mathf.Lerp(minPos, maxPos, timer);

rectTransform.localPosition = new Vector3(posX, posY,
                            posZ);
```

6. Assign the script to the **RedDot** game object.

7. Create another C# script and call it `LerpContinuous.cs`. In this script's `Update()` function, we interpolate the position of the **BlueDot** with itself and the mouse cursor position. We do it every frame. In the `Lerp()` function, we use the `Time.deltaTime` value multiplied by a `public float speed` variable:

```
rectTransform.position =
            Vector3.Lerp(rectTransform.position,
            Input.mousePosition, Time.deltaTime *
            speed);
```

8. Assign the script to the **BlueDot** game object.

9. Play the game to see the effect.

How it works...

We are using the `Lerp()` function in two ways:

- **Standard method**: The `Lerp()` function's `float t` parameter has values from 0 to 1. We've used a timer as out `t` parameter. The `timer` first was increasing to the value of 1. After it reached 1, it was decreasing to 0. This method gives us standard linear interpolation between two values. The `t` parameter is the percentage of the interpolation (for `t = 0.5`, the interpolated value is an average of two input values).

- **Continuous method**: The second method is based on using the output value (in our case the position) as the lower input value in the `Lerp()` function. We call the `Lerp()` function in `Update()` and use `Time.deltaTime` as the `t` parameter. `Time.deltaTime` is a very small value, so each time the function is called, the output value is interpolated toward the end value by a very small fraction. Calling this method in `Update()` results in smooth movement. It is not linear anymore. The **BlueDot** moves faster if it is further away from the cursor and slows down when it gets closer.

 Remember that when you're using the second method, the interpolated value will never truly get to the end position or end value. That's why sometimes we have to implement an `if` statement and check if the interpolated value is close enough to the end value. If so, we can set it to be exactly the same.

The `Lerp()` function is implemented in various classes. These are the most commonly used examples:

- `Mathf.Lerp()`: This interpolates between two float values
- `Vector3.Lerp()`:This interpolates between two vectors (positions for instance)
- `Quaternion.Lerp()`:This interpolates between two rotations
- `Color.Lerp()`:This interpolates between two colors

See also

Two more methods are also worth checking out in Unity's Scripting Reference: `Vector3.Slerp()` and `Vector3.SmoothDamp()`. The first one interpolates a vector spherically (as we would by rotating it) and the second one dampens the change in a vector (a position for instance). It can be used for implementing objects that should smoothly follow another object.

Using the Rotate() function to animate an object

In this recipe, we will use the `Transform.Rotate()` function to create an infinite looping animation of a windmill. We could make the same with the **Animation** View, but sometimes writing a simple script means much less effort than creating a key frame animation.

Getting ready

We need a few models we can rotate in this recipe. As an example, we will use a windmill. It is composed of three game objects: **WindmillBase**, which is the root of the whole windmill, **Windmill** which is parented to the **WindmillBase**, and **WindmillWings** which is parented to the **Windmill**. The **Windmill** game object itself can rotate in the *Y* axis. The **WindmillWings** game object can rotate in its local *Z* axis.

Windmill hierarchy

You can download the example project and go to the `Chapter 10 Miscellaneous\Recipe 03 Using the Rotate function to animate an object` directory. Open the `Example.unity` scene there and play the game. You will see the windmill rotating around the *Y* axis and its wings rotating around their local *Z* axis.

How to do it...

To use the `Rotate()` function for animating objects, follow these steps:

1. Import our windmill to Unity. The model should contain three objects: **WindmillBase**, **Windmill** (parented to **WindmillBase**), and **WindmillWings** (parented to **Windmill**).

2. Place the model in the scene.

3. Create a new C# script and name it `ScriptRotation.cs`. In this script's `Update()` function, we use only one method: `transform.Rotate()`. We have a series of `public` variables to be able to control the rotation speed and axis. The `Rotate()` method can rotate an object in the `World` or `Self` (local) space. We have a `public Space rotationSpace` variable to be able to control it from the **Inspector**:

   ```
   transform.Rotate(rotateAxis * rotationSpeed *
           Time.deltaTime, rotationSpace);
   ```

4. Assign the script to the **Windmill** game object.

5. Set the **Rotation Space** to **World**, and the **Rotation Axis** to (0, 1, 0). This means our object will rotate in the global *Y* axis (the up vector). Set the **Rotation Speed** to your liking (it's in degrees per second; a value of 45-90 should be OK).

6. Assign the same script to the **WindmillWings** game object.

7. Set the **Rotation Space** to **Self** and the **Rotation Axis** to (0,0,1). This means the object will rotate around its local *Z* axis (the forward vector of the object). Again, set the **Rotation Speed** to your liking.

8. Play the game and observe the effect. The **Windmill** game object rotates in the global *Y* axis and the **WindmillWings** game object rotates around its local *Z* axis and follows the **Windmill's** *Y* axis rotation (because of the hierarchy setup).

How it works...

We are using Unity's `Transform.Rotate()` function in this recipe. It allows rotating a transform around any given axis. It rotates the object the number of degrees we set as the function's parameter. We are using `Time.deltatime` to rotate the object X degrees per second. This function also has the `space` parameter, which lets us make a rotation in world or local space. The rest is handled by the hierarchy setup (**WindmillWings** being parented to the **Windmill** game object).

Using this method can save us a lot of time tweaking animations for simple rotating objects. What's more, we can still use **Animation** View to create an animation of the `public float rotationSpeed` parameter of our script. This way we can control the changes of rotation speed with a very simple animation clip, instead of animating the whole transform.

There's more...

Unity has also a `Transform.Translate()` function, which has the same parameters as the `Transform.Rotate()` method but moves our game object instead of rotating it. We can use it to create a similar script and move our object in the scene.

Preparing motion capture files for humanoid characters

Using motion capture files is not always easy. In most cases, we can use them directly (after exporting them to an **FBX** file) for characters using the **Generic** rig type. But we almost always want to use our motion capture files for humanoid characters. The problem occurs when our motion capture rig is not a standard Unity **Humanoid** rig (and again, it is almost always the case). We can expect all kinds of errorsâ©®bones rotating with an offset, deformations in the mesh, and so on.

This recipe shows how to retarget motion capture files onto a rig suitable for Unity humanoid animations. We are going to use Blender 3D.

Getting ready

To follow this recipe, you will need a humanoid character ready to be rigged to a proper Unity **Humanoid** rig. We also need a motion capture animation. You can find a huge free-to-use library of motion capture data on the Carnegie Mellon University's website at `http://mocap.cs.cmu.edu/`. We are going to use the `01_01.bvh` file in this example.

You can also download the example Unity project provided and go to the `Chapter 10 Miscellaneous\Recipe 04 Preparing motion capture files for humanoid characters` directory. You can find the `Example.unity` scene there. If you play the game, you will see a character playing a retargeted motion capture animation. You can find the BVH file in the `Raw data` directory. The final FBX file is in the `Final FBX` directory, and all the `blend` files are located in the `Blend Files` directory.

How to do it...

To use motion capture data for Humanoid characters, follow these steps:

1. First we need to create a rig suitable for Unity's Humanoid characters. In Blender, creating such a rig is quite easy. First enable the **Rigify** add-on and create a new **Human (metarig)** object from the **Armature** section.
2. This rig has almost the same structure as Unity's Humanoid rig, but we need to adjust a few things. First, edit the rig and delete the **heel.L, heel.R, heel.02.L,** and **heel.02.R** bones from the feet.
3. Then delete the **palm.01.L, palm.02.L, palm.03.L, palm.04.L, palm.01.R, palm.02.R, palm.03.R** , and **palm.04.R** bones from the hands.
4. This gives us a proper Unity Humanoid rig. We can also adjust the T-Pose (a **Rigify** rig is created in a more relaxed T-Pose). This step is not a necessity. Name that rig `FinalRig`.
5. Now adjust the bone sizes for your character and skin the character to the rig.
6. Enter **Pose Mode** and click on both shoulders. Enable their Y axis rotation (it is locked by default). This step is important for making the final animation.
7. Import your BVH file (**File | Import | BVH**). You may want to adjust the size of the rig in import settings.
8. Scale the imported BVH rig to roughly match the size of your character. Name the BVH rig **ImportedRig** for better clarity.

9. Now we will create a control rig that we will use to correct any errors. To do so, create an empty object in Blender and name it `Hips`. Create another empty object and name it `HipsTarget`. Make sure both objects have exactly the same position and rotation.

10. Parent **HipsTarget** to **Hips**.

11. To make the objects more visible, set the **Display** of **Hips** to **Cube** and the **Display** of **HipsTarget** to **Sphere**.

12. A pair of those empties is our bone nodeâ◉◉we will create one for each bone of the character:

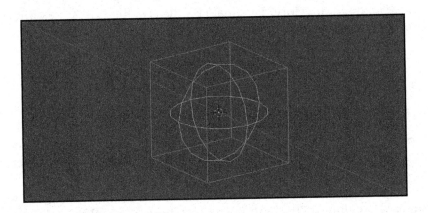

Bone nodeâ□□a pair of two empties

13. Select the **Hips** object and add the **Copy Transforms** constraint to it.

14. Select the **ImportedRig** as the **Target** and its `Hips` bone as the **Bone**.

15. Repeat steps 9-14 for every bone of the **FinalRig** (you can omit the fingers as not many motion capture files have data for fingers anyway). After completing this process, you should have a list of empties reflecting the structure of the **FinalRig**. It should look similar to the following:

- Hips (and **HipsTarget** parented to it)
- Spine (and **SpineTarget** parented to it)
- Chest (and **ChestTarget** parented to it)
- Neck (and **NeckTarget** parented to it)
- Head (and **HeadTarget** parented to it)
- Shoulder.L (and **ShoulderTarget.L** parented to it)
- Shoulder.R (and **ShoulderTarget.R** parented to it)
- LegUp.L (and **LegUpTarget.L** parented to it)

- LegUp.R (and **LegUpTarget.R** parented to it)
- Leg.L (and **LegTarget.L** parented to it)
- Leg.R (and **LegTarget.R** parented to it)
- Foot.L (and **FootTarget.L** parented to it)
- Foot.R (and **FootTarget.R** parented to it)
- ArmUp.L (and **ArmUpTarget.L** parented to it)
- ArmUp.R (and **ArmUpTarget.R** parented to it)
- Arm.L (and **ArmTarget.L** parented to it)
- Arm.R (and **ArmTarget.R** parented to it)
- Hand.L (and **HandTarget.L** parented to it)
- Hand.R (and **HandTarget.R** parented to it)

16. Sometimes our **ImportedRig** has a different structure, for instance it may have more spine bones (three or more). In such case, we should choose the most suitable bone in the **Copy Transform** constraints or add two **Copy Rotation** constraints and interpolate the final rotation of two neighboring bones by setting the **Influence** slider:

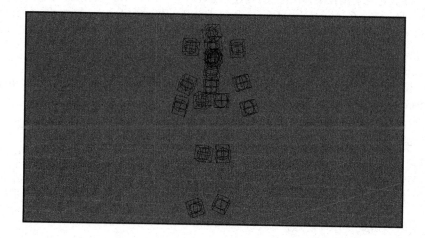

Control rig with Copy Transform constraints

17. Now we need to set the IK for feet. Select the **FinalRig** and go to **Edit Mode**.
18. Copy both foot bones and change their names to **footTarget.L** and **footTarget.R**.
19. Remove their parents and unselect the **Deform** option (they shouldn't deform the mesh).

20. Go to **Pose Mode**.

21. Select the **shin.L** bone and add an **Inverse Kinematics** constraint. Set the **Chain Length** to 2 and choose the **FinalRig** as **Target**, and **footTarget.L** as the **Bone**.

22. Select the **foot.L** bone and add a **Copy Rotation** constraint to it. Choose the **FinalRig** as the **Target**, and the **footTarget.L** as the **Bone**.

23. Repeat steps 21 and 22 for the right leg.

24. Select the **hips** bone and add the **Copy Rotation** and **Copy Location** constraints to it. In both constraints, set the **Target** to **HipsTarget** empty.

25. Select the **Offset** option in the **Copy Location** constraint and move the **hips** bone (in **Pose Mode**) to roughly match the position of the **HipsTarget** empty in the scene.

26. Select the **footTarget.L** bone. Add the **Copy Location** and **Copy Rotation** constraints to it. In both constraints, choose the **FootTarget.L** empty as the **Target**.

27. Select the **Offset** option in the **Copy Location** constraint and move the **footTarget.L** bone (in **Pose Mode**) to roughly match the position of the **footTarget.L** empty in the scene.

28. Repeat steps 26 and 27 for the right foot target.

29. Add a **Copy Rotation** constraint to every other bone (including those with the **Inverse Kinematics** constraint). Set the **Target** for each such constraint to a corresponding empty (for the **shin.L** bone, choose the **LegTarget.L** empty, and so on).

30. You should see the motion of the **ImportRig** being transferred to the **FinalRig**. Additionally, you can move the hips bone and the **footTarget.L** and **footTarget.R** bones to adjust the animation.

31. If you see any errors on the mesh, especially if the limbs of the character are rotated in a weird way, you can rotate the target empties to fix this.

32. You can also rotate the target empties to change the overall pose of the character easily.

33. To finish the retargeting process, save your file as a new one. Select all the bones in the **FinalRig** (in **Pose Mode**), press the space bar, type **Bake Action**, and press *Enter*.

34. In the **Bake Action** window, choose **Visual Keying** and **Clear Constraints**. You can also provide a name for the newly created action. If you click on **OK**, all constraints will be removed and the final animation will be baked.

35. Remember to select the small **F** symbol near this action in the **Action Editor** (this will save the data even if the rig doesn't use it).

36. Remove all the empties and the **ImportedRig** (you may also need to remove its action manually). Save the file.

37. Import the file into Unity and set the rig to Humanoid. The animation should work as intended. You may also choose to export the file to FBX first. If you experience any problems, try with the 6.1 version of the FBX format as it may help:

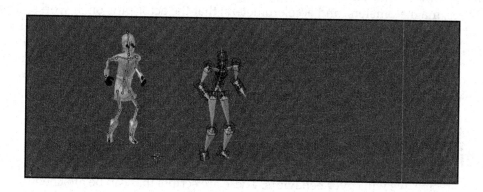

FinalRig on the left and ImportedRig and the empties (control rig) on the right

How it works...

Problems with importing motion capture data can be very frustrating. The most common errors are connected with an inappropriate **T-POSE** of the **BVH** rig. This T-Pose depends on the software the animation was recorded in and exported from. Additionally, BVH rigs can have arbitrary bone hierarchies, with more than two spine bones for instance. A proper Unity Humanoid rig hierarchy was covered in the *Configuring Generic and Humanoid rigs* recipe in Chapter 1, *Working with animations*.

In Blender, the Rigify rig has a proper T-Pose. Thus, the best solution is to retarget the animation from the **ImportRig** to the **FinalRig** (the **Rigify** one). In theory, we could omit creating the control rig (the empties) but those give us more control. The **(...)Target** empties are not constrained to the **ImportRig** bones—they are only parented to the empties that are constrained. This way we can rotate or move the **(...)Target** empties to correct any rotation errors or adjust a pose.

We also use **Inverse Kinematics** for the feet in this setup. This, combined with the **Offset** option in the **Copy Location** constraints (set for the **footTarget.L**, **footTarget.R**, and **hips** bones), allows us to adjust the feet and hips positions. This way we can move the character to the center of the scene quite easily. We can even make it crouch while moving.

See also

If you are on a budget and want to use motion capture data, you can find a lot of free motions on the Carnegie Mellon University's website at http://mocap.cs.cmu.edu/. Another good option is to invest in the Perception Neuron solution (https://neuronmocap.com/)—it is a project successfully founded on Kickstarter. Perception Neuron seems affordable for most indie studios or even individuals. It is a suit with a set of sensors (gyroscopes, magnetometers, and accelerometers) that the actor puts on. It works similar to standard motion capture solutions based on markers. I must say the quality of the recorded motions is mostly very good (it has some problems with rapid motions though). You also have to watch out for large metal objects, speakers, and other sources of magnetic fields in the room. But if you can't afford a motion capture studio session and want to use mocap for your project, it can be a good bet.

Adding behaviors to Mecanim states

In this last recipe, we will cover behaviors. These are scripts that can be attached to Mecanim states. You can use them to turn standard Animator Controllers into logic graphs such as AI trees, quests, and so on.

Getting ready

We are going to create this recipe from scratch and we don't need any special assets. You can download the example project and go to the `Chapter 10 Miscellaneous\Recipe 05 Adding behaviors to Mecanim states` directory. Open the `Example.unity` scene there and play the game. If you play the game, you can press the space bar to change the states in the **Animator Controller** attached to the **Controller** game object. The cycle starts in the **NoBehaviors** state—this is simply an empty state with no additional behavior. If we press the space bar, we transition to **Light1Random**. This state changes the color of the **Light1** light in the scene. If we press the space bar again, the state will change to **WaitAndSwitch**. This state waits for a given time and switches to the next state: **Light2Random**. This one changes the color of the **Light2** light. If we press the space bar again, we will transition to the **RotateObject** state, which rotates an object visible in the scene. Pressing the space bar yet again transitions the controller to the **Light1Random** state again. See the following screenshot for reference:

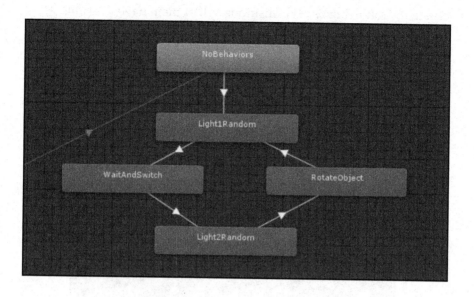

Finished controller

How to do it...

To use behaviors with Mecanim states, follow these steps:

1. First we need to prepare the example scene. Create a **Cube** in the scene.
2. Create two lights and name them **Light1** and **Light2**. Place them near the cube so you can see their effect.
3. Create an empty game object and name it `Controller`.
4. Create a new Animator Controller and name it `LogicController`.
5. Add an Animator component to the **Controller** game object and assign the **LogicController** to it.
6. Open the **LogicController**.
7. Create an empty state and name it **NoBehaviors**. Make it the default state.
8. Create a `Trigger` parameter and name it **Switch**.
9. Create four empty states and name them **Light1Random**, **WaitAndSwitch**, **Light2Random**, and **RotateObject**.

10. Create the following listed transitions. All of them have the same condition: `Trigger` **Switch** parameter and **Has Exit Time** set to false.
    - **NoBehaviors | Light1Random**
    - **Light1Random | WaitAndSwitch**
    - **WaitAndSwitch | Light2Random**
    - **Light2Random | RotateObject**
    - **RotateObject | Light1Random**

11. Select the **Light1Random** state and click the **Add Behaviour** button in the **Inspector**, as shown in the following screenshot:

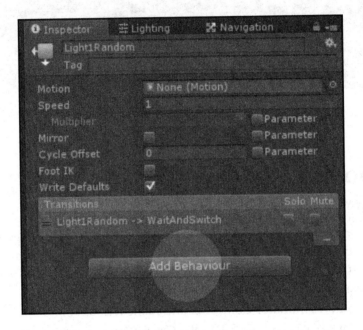

Adding a behavior to a Mecanim state

12. A list with all the available behaviors will appear. Type **LightColorChange** in the search field and press *Enter*. A **Create and add** button will appear. If you click on it, the `LightColorChange.cs` script will be created in the `Assets` folder.

13. Move the script to your script's destination folder.

14. Open the script. Add three global variables to the script: `public string lightGameObjectName`, `public Color color`, and `public bool randomColor`.

15. The script contains several commented out functions. Uncomment the `override public void OnStateEnter()` function. In it we first try to find the game object whose name we store in the `lightGameObjectName` variable. If we find it, we try to get its **Light** component and set the light color to a random value or to a specified value, depending on the `randomColor` flag:

```
GameObject go = GameObject.Find(lightGameObjectName);
if (go != null)
{
    Light light = go.GetComponent<Light>();
    if (light != null)
    {
        if (randomColor)
        {
            light.color = Random.ColorHSV();
        }
        else
        {
            light.color = color;
        }
    }
}
```

16. In the **Animator Controller**, select the **Light1Random** state. In its **Inspector**, set the **Light Game Object Name** to **Light1** and check the **Random Color** checkbox.

17. Select the **WaitAndSwitch** state and add a `WaitAndSwitch` behavior. The `WaitAndSwitch.cs` script will be created. This time add four global variables (with default values): `public string triggerName = "Switch"`, `public float waitTime = 5f`, `bool switched = false`, and `float startTime`. Uncomment the `override public void OnStateEnter()` function, check the time we've entered the state in, and store it in the `startTime` variable. We also set the `switched` flag to `false`:

```
startTime = Time.time;
switched = false;
```

18. Uncomment the `override public void OnStateUpdate()` function and check whether the current time is greater than our `startTime` plus `waitTime`. If so, we set the `Trigger` to transition between states. We also set the `switched` flag to `true` to prevent sending multiple `Triggers`:

```
if (Time.time >= startTime + waitTime && !switched)
{
    switched = true;
```

```
        animator.SetTrigger(triggerName);

    }
```

19. Select the **Light2Random** state in the controller and add the `LightColorChange.cs` behavior to it. Set the **Random Color** checkbox to true and the **Light Game Object Name** to **Light2**.

20. Create a new C# script and call it `LogicController.cs`. This script has three global variables: `public string switchTriggerName = "Switch"`, `public Transform activeObject`, and `Animator anim`. The `anim` variable is set in the `Start()` function. In the `Update()` function of this script, we set the `Trigger` in the Animator Controller when the player presses the space bar. The `Trigger` name is stored in the `switchTriggerName` variable.

21. Assign the script to the **Controller** game object. Then drag and drop the **Cube** game object to the **Active Object** field of the script.

22. Select the **RotateObject** state and add a `RotateObject.cs` behavior to it (you need to create a new one). Move the created script to your destination folder.

23. Open the `RotateObject.cs` script. Add four global variables: `public float rotationSpeed = 45f`, `public Vector3 rotationAxis = Vector3.up`, `public Space rotationSpace = Space.World`, and `LogicController controller`. The first three are used to rotate the object and the last one is a reference to the `LogicController` script. Uncomment the `override public void OnStateEnter()` function and set the reference to the `LogicController` in it:

    ```
    controller =
    animator.gameObject.GetComponent<LogicController>();
    ```

24. Uncomment the `override public void OnStateUpdate()` function and rotate the object that is stored in the `LogicController.activeObject` variable:

    ```
    if (controller == null)
    {
        return;
    }
    if (controller.activeObject == null)
    {
        return;
    }
    controller.activeObject.Rotate(rotationAxis * rotationSpeed *
Time.deltaTime, rotationSpace);
    ```

25. Make sure the Animator component of the **Controller** game object is set to **Always Animate**.

26. Play the game and press the space bar to see the effect. You will need to press the space bar several times to go through the whole cycle.

How it works...

State behaviors can be used to create logic graphsâ⊚⊚these graphs use Animator Controller as a state machine. Animator Controller can work without any Animation Clipsâ⊚⊚empty states can have behaviors as well.

Mecanim state behaviors are scripts that derive from the `StateMachineBehavior` class instead of the `MonoBehavior` class. They have a number of functions we can override. The most useful ones are as follows:

- `OnStateEnter()`: This function is called when the Animator Controller enters this state.
- `OnStateUpdate()`: This function is called every frame when this state is active (is playing). It will be called after `OnStateEnter()` and before `OnStateExit()`.
- `OnStateExit()`: This function is called when the Animator Controller exits this state.

We can still manage the state transitions from a normal `MonoBehavior` script (in our example, it is the `LogicController.cs` script).

Animator Controllers are assets, so they cannot reference objects in the scene. We can work around this by either finding the game objects by name (or tag) or by creating another `MonoBehavior` script that can reference objects in the scene. Our `LogicController.cs` script has an example of this: the `public Transform activeObject` variable. We can get the `LogicController.cs` script component in the behavior (as long as the Animator component is on the same game object). This way we can get to its `activeObject` variable and do an action on this transform.

Index

1

180 degrees turn animation
  creating, with root motion 125, 126, 128

2

2D sprite animation
  exporting, from 3D package 76, 77, 78, 79

3

3D package
  cutscene, importing 239, 240
  object animation, importing 39
  used, for exporting 2D sprite animation 76, 77, 78, 80

A

Action Points
  about 154
  creating 154, 155, 157, 158
actions
  Looped-Action 158
  Post-Action 158
  Pre-Action 158
additive Mecanim layers
  used, for adding motion 214
animated moving platform
  assigning 49
  creating 48, 49
  key elements 50, 51
Animation Events
  used, for drawing weapon 185, 188
  used, for triggering script functions 173, 174, 175
  used, for triggering sound and visual effects 206, 209

working 177
animation flow
  controlling, with parameters 27, 28
animation transitions
  creating, in Animator Controller 23
  working 24, 25
Animation View
  about 41
  camera shakes, creating 209, 211
  curves 45
  day and night cycle, creating 227, 228, 230
  Dope Sheet 45
  light colors, blending 46, 47
  particle system's properties, animating 223, 224, 225
  public script variables, animating 211, 212, 214
  used, for animating camera 232
  used, for changing camera shots 233, 235
  used, for creating flickering light 42, 43, 44
  used, for creating frame by frame sprite animation 81
animation, of multiple objects
  synchronizing 236
animation-driven behavior
  background characters, creating 144, 145, 146
animations
  creating, for better transitions 122, 123, 124, 125
  looping 33, 34
  mirroring 33, 34
  offsetting 34
  playback speed, adjusting 35, 36
  setting, to loop 33
  sound waveforms, using 225, 227
  synchronizing 158, 159, 161
  using, from multiple assets 31, 32, 33
Animator Controller

about 19, 23
Any state 26
Apply Root Motion 22
assigning 20, 21
camera shakes, creating 209, 210, 211
creating 20, 21
Entry and Exit 26
light colors, blending 46, 47
state transition, creating 23
Sub-State Machine, using 170
working 21, 22
Animator state
  active status, checking 183
Animator.SetLookAtPosition() method
  used, for making character to follow object 150,
    151, 153, 154
Any State transitions
  used, for playing hit reaction 177
  using 178
  working 179
appear/disappear animations
  creating 142, 143, 144
automatic doors
  creating 52, 53, 54, 55, 56, 57, 59
  key elements 58
Avatar Masks and Layers
  using 189, 191

B

background characters
  creating, with animation-driven behavior 144,
    145, 146
Blend Shapes
  used, for animating facial expressions 164, 165,
    167
  used, for morphing objects 217, 218
Blend Tree, settings
  1D 110
  2D Freeform Cartesian 110
  2D Freeform Directional 110
  2D Simple Directional 110
  Direct 110
  Mirror 111
  Time Scale 111
Blend Trees

about 106
methods, used for aiming 195, 199
randomized actions, creating 147, 148
used, for blending walk and run animations 106,
  108, 109

C

camera shakes
  creating 209, 210, 211
character joints
  parameters 268
  used, for creating generic ragdoll 266, 267,
    268
character
  animating 51, 52
  edge, grabbing 136, 137, 139
  following, at gaze 150, 151, 153, 154
  jumping 129, 131, 132
  steering, with root motion 117, 119, 120, 121
cloth simulation
  creating 252, 253, 254, 255
critters
  creating, with animation-driven behavior 144,
    145, 146
CutsceneIdle animation 249
cutscenes
  about 231
  importing, from 3D package 239, 240
  playing, in gameplay with root motion 245
  working 241

D

day and night cycle
  creating, with Animation View 227, 228, 230
death trap
  creating 62, 63, 65, 66
destructible objects
  creating 259, 260, 262, 263
dismemberment effect
  creating 271, 272, 273, 274, 275
Dodge animation 182
Double Sided Standard Mobile Legacy Shaders
  package 255

E

elevator triggered
  creating, player input used 68, 69, 70, 71, 72

F

facial expressions
  animating, with Blend Shapes 164, 165, 167
flickering light
  creating, with Animation View 42, 43
frame by frame sprite animation
  creating, with Animation View 81

G

generic ragdoll
  creating, with character joints 266, 267, 268
generic rig
  about 12
  configuring 13, 15, 16

H

Hierarchy
  Planet2 61
  used, for animating local rotation 59, 61
Hinge Joints
  parameters 258
  using 257, 258
hit location, character
  detecting 199, 200, 202
hit reaction 177
Humanoid 241
humanoid characters
  motion capture files, preparing 292, 293, 294, 296
humanoid ragdolls
  creating 262, 263, 264, 265
humanoid rig
  additional bones 17
  advanced animation settings 17
  automatic retargeting 17
  configuration options 14
  configuring 12, 13, 15, 16, 18, 19
  inverse kinematics 17
  look at feature 17

I

IK
  used, for interacting with scene objects 161, 162, 164

J

jump animation
  about 132
  InAir 132
  Jump 132
  Land 132

K

Kinematic 247

L

Lerp() function
  Color.Lerp() function 289
  continuous method 289
  Mathf.Lerp() function 289
  Quaternion.Lerp() function 289
  standard method 289
  used, for animating object 286, 287, 288, 289
  Vector3.Lerp() function 289
LookAt() method
  using 194
  working 194

M

math
  used, for animating object 283, 284, 286
Mecanim states
  behaviors, adding 298, 299, 300, 301, 303
motion capture files
  preparing, for humanoid characters 292, 293, 294, 296, 297, 298
multiple animations
  blending, with Blend Trees 106

N

Nav Mesh Agent component
  character, driving with root motion 132, 133, 134, 135

O

object animation
  importing, from 3D package 39
object
  local position, animating 52, 53, 54, 55, 56, 58
  morphing, with Blend Shapes 217, 218
orbiting planets
  creating 59
Override Animator Controller
  used, for animating different types of characters
    37
  using 37
  working 38

P

parameters, animation flow
  bool 30
  float 29
  int 29
  trigger 29
parameters, Animator Controller
  Avatar 22
  controller 21
  Culling Mode 22
  Update Mode 22
parameters
  used, for controlling animation flow 27, 28
particle system
  properties, animating with Animation View 223,
    224, 225
particles
  animating, with sprite sheets 221, 222, 223
physics engine 251
playback speed, animation
  adjusting 35, 36
player input
  used, for creating elevator triggered 68, 69, 70,
    71, 72
public script variables
  animating, with Animation View 211, 212, 214

Q

Quaternion.LookRotation() method
  used, for making character to follow object 150,

151, 153, 154

R

ragdoll
  force, applying 268, 269, 271
  standing up animation, implementing 275, 276,
    278, 280, 282
randomized actions
  creating, with Blend Trees 147, 148
rig configurations, Unity
  generic rig 11
  humanoid rig 11
  legacy 11
  none 11
Rigid Body character
  driving, with root motion 111, 112, 113, 114,
    116, 117
rigid body joints
  using 256, 257, 258, 259
root motion
  pros and cons 115
  used, for character dodge 181
  used, for creating 180 degrees turn animation
    125, 126, 128
  used, for creating dodge move 180
  used, for driving character with Nav Mesh Agent
    component 132, 133, 134
  used, for driving Rigid Body characters
    movement 111, 112, 113, 114, 116, 117
  used, for steering character 117, 119, 120,
    121
Rotate() function
  used, for animating object 290, 291, 292

S

scene objects
  interacting, IK used 161, 162, 164
skeletal animation
  importing 8, 9, 10, 11, 12
sound and visual effects
  triggering, with Animation Events 206, 209
sound waveforms
  used, for animations 225, 227
SpiderIdle 180
sprite sheets

used, for animating particles 221, 222, 223
Sub-State Machines
  creating 170, 171
  using, in Animator Controller 170
  working 172
subtitles
  synchronizing, with animations 242, 243
Sync option 193

T

trigger position
  animating 62, 63, 65, 67

Turret game object 195

U

Unity
  about 7
  Hierarchy 203

W

wind emitters
  used, for creating realistic effects for foliage 219
  used, for creating realistic effects for particle
    systems 219

CPSIA information can be obtained
at www.ICGtesting.com
Printed in the USA
FSOW04n0752191216
28747FS